Archaeology in Sussex to AD 1500

Archaeology in Sussex to AD 1500

Essays for Eric Holden

Edited by
P L Drewett

1978

Research Report No 29

The Council for British Archaeology

ISBN   0 900312   67   X

The Council for British Archaeology
112 Kennington Road
London SE11 6RE

PRINTED BY DERRY AND SONS LIMITED   CANAL STREET   NOTTINGHAM   ENGLAND

Contents

Preface

The papers published in this volume were all read at a weekend symposium held at Stafford House, Hassocks, East Sussex, from 29 to 31 July 1977. The main purpose of the symposium was to bring together all the archaeologists, both amateur and professional, currently working on the archaeology of Sussex. Fifteen archaeologists presented papers and were asked to summarize their contributions for this volume. By doing so it was thought that we would produce a useful summary of the archaeology of Sussex both for Sussex people and for the archaeological public at large. From the weekend's discussions, and these papers, certain priorities for future archaeological work in Sussex became evident. All will, we hope, be considered in formulating new archaeological policies both by public bodies and private organizations.

During the symposium it became clear that one man was referred to by virtually all the lecturers. This volume is published as a tribute to that man, Eric Holden. Mr Holden's support for others' research is often as great as the time spent on his own research. For this reason, among many others, this volume is dedicated to him by his friends, admirers, and colleagues in Sussex archaeology.

P L Drewett
Institute of Archaeology
University of London

1 October 1977

Notes on Contributors

Fred Aldsworth BA is the Archaeological Officer in the Planning Department of the West Sussex County Council. He formerly worked in the Archaeology Branch of the Ordnance Survey.

Owen Bedwin MA PhD is a Field Officer in the Institute of Archaeology's Sussex Archaeological Field Unit. He is currently engaged on a series of Iron Age excavations in Sussex.

Martin Bell BSc is a student at the Institute of Archaeology where he is undertaking research into Pleistocene land forms and particularly dry valleys. His interest in the Saxon period is closely associated with his eight years' excavating at Bishopstone, the report of which has recently been published as a monograph.

Peter Brandon BA PhD is head of the Department of Geography at the North West London Polytechnic and Editor of the *Sussex Archaeological Collections*. His publications include *The Sussex landscape*.

Henry Cleere BA FSA is the Director of the Council for British Archaeology. He is currently undertaking research into the iron industry of Roman Britain. He was co-founder of the Wealden Iron Research Group.

Alec Down FSA JP is Director of the Chichester Excavations Committee. His many publications on Chichester archaeology include the three monographs *Chichester* 1, 2, and 3.

Peter Drewett BSc FSA is Director of the Institute of Archaeology's Sussex Archaeological Field Unit. He formerly worked in the Inspectorate of Ancient Monuments, Department of the Environment.

Caroline Dudley BA is Keeper of Archaeology at Brighton Museum. Her special interest is the coinage of the late Saxon period.

Ann Ellison MA PhD is a Field Officer with the Committee for Rescue Archaeology in Avon, Gloucester and Somerset. Her recent publications include a monograph (with R Bradley) on her excavations at Rams Hill.

David Freke MA is the Urban Officer in the Institute of Archaeology's Sussex Archaeological Field Unit. He is currently engaged in a series of excavations in Sussex's small towns. His publications include the co-authorship (with Fred Aldsworth) of *Historic towns in Sussex*.

Roger Jacobi MA PhD was until recently a research student at Jesus College, Cambridge, where he re-examined the Mesolithic of Northern Europe.

David Martin is Director of the Rape of Hastings Architectural Survey. His many publications on vernacular architecture include *An architectural history of Roberts-bridge*.

James Money MA FSA is the Director of the Garden Hill Excavation Group. He has excavated and published many important Wealden hill-forts and ironworking sites during the last 30 years.

Joan Sheldon BSc is a lecturer in Environmental Archaeology in the Institute of Archaeology's Department of Human Environment. Her main interests concern the Pleistocene and the interpretation of charcoals from archaeological sites.

Andrew Woodcock MA BSc AMA was formerly Curator of Chichester Museum. He is currently undertaking research into the Palaeolithic in Sussex which has included a re-excavation of the classic raised beach at Slindon. He is now Archaeological Officer in the Planning Department of the East Sussex County Council.

Eric Holden, FSA: A personal appreciation C F Tebbutt

When I came to live in Sussex in 1966, beyond the briefest acquaintance with I D Margary I knew no Sussex archaeologist. However, very luckily for me, a mutual friend mentioned my move to Eric Holden. Most people I imagine would have said, or thought, 'I will try to remember that name; I shall probably come across him sometime.' Not so Eric. My wife and I had not been here long before we were invited to lunch and made to feel very welcome, and I was even given written suggestions for a line of research in the Weald.

Thus began a very pleasant long-term initiation into every aspect of Sussex history, archaeology, folklore, and landscape in the company and enjoying the delightful hospitality of Eric and Hilda Holden. There could have been, I am sure, no better mentors. Eric, I soon found, had an excellent memory and was steeped in a knowledge of Sussex archaeology and archaeologists past and present and what they had accomplished, published and unpublished.

When I began to make my own discoveries his advice and help was invaluable and always freely given. Two days spent helping him to survey Garden Hill fort for me, in a bitter March wind, will never be forgotten. It gave me an admiring insight into his careful, painstaking, and precise method of work under very adverse conditions.

Indeed, I soon found that the Holdens were on friendly terms with all the contemporary Sussex field workers, who did not hesitate to use Eric as a sort of honorary reference library when needing help in their work. I soon recognized as one of his greatest qualities his willingness to give of his encyclopaedic knowledge to fellow workers, even when it involved for him a great expenditure of time and research. Beyond this he would often offer help even before it was asked for when he knew he had something to contribute.

I do not wish to give the impression that Eric's knowledge of archaeology is narrowly confined to Sussex. Both he and Hilda are inveterate attenders at the conferences of national societies, and they have travelled widely to sites over the whole of the British Isles and have visited many of the classical sites of the Mediterranean and the Nile. Thus they have been brought into contact with most of the national figures in the professional archaeological world. This has been of great use to Eric when needing expert opinion on some object, and many of them have benefited from his notes and records on the subjects of their own research.

Controversy regarding the place of the professional and amateur in archaeology has fortunately never reached an acute stage in Britain, but if argument were ever needed to justify the amateur's position then Eric would provide the perfect example. His interests range widely from the palaeolithic to the post-medieval, and one can only say that perhaps he is least interested in the Roman period. The impressive list of his publications appended to this paper well illustrates this and needs no further elaboration. Wisely, as an amateur he has not attempted to become a specialist in any but a few local subjects, but he has been able to use his wide acquaintanceships in the world of specialists to get expert opinions on his excavation finds. The ability to write a polite request letter and to acknowledge help graciously makes it as much a pleasure to give as to receive help from him.

Most of the qualities that have made Eric the good amateur archaeologist that he is are either innate or come from his background. As a successful business man in the building trade he prepared himself by attending evening classes in all aspects of his trade including technical drawing, surveying, and the handling of tools in a craftsmanlike fashion. How better to understand primitive people than oneself to know the use and feel of handtools, the sensitive touch of wood, and the problems of building construction in all sorts of materials. As he had prepared himself for his business by study and training, so, when he decided to adopt archaeology as a hobby, he took a two-year course at the Institute of Archaeology in London to enable him to carry out an excavation expertly and intelligently and adequately to publish the results. His serious attraction to the subject did not start, as with many of us, as a teenage enthusiasm but came later in life when he was thinking of retiring. It probably came first as an interest in the art of surveying and drawing, exemplified by his admiration for the work of Robert Gurd, who was employed by Cecil Curwen to illustrate his published works. All the plans and drawings for the first edition of Curwen's *Archaeology of Sussex* were done by Gurd, but additional plans for the current (1954) edition, published after Gurd's death, were done by Eric, ie those of Black Patch and Itford Hill. Not only does he draw maps, plans, pottery, and flint artefacts with remarkable accuracy but his essays into other forms of pictorial art also show that he is an artist with a rare touch.

He had joined the Sussex Archaeological Society as a life member in 1948, but probably the first important dig at which Eric and Hilda worked was the Itford Hill Bronze Age settlement excavated by G A Holleyman and G P Burstow in 1949–53. For this Eric did all the plans and survey work. Then in the early 1950s he started his own dig, a rescue operation at the site of the medieval village of Hangleton, about to be engulfed by Hove. Interest in medieval villages was then a very new part of archaeology, and this was the first of its kind in Sussex and one of the first in the country. This whetted Eric's interest in medieval archaeology and was followed by a dig at a Saxon and medieval site at Old Erringham and later another, in partnership with K J Barton, at Bramber Castle.

Perhaps one of Eric's most spectacular discoveries was at Itford Hill to which he returned in 1971 when the original site, although scheduled, was threatened. Scattered Bronze Age pottery and a low mound indicated a barrow about to be destroyed by ploughing, and Eric decided to excavate the barrow. In this excavation and its publication a form of barrow construction unique in Sussex was described in detail and, most surprisingly, a sherd from the Itford Hill settlement, where he had worked 20 years before, was found to belong to a broken cremation urn placed in the barrow. This is believed to be the first time a Bronze Age settlement could be securely linked to a nearby barrow.

After the Itford Hill dig poor health made Eric decide not to undertake further major excavations, at least until all his past work had been prepared for publication. However, with improving health resulting from a change to a strict vegetarian diet, he has been able to undertake a number of research investigations and to publish several shorter papers on his results.

In the above brief notes I have not yet mentioned Eric's important administrative work in the cause of Sussex archaeology to which, with his business training, he is well suited. This has been, first, as secretary of the SAS Archaeological Committee which he ran for many years with zeal and efficiency. A second activity is as local correspondent of the Department of the Environment, to which he has recommended many sites for scheduling, and has kept them informed when scheduled sites were threatened or were already being damaged or destroyed. He has also worked closely with the Archaeology Division of the Ordnance Survey and has looked after the maps on which new sites are recorded. His unique knowledge of Sussex archaeology made him the obvious choice for appointment to the Department of the Environment's South-East Regional Advisory Committee and also the Management Committee of the Sussex Archaeological Field Unit. His outstanding contribution to archaeology was recognized by his election to the Council of the Sussex Archaeological Society in 1957 and to a Fellowship of the Society of Antiquaries of London in 1962.

It would be impossible to complete this short appreciation without paying tribute to Hilda, who has been a helpmate indeed in so many of Eric's archaeological activities. Not only has she nursed him back to health, but she has also provided endless hospitality to many friends of like interests. Her sharp eyes make her the perfect field worker: no flint or sherd within range can escape her, or unusual field contour or cropmark remain undiscovered. I can only end by wishing them both a long life together, fruitful in new discoveries in the hobby they love.

Selected bibliography of E W Holden's publications Compiled by C Cartwright and C F Tebbutt

Sussex Archaeological Collections
'Excavations at the deserted medieval village of Hangleton,' Part 1, **101** (1963), 54–181
'Slate roofing in medieval Sussex', **103** (1965), 67–78
Barton, K J and Holden, E W, 'Excavations at Michelham Priory', **105** (1967), 1–12
'The excavation of a motte at Lodsbridge Mill, Lodsworth', **105** (1967), 103–25
Roe, D A and Holden, E W, 'Two recently discovered Lower Palaeolithic handaxes from Northease Farm, Rodwell, and a note on Sussex Palaeoliths', **106** (1968), 206–12
Holden, E W, Evison V I and Ratcliffe-Densham, H B A, 'Anglo-Saxon burials at Crane Down, Jevington', **107** (1969), 126–34
'Militia Camps in Sussex, 1793, and the situation of "Wick" Church', **108** (1970), 82–5
'A sandstone roundel and Mesolithic flints from Bognor Common, Fittleworth', **109** (1971), 4–7
'Some notes on the Long Man of Wilmington', **109** (1971), 37–54
'A Bronze Age cemetery-barrow at Itford Hill, Beddingham', **110** (1972), 70–117
'Sussex Bronze Age pottery', **110** (1972), 125
'Mound at Forest Row', **110** (1972), 126
'Earthworks at Buxted', **110** (1972), 127
'The possible remains of a Neolithic causewayed camp on Offham Hill, Hamsey, near Lewes', **111** (1973), 109–10
Holden, E W and Roe, D A, 'The Ade Collection of flints, and a Palaeolithic handaxe from Hassocks', **112** (1974), 1–8
'Ancient monuments in Sussex', **112** (1974), 152
'Flint mines on Windover Hill, Wilmington', **112** (1974), 154
'Charcoal burials at East Hill, Hastings', **112** (1974), 160–1
'A medieval plumb-bob from Ansty', **112** (1974), 161–2
Holden, E W and Bradley, R J, 'A late Neolithic site at Rackham', **113** (1975), 85–103
'New evidence relating to Bramber Bridge', **113** (1975), 104–117
'Bowl barrow at Westdean, near Eastbourne', **113** (1975), 186
'Itford Hill flint artefacts', **113** (1975), 187
'Sandstone extraction at Eastbourne', **113** (1975), 187–9
'A possible moated site and medieval salterns at Bramber', **113** (1975), 191
'Excavations at Old Erringham, West Sussex, Part 1: The Saxon weaving hut', **114** (1976), 306–21

Sussex Notes and Queries
'Earthworks at Court Hill', **13**, 8 (1950–3), 183–5
'Sussex barrows', **15**, 4 (1958–62), 126–7
'Roman coins', **15**, 4 (1958–62), 129
'Sussex barrows', **15**, 5 (1958–62), 175
'St Mary's, Bramber', **15**, 7 (1958–62), 238–40
'Sussex barrows', **15**, 8 (1958–62), 270–1
'Salt works at Botolphs', **15**, 9 (1958–62), 304–7
'Deserted medieval villages', **15**, 9 (1958–62), 312–15
'Manxey, Pevensey', **15**, 9 (1958–62), 20
'Crested ridge tiles', **15**, 9 (1958–62), 322
'Aldingbourne: excavations at Tote Copse', **15**, 10 (1958–62), 332–3
'Botolph's Seal', **15**, 10 (1958–62), 353
'Saxo-Norman remains at Telscombe', **16**, 5 (1963–7), 154–8
'Hangleton medieval excavations, Part 1', **16**, 5 (1963–7), 160–2
'Lava quern stones from Selmeston and Lewes', **16**, 6 (1963–7), 187–91
'Flint artefacts from Arlington and Hailsham', **16**, 7 (1963–7), 221–5
Barton, K J and Holden, E W, 'Excavations at Bramber Castle: First season's work 1966', **16**, 8 (1963–7), 256–8
'Possible medieval salt pans at Pett Level', **16**, 9 (1963–7), 301–4
'Polished flint axe from Hellingly', **16**, 9 (1963–7) 321
Barton, K J and Holden, E W, 'Excavations at Bramber Castle: Second season's work 1967', **16**, 10 (1963–7), 333–5
'Lewes Castle', **17**, 6 (1968–71), 184–8
Holden, E W and Dunning, G C, 'Polychrome ware from Old Erringham Farm, near Shoreham-by-Sea', **17**, 6 (1968–71), 192–3

Archaeological Journal
'A note on sawpits', **132** (1975), 231
Holden, E W and Barton, K J, 'Excavations at Bramber Castle, 1966–7' (forthcoming)

The environmental characteristics of the county of Sussex are particularly dependent on the geological structure of the Weald. The broad concept of an eroded Chalk anticline leaving infacing escarpments of North and South Downs overlooking the intervening Younger Cretaceous sediments has become very well known since first described by John Farey in 1806. Geological research in the subsequent years has inevitably revealed greater complexity. New minor anticlines, synclines, and faults have been discovered (Lake, 1975) to add to well known examples such as the inverted reliefs of the Mount Caburn syncline and the Glynde Reach anticline. The Central Wealden sands and clays were thought by Allen (1959) to have been laid down in a series of alternating lacustrine and deltaic facies deposited in a sedimentary environment caused by minor regressions and transgressions of the Cretaceous sea. Allen (1975) now postulates these sediments as having an origin in a subsiding *Graben* basin margined by active horsts and spasmodically open to the sea. Essentially, however, the lithology of the sediments remains the same and their variability, together with the topography of the area, gives rise to the geographical divisions shown on Fig 1.

The soils at present occurring in the Weald (Fig 2) have recently been re-mapped by McRae and Burnham (1975). When considering their potential for land-use we must bear in mind that prehistoric farming changed their status, and a present-day assessment of capacity may not hold for the Postglacial Climatic Optimum. This applies both to the thin rendzina soils on the Downs (Limbrey, 1975) and to the podzols and gleyed soils of the sandy subsoils (Dimbleby, 1962). In some areas of Sussex the soils vary locally, particularly at the base of high ridges such as those of the Central or High Weald as well as at the foot of Chalk escarpments, where Drift deposits mask underlying clay or acid sandstones.

Pleistocene conditions in Sussex

When considering the environmental history of an area the changing climatic conditions through the Pleistocene make a convenient starting point. Until recently it was generally held that Sussex never lay under an ice-sheet but only suffered the rigours of a periglacial climate. In 1975, however, Kellaway *et al* suggested that 'the crude concept of "periglacial southern Britain" is out of date' and that some geomorphological features in the area can only be explained in terms of subglacial conditions. Their evidence comes mainly from the floor of the English Channel which, by seismic profiling and coring, has been shown to possess a relatively flat bedrock surface bounded by underwater cliffs in the vicinity of Beachy Head, the Isle of Portland, and further west in Devon and Cornwall. Submerged 'palaeovalleys' dissect this surface, only some of them being extensions of modern estuaries. Others are discrete deeps or fosses of circular, crescentic, or elongated form incised into the bedrock to a depth of 70–100 m. These closed systems closely resemble the subglacial tunnel valleys known from terrestrial locations in formerly glaciated regions. The infilling of one of the largest, Fosse Dangeard in the Straits of Dover, has been studied by Destombes *et al* (1975). A pollen analysis by Morzadec-Kerfourn suggests that the upper 50 m or so of the deposit dates from the Brørup (Chelford) interstadial of the Last Glaciation, though the spectrum is not very distinctive.

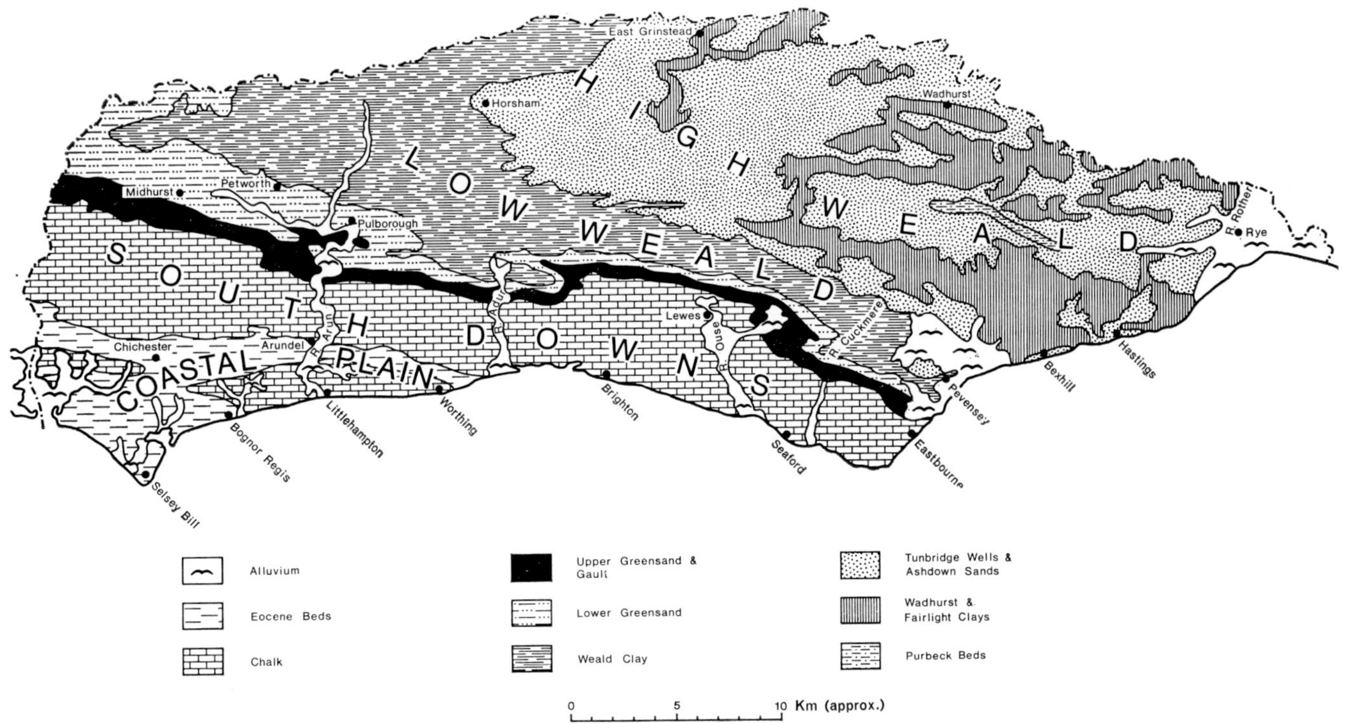

Alluvium	Upper Greensand & Gault	Tunbridge Wells & Ashdown Sands
Eocene Beds	Lower Greensand	Wadhurst & Fairlight Clays
Chalk	Weald Clay	Purbeck Beds

0   5   10 Km (approx.)

Fig 1 Simplified geological map of Sussex (based on Geological Survey Memoir)

The lower 80 m would thus represent the Last (Eemian or Ipswichian) Interglacial and, if the infilling followed immediately after erosion, the glacier would date from the Wolstonian. Whether the similar deeps in the English Channel were also formed in this glaciation or an earlier, pre-Hoxnian phase is not clear and the breaking through of the Channel barrier, probably in the Ipswichian Interglacial, would complicate the situation in the Straits. The unusual climatic conditions caused by a low glacial sea level and consequent exposure of a much extended western continental shelf may well have led to a tongue of ice moving eastwards along the English Channel to reach Beachy Head without impinging to any great extent on present inland Sussex, though workers in other areas of southern Britain do not find evidence for it (Mitchell, 1977). Kellaway would, however, like to invoke a glacial origin for the much earlier clay-with-flints on the South Downs and draws attention to the valley bulges and cambering found in many areas of southern Britain (Kellaway, 1972).

In many ways the revolutionary idea of a Channel glacier would solve some of the long-standing geomorphological problems such as the presence of large erratics of western and northern provenance found in places along the southern coast, such as those near Selsey (Pagham erratics). They have been explained as ice-rafted boulders but in fact lie at a height incompatible with their deposition by a low glacial sea-level. The problem lies in the dating of the glacial phase producing these phenomena, since the allocation by Kellaway of the Goodwood or Slindon 'raised beach' (c 30 m OD) to a glaciofluvial deposit of the Wolstonian Glaciation raises chronological problems for the contained (and in some cases unrolled) Acheulian tools (Woodcock, this volume).

The lower 8 m beach, formerly to be seen along extensive stretches of the south coast, but now mainly visible only at Black Rock, Brighton, is assigned by most workers to the Ipswichian Interglacial. Deposits on the plain near Chichester and at Selsey Bill have been attributed to the same high sea-level, but Hodgson (1964) has shown that these deposits of sands, pebbles, and loams lie on surfaces ranging from 2·7 to 15 m (8–47 ft) OD with no recognizable break between them. The assigning of beaches or terraces to interglacial phases on altimetric grounds alone has always been fraught with difficulties (Zeuner, 1959), and Hollin (1977) has recently suggested that some beach deposits of the Ipswichian Interglacial may derive their cold faunal content from the fact that an ice-surge from the Antarctic produced a high sea-level and also acted as a trigger for the beginning of the following glacial phase.

The chronology of the Pleistocene in general and, in particular, the correlation of interglacial phases both within these islands and between Britain and continental countries is presently undergoing serious revision (Shotton, 1977). It is not possible to give details in this context, but studies of deep-sea cores (Shackleton and Opdyke, 1973; 1976) and palynological work (Turner, 1975) are indicating many more interglacial phases than the four well known ones of Flandrian, Ipswichian, Hoxnian, and Cromerian.

Geomorphologists seem to agree that during the last glacial phase (Devensian or Weichselian) southern Britain experienced only periglacial climatic conditions and was not covered by ice except for minor upland ice-fields. Relict land forms and deposits from this period abound. It has long been suggested that the shape and, possibly, the initiation of dry valleys and coombes can be attributed to periglacial conditions (Reid, 1887; Bull, 1936; 1940; Small, 1970; Sparks, 1949). The soliflucted deposit known as Head or Coombe Rock occurs in many sections in Sussex, both in valleys and at the foot of escarpments. The pressure-changes set up in the 'active layer' in a permafrost zone during the summer melt and subsequent re-freeze result in cryoturbations or involutions which can be seen in many parts of the cliffs along the south coast, particularly along the under-cliff walk from Brighton to Rottingdean and at Birling Gap (Williams, 1971).

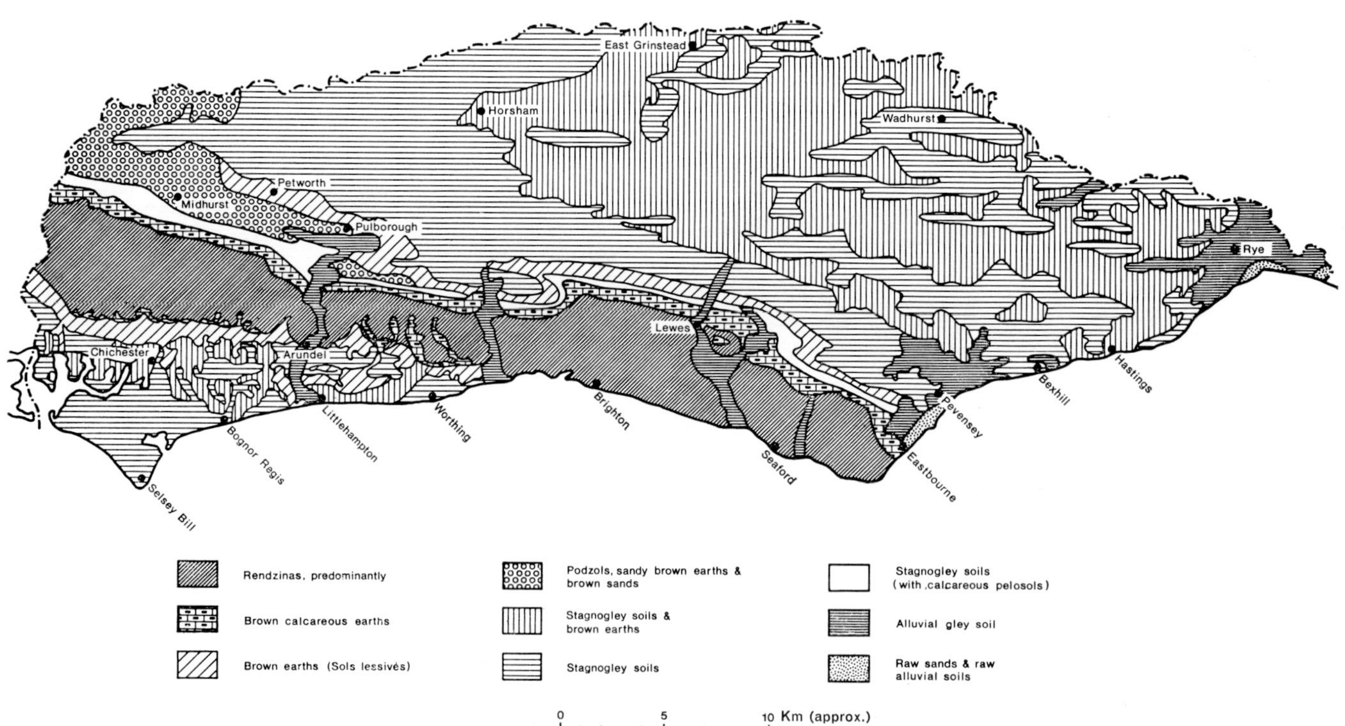

Fig 2 Sussex soils. Based on McRae and Burnham (1975) and Hodgson (1967)

Another periglacial feature which has been recently recognized in Sussex is the so-called stone stripes where troughs in the Chalk are filled with dark grey or brown soil. These are generally shallower (1 m or so deep) than involutions and, as their name implies, linear in shape and spaced between 1 m and 10 m apart. First recognized by Williams (1971) at Saltdean, they have also been found at Newhaven (Bell, 1976) and on Bullock Down. They show fewer signs of internal sorting than similar ones in sands and gravels in areas such as East Anglia (Sparks and West, 1972) and do not appear to show well in aerial photographs. The processes of formation are not well understood and postglacial chemical weathering has clearly affected the form of the trough, but the upstanding flints within the troughs indicate that freeze/thaw pressures are involved and suggest a periglacial origin. Watt *et al* (1966) give a detailed account of those found in the Breckland, where a geological *sine qua non* for their presence seems to be a superficial covering of relatively thin (maximum $2 \cdot 5$ m) sandy or loamy Drift overlying the Chalk. The stripes disappear where the covering increases in depth or where it rests on till rather than Chalk. A recent summary of these and other periglacial features in southern Britain can be found in Bell (1975). Fossil pingos, known from elsewhere in Britain (Mitchell, 1973; Watson, 1971) have not been reported from Sussex.

Just which part of the last glacial phase gave rise to the phenomena described above is difficult to say. It seems doubtful whether any glacial or periglacial features can be assigned to the early part of the Devensian in Britain. The oxygen-isotope curve of Shackleton and Opdyke (1973) shows an abrupt change at 80,000 BP, suggesting a rapid build-up of ice somewhere in the northern hemisphere, but the greatest extent of ice-sheets in Britain was about 20,000 BP, with the sea-level at its lowest (-130 m) about 15,000 BP. This was also the period of greatest loess deposition in southern and eastern Britain. Conditions were cold enough (at least $-8°$C annual average) for permafrost and ice-wedges to occur in the Midlands at the Devensian type-site of Four Ashes before 42,000 BP. Williams (1975) suggests, however, that involutions occur under somewhat different climatic conditions than do ice-wedges, though it is difficult to envisage their formation except in the presence of permafrost. They are difficult to date stratigraphically as their main distribution is beyond the moraines in the south and west. A rather late phase of the Devensian seems most likely, and this is supported by molluscan evidence from the involutions under the South Street Long Barrow in Wiltshire where Evans (1972) found a snail fauna characteristic of late Devensian subarctic conditions.

Even under such apparently adverse climatic conditions, Man was present in southern Britain, as the flints found within the involutions at Newhaven show. The summer temperatures, however, may well have been at least as high as today even when the ice-sheet reached East Anglia and the Midlands (Lamb, 1977).

Conditions cold enough to lead to large-scale solifluction continued into the late Devensian stages I and III, as shown by Kerney (1963) for sites in south-east England. Recent studies along the Sevenoaks Bypass (Weeks, 1969) have confirmed that Zone III was cold enough to produce large-scale periglacial erosion as solifluction lobes lie on top of an Allerød soil there, as at Brook and Halling at the foot of the North Downs escarpment (Kerney *et al*, 1964). The molluscan evidence from Brook suggests that conditions during Zone III were somewhat warmer but wetter than Zone I, and this is supported by molluscan

studies at Cow Gap and Beddington Chalk Pit in Sussex (Williams, 1971).

The Flandrian Period

It seems clear that these late glacial conditions generally saw the hill sides swept bare of superficial deposits so that the history of soil development both on the slopes and on the accumulated deposits at the base started from about 8,000 BP. Pedogenesis and plant succession are very interdependent processes so that, with increased temperatures during the early Flandrian, a natural succession occurred through more or less ephemeral serial stages towards increasingly long-lived and persistent communities. By about 6,000 BP a dynamic equilibrium was attained between biological communities, the maturity of the soils and the climate. For most of Britain the vegetation type represented by this stage was forest and all indigenous tree species had arrived, except possibly beech. Subsequent introductions in Roman and later periods were by the hand of man (Mitchell, 1974). A convenient term for this virgin forest is 'Wildwood' (Rackham, 1976).

In Sussex the Wildwood was found as much on the siliceous rocks of the Greensand and Hastings Sands, now covered in heathland, as on the Chalk Downs. Increasing numbers of pollen analyses have made us aware of man's effect on the landscape even before the introduction of farming. After clearance by fire or axe the natural regeneration is often prevented either by grazing domestic animals or by deterioration of the soil, so that the structure breaks down and the A-horizon is easily removed by wind or water erosion. This is particularly true in so-called 'brittle environments' (Dimbleby, 1976) where bedrocks poor in nutrients occur (Dimbleby, 1962). In order to prove that the same changes as known elsewhere have occurred in prehistoric Sussex more research into palaeosols is required. The necessary requisites are soils buried by sediments either naturally or by man so that the floral and faunal content of the ancient landscape is preserved. The anaerobic conditions of water-logged sites are the best situations in which biological remains survive, but only isolated valley peats are found in Sussex, where the rising sea level of the Flandrian has led to flooding in the valleys, particularly within and just beyond the gaps in the Downs through which the rivers flow. Such an area lies in the Ouse valley near Lewes where a succession through the Vale of the Brooks was studied by Thorley (1971). Radiocarbon dating shows that the peat growth started in the Mesolithic period and continued to the Bronze Age. On the other hand, the growth of peat in the Pevensey Levels was shown by Barnes (1974) to have taken place mostly in the medieval period. How closely the growth of peat can be related to rising sea-level remains a debatable point as shown by Akeroyd (1972), and workers disagree as to whether the general sea-level during the Flandrian was ever higher than the present-day OD level.

The acid soils on siliceous parent rocks of the Weald also preserve pollen grains well and their low pH means that the soil horizons and therefore the included grains remain unmixed by worms and other soil microfauna. A number of pollen diagrams have been published which reflect the general characteristics of the history of floral changes in southern Britain. The climax forest present by the Atlantic seems to be of the type known as mixed oak, with oak as dominant species and elm, ash, alder, and lime making up the main tree spectrum, with hazel as chief underwood species. In some areas of the Lowland Zone of Britain, however, lime or linden can be shown to be particularly abundant before the elm decline (Moore, 1977), and

Iversen considers that it has been underrated as a component of the Wildwood. Although insect-pollinated, lime produces large quantities of pollen (Godwin, 1975) so that its interpretation in pollen diagrams is a problem. Several sites in East Anglia and the south-east have recently shown pollen frequencies for lime of 30–50% arboreal pollen, particularly on sandy or gravelly soils. On the other hand, Dimbleby's diagrams from Lower Greensand sites in the Weald (Iping and Rackham, mentioned below) do not reflect this tendency. Rackham (1976) reports that such lime-dominated woods still exist in some areas of Britain, particularly in East Anglia and Derbyshire but, on the whole, lime can be shown to have been a victim of man's interference with the woodland and to be replaced by ash, elm, and other trees from the Iron Age onwards. It would, of course, be very valuable to Mesolithic man in the Atlantic woods for its bast, which was used in the making of nets and other cordage. Its leaves, too, could be used as fodder for deer in the same way as has been suggested for ivy (Simmons and Dimbleby, 1974) which also appears with high frequencies in pollen diagrams of this period.

Two sites are particularly important for tracing the history of changing pedological and vegetational conditions on the Greensand of Sussex. Iping Common Mesolithic site was excavated by Keef (Keef *et al*, 1965), and here the pollen analysis showed that man was already starting the process of deforestation in the Boreal period. This led to increased podzolization of the soil which went hand-in-hand with increasing extent of heather (*Calluna*) at the expense of tree-cover. The subsequent burial of the Mesolithic horizon by wind-blown sand indicates the final collapse of the soil structure leading to secondary erosion by natural agencies. The relatively small numbers of people in the Boreal and Atlantic periods ensured that clearance was on a small scale, so that at Rackham (Holden and Bradley, 1975; Dimbleby and Bradley, 1975) the lowest levels showed a predominance of trees (oak, alder, birch, hazel) in the early Sub-boreal but these conditions changed to a dominant *Calluna* heathland at the end of the Sub-boreal. Late Neolithic flints were found part-way down the profile but, unlike the implements in the Iping Common section, not associated with any recognizable land surface, and it seems possible that this strongly leached acid podsol was originally a forest brown earth with a high enough pH for earthworms to flourish. Their casts on the surface would gradually bury the Neolithic working floor, which was situated probably in a clearing in the original forest. The subsequent deforestation and extension of *Calluna* in the area, possibly in the Bronze Age, led to increasing leaching of the bases until at about a pH of 5·5 earthworms could no longer function and the present-day podsol was initiated. These two sites demonstrate the importance of understanding pedological processes when interpreting the position of artefacts on archaeological sites.

In view of the possible re-evaluation of the importance of the High Weald as a habitat for prehistoric man which emerged from the Conference discussions, it would clearly be interesting to know the vegetational history of this area. Unfortunately, relatively little palynological work has been done and environmental studies of buried soils depend on archaeological reconnaissance in this hitherto blank area on most distribution maps before the Roman period. The presence of beech (*Fagus*) from the rock-shelters at High Rocks (Money, 1960; 1962) suggests a very interesting arboreal community, as this tree is not known elsewhere on acid soils at such an early period and is generally considered to be infrequent before Zone

VIII. The Iron Age camp site at High Rocks, however, showed an absence of beech but high counts for lime in the soil beneath the ramparts and in that between ramparts of Phase I and Phase II (Money, 1968), suggesting that the beech had died out and not recolonized the area until late in the Iron Age. Further elucidation of this point must await a more complete sequence of pollen samples from Central Wealden sites. It seems clear that the main exploitation of the Wildwood occurred from the late centuries BC onwards in connexion with ironworking. Commercial management of the woods has been suggested by Cleere (1976) and the coppiced woods of the Weald may well go back to the Roman period (Rackham, 1976). Coppicing and lopping alone do not lead to deforestation and, in fact, prolong the life of a tree, as pointed out by Rackham (1974).

Palaeoecology of the Chalk Downs

The pedological and vegetational history of the Chalk is more difficult to elucidate because pollen does not survive in any great quantity from basic soils. Charcoal is found on many sites, as also from acid soils, and the tree species can be identified at least to generic level. The results can generally only be analysed on a presence/absence basis, because the number or weight of pieces cannot be related with any certainty to proportion of trees on the site or growing nearby. Its main interest lies in a comparison between trees identified and those shown in the pollen diagram. Abnormal conditions do sometimes allow pollen to persist on Chalk sites, usually where less calcareous sediments lay on the Chalk, for example the loess of Last Glaciation age at Lullington Heath or on the spreads of clay-with-flints and other Tertiary relict deposits. Work by Evans and Dimbleby (1974) has shown that analyses of pollen and molluscs from such basic soils sometimes do not produce identical results when examined in detail, and these discrepancies may be partly a reflection of the fact that any pollen surviving in a buried soil is likely to represent the latest assemblage before burial, since it has a short life in calcareous soils whereas snail shells will accumulate over a long period.

Nonetheless, molluscan analyses have produced some interesting results from archaeological sites in Sussex. Thomas (in Drewett, 1977) has shown that the causewayed camp at Offham was built in a clearing in woodland and that this woodland persisted through to the construction of a second bank and ditch at a later date. Large quantities of open-country molluscan forms suggesting widespread deforestation only appeared in the ditch-fill at a period roughly within the Bronze Age. On the other hand, molluscan studies from the Alfriston oval barrow (Thomas, in Drewett, 1975) suggested that open grassland obtained on this part of the Downs sometime in the third millennium BC before the barrow was constructed. In this case, the upper layers of the soil had probably been removed before the construction of the barrow, and this soil removal often occurs on archaeological sites thereby making environmental interpretation of the surviving organic remains very difficult (Evans, 1972, 244). From what little information we have available it appears that Chalk downland in south-east Britain provided a contrast with the rest of the British Isles (Turner, 1970) by the end of the Sub-boreal, in that open grassland was maintained with little woodland regeneration, probably due to a breakdown in the structure of the soil and the grazing of domestic stock. This clearance was intensified in the Iron Age and Romano-British period with ploughing of the hillsides and subsequent accumulation of surface soil in valleys at the foot of slopes.

Beyond this point the environmental history of the Downs and, indeed, of the whole of Sussex can be mainly traced in medieval documentation and becomes a matter for local studies of an historical nature (Brandon, 1975).

References

Akeroyd, A V, 1972　'Archaeological and historical evidence for subsidence in southern Britain', *Phil Trans Roy Soc London*, **A272**, 95–133

Allen, P, 1959　'The Wealden environment: Anglo-Paris basin', *ibid*, **B242**, 283–346

Allen, P, 1975　'Wealden of the Weald: a new model', *Proc Geol Ass*, **86** (1976), 389–436

Barnes, M, 1974　*Vegetational history of the Pevensey Marshes, Sussex*, unpublished MA thesis, Univ London Inst Archaeol

Bell, M, 1975　*Sediment analysis and periglacial landforms as evidence of the environment of southern England during the Last Glaciation*, unpublished BSc thesis, Univ London Inst Archaeol

Bell, M, 1976　'The excavation of an early Romano-British site and Pleistocene land-forms at Newhaven', *Sussex Archaeol Collect*, **114**, 218–305

Brandon, P, 1975　*The Sussex landscape*, London

Bull, A J, 1936　'Studies in the geomorphology of the South Downs', *Proc Geol Ass*, **47**, 99–129

Bull, A J, 1940　'Cold conditions and landforms in the South Downs', *ibid*, **51**, 63–71

Cleere, H, 1976　'Some operating parameters for Roman Ironworks', *Bull Inst Archaeol*, **13**, 233–46

Destombes, J P, Shephard-Thorn, E R, and Redding, J H, 1975　'A buried valley system in the Straits of Dover', *Phil Trans Roy Soc London*, **A279**, 243–56

Dimbleby, G W, 1962　*The development of British heathlands and their soils*, Oxford

Dimbleby, G W, 1976　'Climate, soil and man', *Phil Trans Roy Soc London*, **B275**, 197–208

Dimbleby, G W and Bradley, R J, 1975　'Evidence of pedogenesis from a Neolithic site at Rackham, Sussex', *J Archaeol Sci*, **2**, 179–86

Drewett, P, 1975　'The excavation of an oval burial mound of the third millennium bc at Alfriston, East Sussex, 1974', *Proc Prehist Soc*, **41**, 119–52

Drewett, P, 1977　'The excavation of a Neolithic causewayed enclosure on Offham Hill, East Sussex', *ibid*, **43**, 201–42

Evans, J G, 1972　*Land snails in archaeology*, London

Evans, J G and Dimbleby, G W, 1974　'Pollen and land snail analysis of calcareous soils', *J Archaeol Sci*, **1**, 117–33

Farey, J, 1806　'Geological section of the country from London to Brighton', Ms in Inst Geol Sci, London

Godwin, H, 1975　*A history of the British flora*, 2 edn, Cambridge

Hodgson, J M, 1964　'The low-level Pleistocene marine sands and gravels of the West Sussex Coastal Plain', *Proc Geol Ass*, **75**, 547–61

Holden, E W and Bradley, R J, 1975　'A late Neolithic site at Rackham', *Sussex Archaeol Collect*, **113**, 85–103

Hollin, J, 1977　'Thames interglacial sites, Ipswichian sea-levels and Antarctic surges', *Boreas*, **6**, 33–52

Keef, P A M, Wymer, J J, and Dimbleby, G W, 1965　'A Mesolithic site on Iping Common, Sussex, England', *Proc Prehist Soc*, **31**, 85–92

Kellaway, G A, 1972　'Development of non-diastrophic Pleistocene structures in relation to climate and physical relief in Britain', *Proc 24th Int Geol Congr Montreal*, Sect 12, 136–46

Kellaway, G A, Redding, J H, Shephard-Thorn, E R, and Destombes, J P, 1975　'The Quaternary history of the English Channel', *Phil Trans Roy Soc London*, **A279**, 189–218

Kerney, M P, 1963　'Late-glacial deposits on the Chalk of south-east England', *ibid*, **B246**, 203–54

Kerney, M P, Brown, E H, and Chandler, T J, 1964　'The Late-glacial and Post-glacial history of the Chalk escarpment near Brook, Kent', *ibid*, **B248**, 135–204

Lake, R D, 1975　'The structure of the Weald—a review', *Proc Geol Ass*, **86** (1976), 549–57

Lamb, H H, 1977　'The late Quaternary history of the climate of the British Isles', in Shotton, F W (1977)

Limbrey, S, 1975　*Soil science and archaeology*, London

McRae, S G and Burnham, C P, 1975　'The soils of the Weald', *Proc Geol Ass*, **86** (1976), 593–610

Mitchell, A, 1974　*A field guide to the trees of Britain and Northern Europe*, London

Mitchell, G F, 1973　'Fossil pingos in Camaross Townland, Co Wexford', *Proc Roy Ir Acad*, **73B**, 269–82

Mitchell, G F, 1977　'Raised beaches and sea-levels', in Shotton, F W (1977)

Money, J H, 1960; 1962　'Excavations at High Rocks, Tunbridge Wells', *Sussex Archaeol Collect*, **98**, 214; **100**, 151

Money, J H, 1968　'Excavations in the Iron Age hill-fort at High Rocks, near Tunbridge Wells, 1957–1961', *ibid*, **106**, 158–205

Moore, P D, 1977　'Ancient distribution of lime trees in Britain', *Nature*, **268**, 13–14

Rackham, O, 1974　'The oak tree in historic times', in *The British Oak* (eds M G Morris and F H Perring), London, 62–79

Rackham, O, 1976　*Trees and woodland in the British landscape*, London

Reid, C, 1887　'On the origins of dry valleys and of coombe rock', *Quart J Geol Soc*, **43**, 364–73

Shackleton, N J and Opdyke, N D, 1973　'Oxygen isotope and palaeomagnetic stratigraphy of equatorial Pacific core V28–238: oxygen isotope temperatures and ice volumes on a 10^5 and 10^6 year scale', *Quatern Res*, **3**, 39–55

Shackleton, N J and Opdyke, N D, 1976　'Oxygen isotope and palaeomagnetic stratigraphy of equatorial Pacific core V28–239: Late Pliocene to Latest Pleistocene, in Investigations of late Quaternary paleoceanography and paleoclimatology' (eds R M Cline and J D Hays), *Mem Geol Soc Am*, **145**, 449–64

Shotton, F W, 1977　*British Quaternary studies: recent advances*, Oxford

Simmons, I G and Dimbleby, G W, 1974　'The possible role of ivy *(Hedera helix* L.) in the mesolithic economy of Western Europe', *J Archaeol Sci*, **1**, 291–6

Small, R J, 1970　*The study of landforms*, Cambridge

Sparks, B W, 1949　'The denudation chronology of the dip-slope of the South Downs', *Proc Geol Ass*, **60**, 165–215

Sparks, B W, and West, R G, 1972　*The Ice Age in Britain*, London

Thorley, A, 1971　'Vegetational history of the Vale of the Brooks', *Inst Brit Geogr Conf*, Part 5, 47–50

Turner, C, 1975　'The correlation and duration of Middle Pleistocene interglacial periods in north-west Europe', in *After the Australopithecines* (eds K W Butzer and G L Isaac), The Hague, 259–308

Turner, J, 1970　'Post-Neolithic disturbance of British vegetation', in *Studies in vegetational history of the British Isles* (eds D Walker and R G West), Cambridge, 97–116

Watson, E, 1971　'Remains of pingos in Wales and the Isle of Man', *Geol J*, **7**, 381–92

Watt, A S, Perrin, R M S, and West, R G, 1966　'Patterned ground in Breckland: structure and composition', *J Ecol*, **54**, 239–58

Weeks, A G, 1969　'The stability of natural slopes in south-east England as affected by periglacial activity', *Quart J Engng Geol*, **2**, 49–61

Williams, R B G, 1971　'Aspects of the geomorphology of the South Downs', *Inst Brit Geogr Conf*, Part 5, 35–42

Williams, R B G, 1975　'The British climate during the last Glaciation: an interpretation based on periglacial phenomena', in *Ice Age: Ancient and Modern* (eds A E Wright and F Mosely), Liverpool, 95–120

Zeuner, F E, 1959　*The Pleistocene Period*, 2 edn, London

The Palaeolithic in Sussex Andrew Woodcock

The Lower and Middle Palaeolithic in Sussex

The Palaeolithic period in Sussex has received relatively little attention in recent years, the only general accounts of the period being those by Grinsell (1929), Curwen (1954), and Holden and Roe (1968), and the time would therefore seem ripe for an up-to-date re-examination in the light of recent discoveries.

Overall, Sussex has yielded relatively few Palaeolithic implements when compared with the amount of material discovered in adjacent counties and much undoubtedly still awaits discovery. This paper does not aim at giving a comprehensive gazetteer for the county, for this has already been provided (Roe, 1968a; Woodcock, 1978), but through selected examples to attempt to construct a chronological and typological framework within which the Sussex material can be set.

Before this can be done it is perhaps as well first of all to examine some of the limitations with which the Palaeolithic archaeologist is faced. Despite the very large numbers of Palaeolithic artefacts that have been recovered—and Roe (1968a) in his *Gazetteer of British Lower and Middle Palaeolithic sites* listed over 91,000 artefacts from some 3,000 sites—pitifully few of these sites have proved capable of producing information of a substantial nature. In order to see why, we have only to look at the last 300,000 years or so, the period during which we have evidence for Palaeolithic man in Britain, and examine the geological changes that have taken place. Britain has been subjected to a series of glacial periods, although in all probability

the ice itself never reached Sussex (for a contrary view, see Kellaway *et al*, 1975). The periglacial conditions that would have existed, however, gave rise to thick sheets of Coombe Rock, formed as an accumulation of material sludging down the slopes of the Downs, so resulting in enormous changes in topography. The large amount of ice locked up in the expanded polar caps and other ice accumulations during the cold glacial periods would have caused a great reduction in the sea level, leading to severe downcutting in the lower reaches of the river valleys. The warmer interglacial periods which separated these glaciations, times when climatic conditions would have allowed man to occupy Sussex, saw sea levels up to some 30 m higher than those of the present day, so rendering large areas of the lower-lying parts of the Weald unsuitable for settlement. This effect can be clearly seen on the distribution map, where finds in the Wealden area are particularly sparse. It is no wonder then, in the light of such events, that the vast majority of Palaeolithic artefacts in Sussex derive from geologically disturbed contexts in which material from several distinct occupations has frequently been mixed together. The prospects of obtaining *in situ* sites are therefore extremely poor. Luckily, however, Sussex is blessed with one or two such sites, about which more will be said later.

The bulk of the material available for study derives not from controlled archaeological excavation but from collections formed more or less casually in the course of quarrying operations before the advent of modern mechanical methods. Under such circumstances, collection

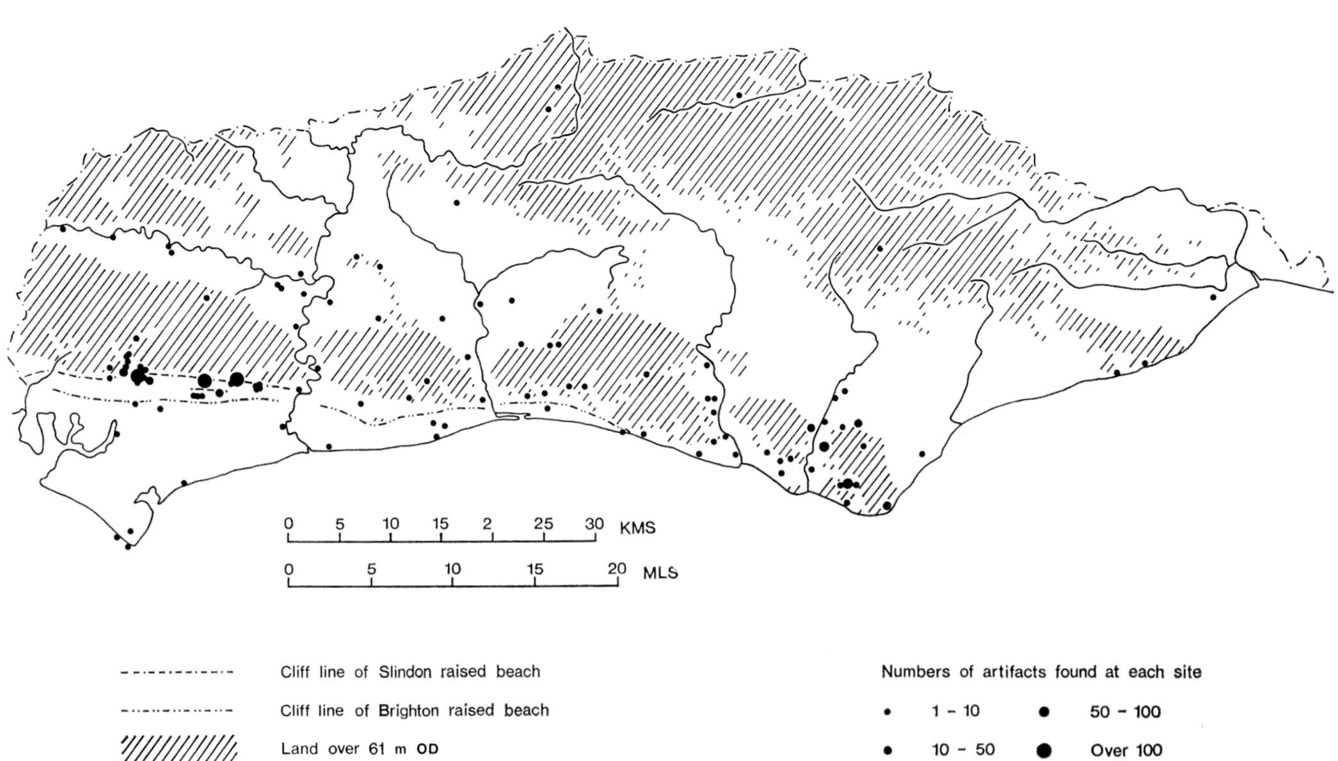

Fig 3 Distribution map of Lower and Middle Palaeolithic sites in Sussex

frequently took place in a highly selective manner with a bias towards the finer and more saleable items. For this reason true and complete assemblages of material are rare. It is also inevitable that the distribution map of Palaeolithic finds in Sussex (Fig 3), whilst illustrating general trends, will also reflect the areas of operation of the various collectors and researchers who have been active in the area. Neither must it be forgotten that the map illustrates the accumulated evidence for man's activity over many tens if not hundreds of thousands of years, and no attempt has been made here to separate out finds from one particular period.

The complexities and uncertainties of Pleistocene geology are such that the majority of sites can only be dated within the broadest of limits. For the purpose of this paper the recently agreed sequence of Hoxnian Interglacial, Wolstonian Glaciation, Ipswichian Interglacial, and Devensian Glaciation (Mitchell *et al*, 1973) will be used, for this is not the place to consider arguments as to the validity of such a sequence. For most of the artefacts it is the typology of the implements themselves, with all its attendant pitfalls, that is our best or only clue as to date. Typological series must always be treated with caution, for certain forms of implement are found almost universally throughout the Palaeolithic, whilst an apparently crude implement may merely be the result of hurried or inexperienced workmanship and need not indicate an early date.

It is difficult to state with any degree of certainty which is the earliest Palaeolithic material from Sussex. So far no certain traces of Clactonian material with its thick flake tools, choppers, and cores has been discovered, although the foreshore at Rainbow Bar near Fareham in Hampshire (Draper, 1951; Wymer, 1968) has yielded considerable quantities. It may be significant, therefore, that one of the typologically earliest Sussex handaxes comes from the foreshore also, at Selsey (Fig 4, no 1; Woodcock, 1978; Lewes BHM). This large, heavy, stone-struck, pointed handaxe is deeply mud-stained and appears to have come from *beneath* the well known later Ipswichian deposits. Although typology must be used with caution, this implement is undoubtedly of archaic appearance and is in many ways similar to 'Earlier Acheulian' examples from such sites as Fordwich in Kent (Roe, 1968b; 1975). Also apparently early is an intriguing group of artefacts from the 'clay-with-flints' capping the Downs 180 m above Folkington near Eastbourne (Todd, 1934; 1936; BM). These are remarkable for their degree of abrasion and lustrous black staining, quite unlike anything found on any of the other known hill-top Palaeolithic sites from Sussex. The assemblage contains at least four bifacially worked tools.

The gravels of the Sussex rivers have produced only a scatter of implements. Most are in an abraded condition and lack adequate documentation. This scarcity of material is largely due to the lack of extensive gravel working at the end of the last century, when the bulk of the Palaeolithic material now surviving in Britain was collected. R Garraway Rice, that famous collector of Sussex material, records a number of implements from the Pulborough area and the valley of the Arun, as at Arundel, Burpham, and South Stoke (Garraway Rice, 1905; Lewes BHM). Handaxes are also known from the gravels of the Adur, as at Henfield (Roe, 1973; BM, Lewes BHM), the Ouse, as at Lewes (Woodcock, 1978; Lewes BHM), and the Cuckmere, as at Arlington (Woodcock, 1978; Lewes BHM).

The study of Palaeolithic man in Sussex is, however, very much concerned with the question of the raised beaches and their associated deposits. These relics of ancient coastlines, deposits lying directly on marine platforms cut into the older Tertiary and Cretaceous rocks now left inland, record the former higher sea-levels of the Hoxnian and Ipswichian interglacials.

The highest and oldest of these beaches is the 'Slindon' or '100 ft' raised beach, which marks the time of maximum marine transgression during the Hoxnian interglacial when the world sea-level was over 30 m above that of the present day. Although little trace of the deposits can be seen casually on the ground, exposures in numerous gravel pits have revealed their considerable extent and complexity. Their most northerly limit is marked by a substantial, though now buried, cliff cut into the chalk which still reaches a height of up to 6 m in places, as at Amey's Eartham Pit, Boxgrove, near Chichester (Woodcock, 1978). This cliff-line can be traced from north of Funtington to Lavant and Slindon and as far east as Arundel. At the foot of the cliff are preserved the remains of a shingle beach which in various places contains abraded artefacts including handaxes, as at Slindon (Calkin, 1934). The actual maximum height of this beach is *c* 40 m OD. Traces of a further shingle bank survive at a slightly lower elevation (*c* 25 m OD) between Aldingbourne and Arundel (Fowler, 1932; Calkin, 1934), which probably represents a temporary pause in the regression of the sea. This too has yielded artefacts, much abraded but including at least one handaxe (Calkin, 1934; BM, Chichester Mus, Cambridge A and E). Associated with the shingle beaches are thick deposits of so-called 'lug-sands' (the Slindon sands) remarkable for their fine particle size, laminated structure, and preservation in places of trace fossils. In their upper levels these sands gradually change to a more clayey consistency, ending abruptly in a thin dark-brown band. These changes represent the drying out of the sands which were originally deposited in an intertidal environment, and the establishment of a stable land surface. This sequence is best illustrated at Amey's Eartham Pit, Boxgrove (Woodcock, 1978), certainly one of the most important and prolific sites so far discovered in Sussex. At this pit the dark-brown band has produced a small quantity of artefacts, *in situ*, and in mint condition, including two handaxe roughouts abandoned at an early stage in their manufacture (Chichester Mus).

Above this horizon is a laminated brickearth deposit ranging from a few centimetres to over 2 m in thickness, the surface of which is much weathered and channelled. On this surface, and in the fill of the channels at the same pit, considerable quantities of Palaeolithic material have been found. So far some 400 artefacts have been recovered, including over 40 handaxes and handaxe roughouts at all stages of manufacture (Fig 4, nos 2–4; Chichester Mus). The heavy patination, considerable weathering, and evidence of later retouch shown by some of the artefacts suggests that they may have accumulated over some thousands of years. This material most probably represents the sporadic exploitation by Palaeolithic man of readily available supplies of fresh flint from the abandoned Pleistocene cliff, sometime after the Hoxnian maximum. It is most likely that the fresh artefacts found on the surface of the raised beach at Slindon are of approximately the same date. This site, in the north-west corner of Slindon Park, is perhaps the best known of the Palaeolithic sites in Sussex. The first discoveries were made by Curwen (1925) and Fowler (1929), followed subsequently by a more detailed examination by Calkin in the 1930s (1934). The bulk of the material was found lying on the surface of the beach. Although the exact number of artefacts discovered is not known, there were at least 45 handaxes

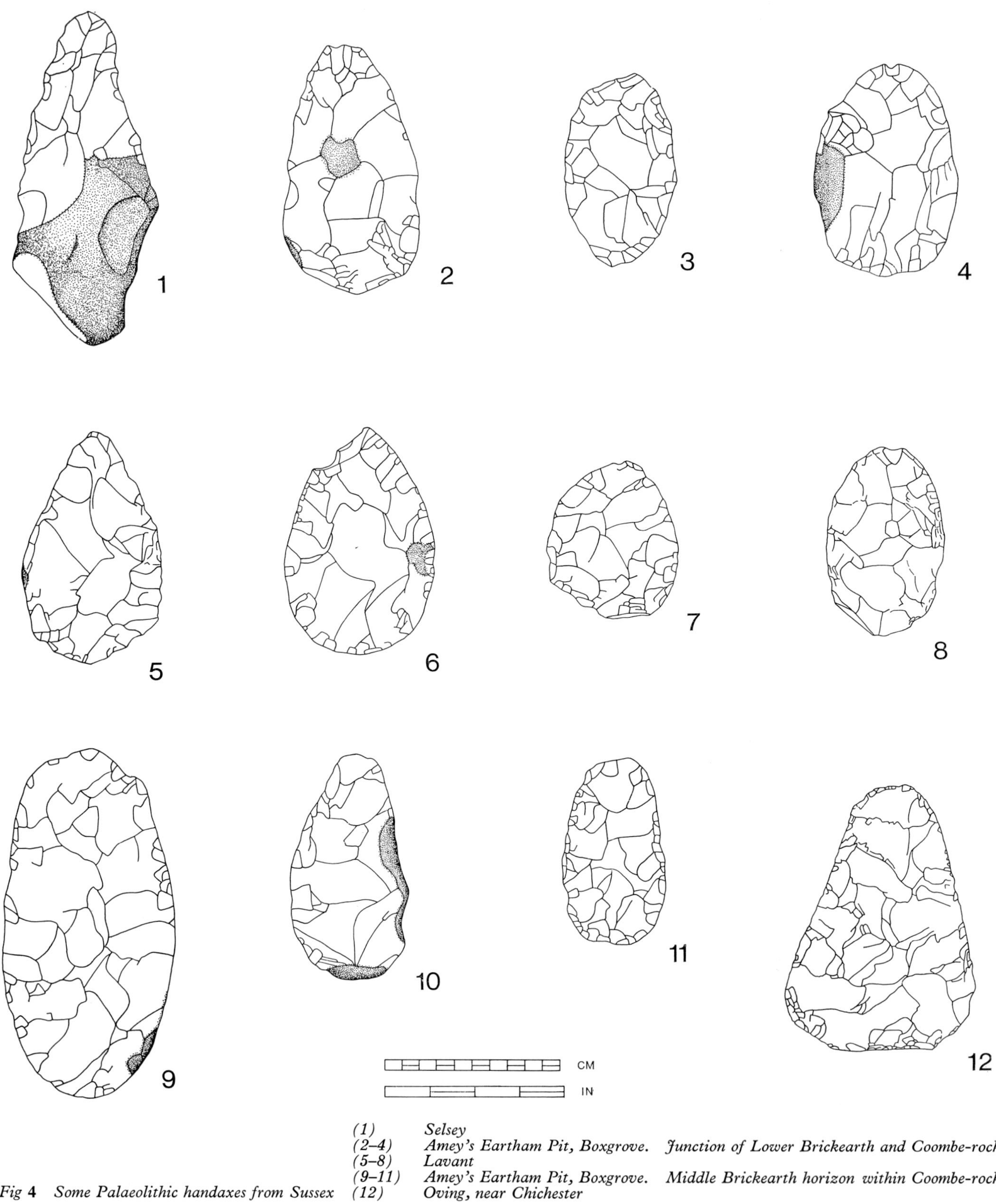

<table>
<tr><td>(1)</td><td>Selsey</td><td></td></tr>
<tr><td>(2–4)</td><td>Amey's Eartham Pit, Boxgrove.</td><td>Junction of Lower Brickearth and Coombe-rock</td></tr>
<tr><td>(5–8)</td><td>Lavant</td><td></td></tr>
<tr><td>(9–11)</td><td>Amey's Eartham Pit, Boxgrove.</td><td>Middle Brickearth horizon within Coombe-rock</td></tr>
<tr><td>(12)</td><td>Oving, near Chichester</td><td></td></tr>
</table>

Fig 4   Some Palaeolithic handaxes from Sussex

and handaxe roughouts, together with over 300 waste pieces now widely scattered in museum collections (notably BM, Cambridge A and E, Chichester Mus, Lewes BHM, Worthing Mus). Recent excavations by the author (Woodcock, 1978; Chichester Mus) have produced a further four handaxes and over 200 waste pieces, and suggest that the bulk of this material is actually later in date than the beach, and not contemporary with its formation as was previously thought, although it must be admitted that the time-interval between the two events is not yet clear. None of the artefacts shows evidence for a Levallois element amongst the industry, those flakes previously claimed as such (Calkin, 1934) being merely handaxe trimmers.

A further very interesting series of artefacts, including over 50 handaxes, have been found in the Lavant area north of Chichester (Fig 4, nos 5–8; Woodcock, 1978; Chichester Mus) and although some are clearly beach-rolled, many remain in a fresh condition. Most were found at the end of the last century and the circumstances of their discovery are not always clear. They do, however, seem once again to reflect Palaeolithic man's use of easily accessible sources of flint at the end of the Hoxnian period, contemporary with and subsequent to the maximum transgression of the sea.

The industries represented by the material from Lavant, Boxgrove, and Slindon are remarkably similar, and can be classified typologically as 'Late Middle Acheulian', if we follow the terminology of Wymer (1968) and Waechter (1973). The handaxes are characteristically 'ovate' forms, with flat ovate, cordate, and subcordate shapes predominating, the standard of workmanship and the refinement of the implements being high. They show an almost total absence of S twists, and a relatively low percentage of the handaxes have tranchet cutting edges. This material is quite unlike that from the Swanscombe Middle Gravels, for intance (Ovey, 1964; Wymer, 1968), with its high percentage of pointed forms, with which it has been traditionally equated on altimetric grounds (Calkin, 1934). Nor does it entirely match the implements from the Upper Loam at Swanscombe (Waechter, 1973) with its many twisted forms. Its strongest affinities seem to lie with series like the later Acheulian material from the Highlands Farm Pit, Henley-on-Thames (Wymer, 1961; Roe, 1968b) for which Wymer has suggested a date late in the Hoxnian period, or during the Wolstonian.

The deposits of the 'Slindon' raised beach are covered by a thick blanket of Coombe Rock which shows at least two major phases of deposition, separated by a thin layer of Brickearth as at Amey's Eartham Pit, or elsewhere by an erosion horizon as at West Stubbs Copse Pit, Tortington (Woodcock, 1978). From this Brickearth layer at Amey's Eartham Pit have come seven handaxes, together with over 30 waste pieces (Fig 4, nos 9–11; Chichester Mus). All are in a fresh condition and show an exceptionally high standard of workmanship. Elongated ovates and subtriangular handaxes predominate, characterized by straight edges and a cutting tip formed by tranchet blows from opposing directions. Two further handaxes are known from West Stubbs Copse Pit, Tortington (Woodcock, 1978; Worthing Mus) which appear to have come also from this horizon. These finds seem most likely to date from an interstadial within the Wolstonian glaciation itself.

The 'Brighton' or 25 ft raised beach in Sussex is also marked by a now buried cliff-line which can be traced eastwards from Westbourne to Hambrook, Chichester, and Westhampnett, then just south of the A27 to Arundel and Brighton. The deposit is now recognized as a composite one which varies from compact shingle and flint pebbles, through sand and pebbly sand, to almost pebble-free bedded sands. The deposits have been much studied at various locations (Sparks and West, 1960; Hodgson, 1964) and can be securely dated to the Ipswichian interglacial. The association of the 'Brighton' raised beach with archaeological material of 'Mousterian of Acheulian Tradition' (hereafter MAT) including *bout coupé* and flat subtriangular handaxes is well known (Shackley, 1976). Unfortunately, little material is known from Sussex and

only one handaxe from Brighton (Smith, 1915; BM) is known to have been found within the beach itself, and this specimen is much abraded and typologically inconclusive. Two significant handaxes have, however, been found in the deposits which overlie the beach. The first from Broadwater, Worthing (Evans, 1968; Worthing Mus) certainly approaches the *bout coupé* form, whilst the second from Oving near Chichester (Fig 4, no 12; Curwen, 1946; Lewes BHM) is one of the finest examples of a flat subtriangular handaxe yet found in Sussex.

The South Downs have produced quantities of hill-top palaeoliths, and the freshest of these probably date to the last Ipswichian interglacial and beginning of the Devensian glaciation. All are surface-collected and most inadequately documented. There are, however, several examples of handaxes which would fit quite happily within a MAT assemblage. The Downland to the west of Eastbourne has been particularly prolific in producing implements of this type, as at Friston, for example (BM, Lewes BHM). Garraway Rice records over 150 as having been said to have been found in this part of Sussex (Garraway Rice, 1911), though the whereabouts of most is not known. That material which does survive includes *bout coupé*, finely made ovates, and subtriangular handaxes. Similar subtriangular forms, well made and with an axe-like shape certainly related to the *bout coupé* forms, are known from Alfriston (Roe, 1974; BM, Lewes BHM, London Mus) and nearby at Alciston (Roe, 1974; Lewes BHM). Another fine *bout coupé* handaxe has been found at Wilmington Hill (Curwen, 1954; Lewes BHM). Away from the South Downs *bout coupé* or *bout coupé*-like handaxes are known from Woods Hill, West Chiltington (Garraway Rice, 1920; Worthing Mus), and nearby at Beedings, near Pulborough (Curwen, 1938; Lewes BHM), as well as from the sandy heathlands flanking the River Rother at West Heath, Harting (Woodcock, 1978).

Finds of Levallois material in Sussex are scarce. Most examples have been surface-collected and although they have often been found in comparable situations to the MAT material, for instance the examples from Beachy Head near Eastbourne (BM, Lewes BHM), Friston (Lewes BHM), and Peacehaven (Lewes BHM), there is insufficient evidence to say whether they are directly related. One or two examples of possible Levallois material are known from the foreshore at Selsey (BM NH) which may be associated with the Ipswichian deposits there.

It is therefore possible from a study of Lower and Middle Palaeolithic finds from Sussex to produce a basic sequence within which the history of man's occupation of the county can be fitted. Although limitations of space do not permit discussion of the many problems involved in any depth, this paper has I hope served not only as a statement of what is known, but also demonstrated that further research is badly needed and important discoveries undoubtedly await future workers.

The Upper Palaeolithic in Sussex

The Last Glaciation, a period which probably lasted from approximately 70 000 to 8 000 BC, was not an episode of uniformly cold climate, but a complex sequence of cold stadial periods and warmer interstadial periods when at times the summer temperature approached that of the present day. The large amount of water locked up in the ice sheets resulted in a world-wide lowering of the sea-level, so that Britain became part of the continent of Europe. Thus both man and the large herds of animals upon which his existence depended could move freely into Britain during the milder periods.

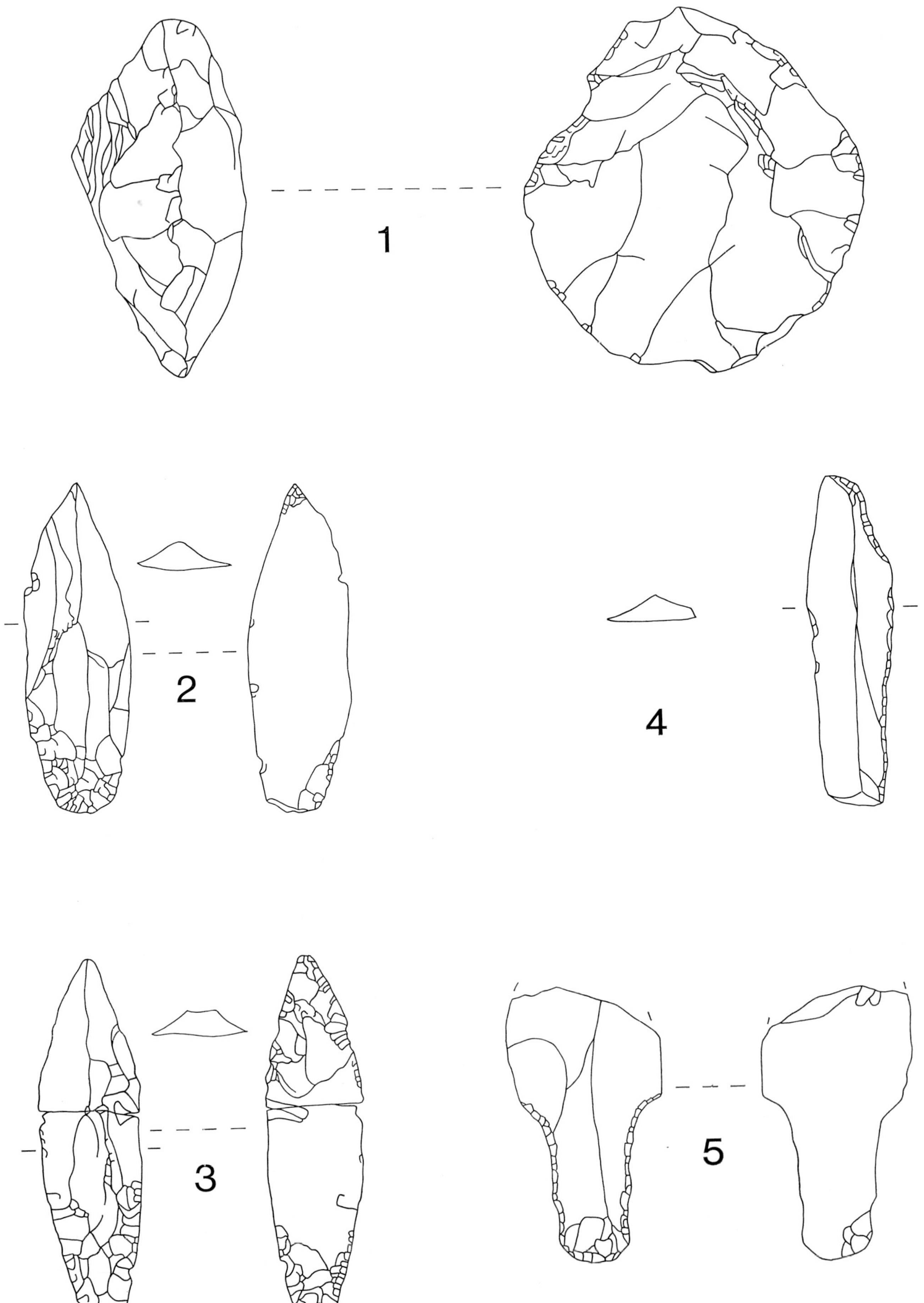

Archaeological sites dating to the Last Glaciation are far from common in Britain and indeed there are only four sites in Sussex which can be ascribed to this period with any degree of certainty. For all but one of these sites implement typology is the only clue as to date. The first of the Sussex sites to be considered is an exception, for it is solely on geological grounds that it is included within this group. The material consists of 156 pieces of waste (including conjoinable groups of flakes) and one possible tool (Fig 5, no 1), discovered *in situ* at Newhaven (Bell, 1976). The artefacts were found within the silt fill of ice-wedge features formed in the underlying Coombe Rock. The excavator concluded that they could only have been dropped at a time when loess was being deposited and that because of this the site was probably occupied somewhere between 28 000 and 14 000 BC. All the artefacts are in mint condition and many of the flakes have small bulbs of percussion consistent with the use of a soft hammer technique. The bifacial implement/core is unfortunately typologically inconclusive and it is not clear whether it represents an unfinished handaxe, an attempt to produce a prepared core, or is merely the end result of flake production. The possibility cannot, however, be ruled out that the artefacts are in fact somewhat earlier in date, for the debitage is not what one would perhaps expect from industries of this date.

A most interesting group of artefacts (a selection of which are preserved within the Piffard Collection in Lewes Museum) were discovered at the end of the last century by Dr John Harley whilst quarrying stone beside the drive to his house at 'Beedings', north of Nutbourne near Pulborough (Curwen, 1949). The material consisted of some 2,300 artefacts, mainly long flakes and blades, some scrapers and burins, but most important a number of bifacially worked 'leaf-points' (Fig 5, nos 2 and 3). A certain admixture of Mesolithic and later material also appears to have been found. Although this material has variously been considered as a forgery or spurious import from the continent, the discovery may well be genuine, and if so must represent one of the most important finds of British Proto-Solutrian material yet discovered. It is tempting to regard the artefacts as the debris from a now destroyed rockshelter, for the driveway to the house terraces the steep slope formed where the Lower Greensand beds outcrop and overlook the Wealden Clay.

Also within the Piffard Collection in Lewes Museum is a 'shouldered-point' said to have come from Old Faygate (Fig 5, no 4). It is made on a flint blade which has acquired a bluish patina. It is broken at its basal end and shows some recent damage along its edge. It does, however, seem to be of Upper Palaeolithic date.

Less certain is the base of a possible 'tanged-point' found at Newhouse Farm, High Hurstwood, near Uckfield (Fig 5, no 5). It is made from orange-brown flint and the tang is undoubtedly a genuine feature of the implement, though it could possibly be of Neolithic date.

This then is our sum total of Upper Palaeolithic sites in Sussex and further fieldwork is badly needed. Other river valley locations similar to Newhaven and rock-shelter sites similar to 'Beedings' may well contain *in situ* assemblages of implements, and their discovery can only benefit the study of the Upper Palaeolithic in this country.

Acknowledgements

I am indebted to both Martin Bell and Roger Jacobi for their help in providing information during the preparation of the second part of this paper.

Abbreviations used in the text

BM	British Museum (London WC1)
BM NH	British Museum (Natural History), South Kensington (London SW7)
Cambridge A&E	University Museum of Archaeology and Ethnology, Cambridge (Cambridgeshire)
Chichester Mus	Chichester District Museum, Chichester (West Sussex)
Lewes BHM	Barbican House Museum, Lewes (East Sussex)
London Mus	The Museum of London, London Wall (London EC2)
Worthing Mus	Worthing Museum and Art Gallery (West Sussex)

References

Bell, M G, 1976   'The excavation of an early Romano-British site and Pleistocene landforms at Newhaven, Sussex', *Sussex Archaeol Collect*, **114**, 218–305

Calkin, J B, 1934   'Implements from the higher raised beaches of Sussex', *Proc Prehist Soc*, **7**, 333–47

Curwen, E, 1925   'Palaeolith from raised beach in Sussex', *Antiq J*, **5**, 72–3

Curwen, E C, 1938   'Some noteworthy flints from Sussex', *Sussex Archaeol Collect*, **73**, 198–200

Curwen, E C, 1946   'A handaxe from the Chichester gravels', *Proc Prehist Soc*, **12**, 172–3

Curwen, E C, 1949   'A flint dagger factory near Pulborough, Sussex', *Antiq J*, **29**, 192

Curwen, E C, 1954   *The Archaeology of Sussex*, 2 edn, 26–46

Draper, J C, 1951   'Stone industries from Rainbow Bar, Hants', *Archaeol News Letter*, **3**, 147–9

Evans, K J, 1968   'Worthing Museum Archaeological Notes for 1965 and 1966', *Sussex Archaeol Collect*, **106**, 140–1

Fowler, J, 1929   'Palaeoliths found at Slindon', *ibid*, **70**, 197–200

Fowler, J, 1932   'The "100 ft" raised beach between Arundel and Chichester, Sussex', *Quart J Geol Soc*, **88**, 84–99

Garraway Rice, R, 1905   'Palaeolithic implements from the terrace gravels of the River Arun and Western Rother', *Proc Soc Antiq*, **20**, 197–207

Garraway Rice, R, 1911   *ibid*, **23**, 372

Garraway Rice, R, 1920   *ibid*, **32**, 78–82

Grinsell, L V, 1929   'The Lower and Middle Palaeolithic Periods in Sussex', *Sussex Archaeol Collect*, **70**, 172–82

Hodgson, J M, 1964   'The low-level Pleistocene marine sands and gravels of the West Sussex Coastal Plain', *Proc Geol Ass*, **75**, 547–61

Holden, E W and Roe, D A, 1968   'Two recently discovered Lower Palaeolithic handaxes from Northease Farm, Rodmell, and a note on Sussex Palaeoliths', *Sussex Archaeol Collect*, **111**, 206–12

Kellaway, G A, Redding, J H, Shephard-Thorn, E R, and Destombes, J P, 1975   'The Quaternary history of the English Channel', *Phil Trans Roy Soc*, **A279**, 189–218

Mitchell, G F, Penny, L F, Shotton, F W, and West, R G, 1973   'A correlation of quaternary deposits in the British Isles', *Geol Soc London Special Report* **4**, 1–99

Ovey, C D (ed), 1964   'The Swanscombe skull—a survey of research on the Pleistocene site (which includes a full bibliography)', *Roy Anthrop Inst*, 1–215

Roe, D A, 1968a   *A Gazetteer of British Lower and Middle Palaeolithic sites*, CBA Res Rep **8** (The Sussex sites are listed on 295–305)

Roe, D A, 1968b   'British Lower and Middle Palaeolithic handaxe groups', *Proc Prehist Soc*, **34**, 1–82

Roe, D A, 1973   'Palaeolithic flints from Henfield,' *Sussex Archaeol Collect*, **111**, 108–9

Roe, D A, 1974   'The Ade Collection of flints and a Palaeolithic handaxe from Hassocks', *ibid*, **112**, 3–5

Roe, D A, 1975   'Early Acheulian in Britain', *Proc Prehist Soc*, **41**, 1–9

---

(1)   *Bifacial implement from Newhaven (1/2)*
(2 and 3) *Leaf-points from Beedings, near Pulborough (1/2)*
(4)   *Shouldered-point from Old Faygate (1/1)*
(5)   *Tanged-point from High Hurstwood, near Uckfield (1/1)*

Fig 5   Some possible Upper Palaeolithic implements from Sussex (facing page)

Shackley, M L, 1976   *A study of the Mousterian of Acheulian tradition industries of Southern England*, PhD thesis, Univ Southampton

Smith, R A, 1915   *Proc Geol Ass*, **26**, 4

Sparks, B W and West, R G, 1960   'Coastal interglacial deposits of the English Channel', *Phil Trans Roy Soc*, **B243**, 95–133

Todd, A E, 1934   'Early flake implements from the "clay-with-flints" on the Eastbourne Downs', *Proc Prehist Soc East Anglia*, **7**, 419–20

Todd, A E, 1936   'Early Palaeoliths from the summit of the South Downs', *Proc Prehist Soc*, **2**, 140–3

Waechter, J d'A, 1973   'The Late Middle Acheulian industries in the Swanscombe area', in *Archaeological theory and practice* (ed D E Strong), Seminar Press, 67–86

Woodcock, A G, 1978   *The Lower and Middle Palaeolithic Periods in Sussex*, PhD thesis, Univ Leicester (forthcoming)

Wymer, J J, 1961   'The Lower Palaeolithic succession in the Thames Valley and the date of the Ancient Channel between Caversham and Henley', *Proc Prehist Soc*, **27**, 1–27

Wymer, J J, 1968   *Lower Palaeolithic archaeology in Britain as represented by the Thames Valley*, John Baker, London, 1–429

Roger Jacobi

In sharp contrast to the 3000 years of the late-glacial for which it is possible to record with certainty only one find from Sussex—a shouldered point from Old Faygate near Horsham—material representing the 4500 radiocarbon years of the Mesolithic can be produced from some 500 find-spots, ranging in quality from parish references in the case of old collections, notably that made by Garraway Rice from areas of the Downs, to the specific field or eight-letter grid references of more recent workers.

While sites with microliths still cluster on the Lower Greensand, survey work has revealed equally significant concentrations of flint material on the Weald Clay (Standing, 1964) and the Ashdown Sands (Tebbutt, 1975) and, rather fewer, on the Chalk (Bell and Tatton-Brown, 1975) noticeably on the capping 'Clay-with-Flints'. Very clearly the largest sites, or clusters of sites, centre on permanent springs and where possible combine this choice with what one can suspect to have been a well drained subsoil. On the chalk the association of sites with patches of 'Clay-with-Flints', an association observed also in the other counties of south-eastern Britain, could reflect the water-retentive properties of this deposit, if these patches do not simply represent the last remnants of an otherwise eroded soil cover.

While arguments have been presented to suggest that the large number of find-spots on the Lower Greensand reflects the choice of a '. . . relatively penetrable . . .' (Wooldridge and Goldring, 1953, 173) dry scrub or woodland for hunting—possibly that most susceptible to fire management—site catchment analysis suggests that within Sussex only 9·7 m² of the Ashdown sands between Wadhurst and Hawkhurst on the Kent–Sussex border had not been taken into the 'home territory' (at a 6 mile/10 km radius) of a known Mesolithic site, at one moment or another within the period. If the distribution of 'settlements' shows *some* selectivity towards a particular geological deposit, it is clear that 'exploitation' involved all geological deposits (Jacobi, 1977a).

Equally it remains hazardous to speculate on differences in woodland types as between one deposit and another given that the course of development of soil profiles on each remains largely unknown, beyond the fact that by the Atlantic many profiles on the Lower Greensand had become sufficiently acidic to allow the preservation of pollen grains, while soils on the chalk may, it has been suggested, formerly have been deeper than at present (Thorley, 1971), sufficiently so, to allow the growth of pine woodland. Indeed, with the exception of the diagram from the Vale of the Brooks, near Lewes, the source of whose pollen input must remain debatable, the pollen record is at present confined to the Lower Greensand, and within the Weald only certainly extends back beyond the Atlantic in basin peats accumulated near Elstead in Surrey (Seagrief and Godwin, 1960). With the exception of Elstead, the pollen record for the succeeding Atlantic derives entirely from analyses in mineral profiles whose increased acidity may often be the end product of previous human intervention—an intervention which, within the latter portion of the Mesolithic, the earliest period represented in the pollen diagrams, was to lead locally to the establishment of hazel woodland or even heath conditions (Dimbleby, 1960; Keef *et al*, 1965, 87–88).

Only three radiocarbon dates are available for Mesolithic sites in Sussex: Q1312 = 4850 bc $\pm$ 100 for Hermitage Rocks near High Hurstwood (East Sussex: Tebbutt, 1975, 41) and a pair of dates of BM 40 = 3700 bc $\pm$ 150 and BM 91 = 3780 bc $\pm$ 150 for High Rocks shelter F—Periods II and III respectively (Money, 1960, 212; 1962). That these latter dates refer to the microlithic material found in the shelter and not the sherds of 'Whitehawk Ware' found at the same level is confirmed by thermoluminescence dates on samples of the pottery which place it well within the accepted age-range of the Neolithic. Exploitation of the 'High Weald' by Mesolithic groups into the 4th millennium bc appears confirmed by the latest in a series of determinations for the Stonewall shelter near Tunbridge Wells, use of which had begun before 6000 bc. No Sussex site is strictly speaking 'dated' by means of pollen analysis, although it remains a probability that at Iping (site I) the flint material had become buried within the mineral soil *before* the pollen record opens, arguably as early as the later Boreal.

No contemporary artefacts of bone or antler have been identified from Sussex, or indeed from anywhere within the Weald. Similarly with the exception of a single broken metacarpal from the base of pit 13 at Farnham, attributable to either sheep (Rankine, 1936, 43) or roe-deer (C Grigson, 1976, *pers comm*), faunal material is recorded from no site inside the Weald; the organic debris recovered by Abbott (1896) from the fissures of the Hastings 'kitchen-midden' site (apparently together with Mesolithic artefacts) was, perhaps, more convincingly associated with the sherds of early medieval coarse wares excavated at the same time. The hazel nut shells from Selmeston (Clark, 1934a, 140) and Iping Fitzhall are too few either to argue for collection of plant foods or to act as any form of seasonal indicator.

Thus as representative of this period in Sussex we have solely a series of flint industries, the microlithic components of some 16 of which are suitable in terms of sample size (at least) for any form of statistical analysis. This group includes, of course, the enormous collections of material amassed by Attree and Piffard from surface sites east of Horsham, and which Clark used as a basis for his arguments in defining the existence of a distinctive microlithic technology within the Weald—the 'Horsham culture' (Clark and Rankine, 1939, 95–6).

To help evaluate the Sussex microlithic material, typological data on these 16 samples—the numbers of each microlith shape identified (these *shapes* and their *classification numbers* can be recovered from the key to Fig 6)—have been combined in the following study with similar information for 28 selected sites/samples from Kent, Surrey, and eastern Hampshire, largely from sites on the Lower Greensand belt of the Weald. Also included, for reasons which will become apparent, are the microlithic assemblages from Thatcham sites I, II, IIIA (Wymer, 1962) and site VII (in preparation), also the patinated series from Downton (Jacobi, 1973, 238), a total of 49 samples.

Selected for inclusion are assemblages which, with the exception of surface collections from Wonham (Ellaby, 1977) and Flanchford (Ellaby, 1976), near Reigate, derive from excavated contexts, either pits (as at Farnham or

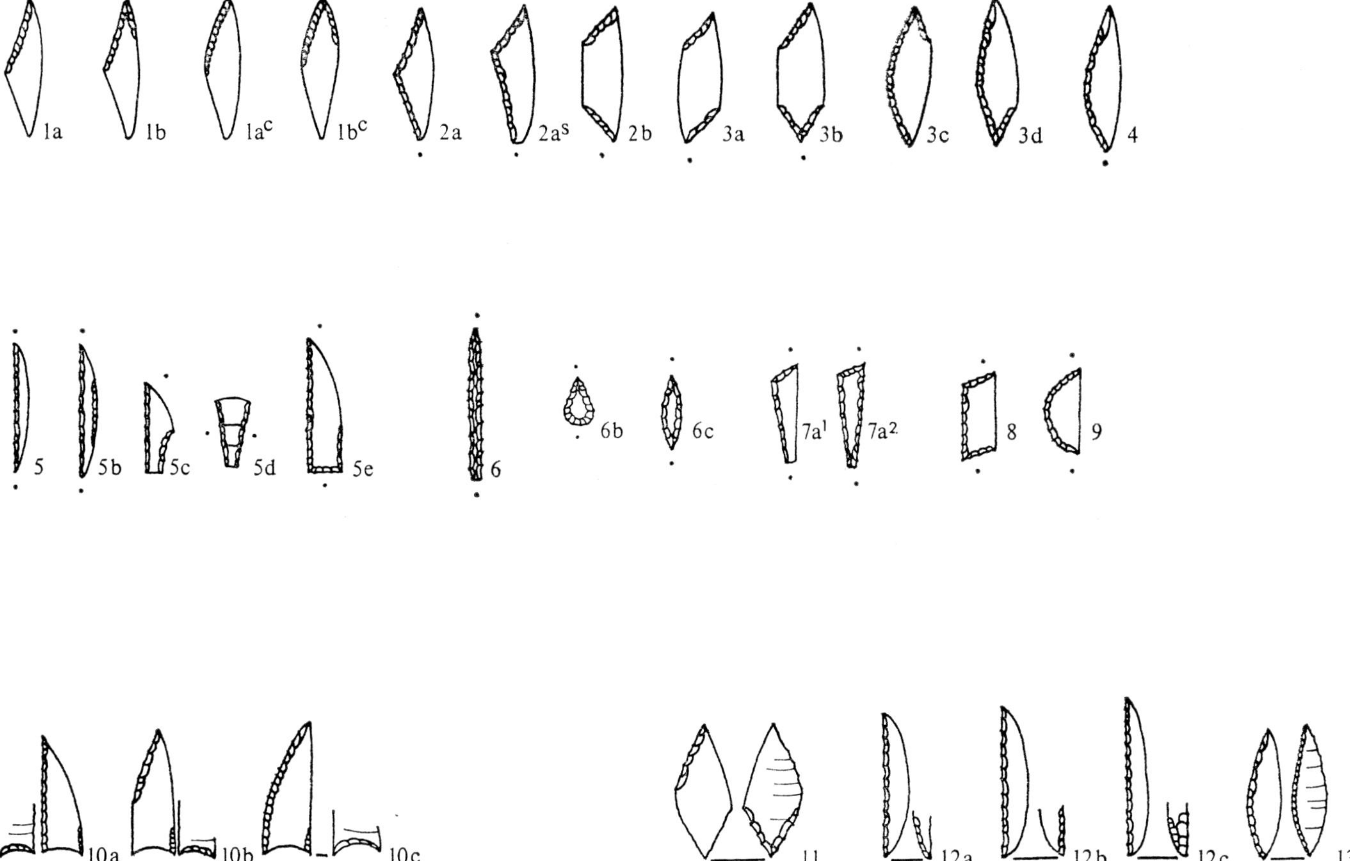

Fig 6   *Wealden Mesolithic: blade microliths and points (1–4) broad-blade microliths;   (5–9) narrow-blade microliths;   (10) hollow-based points;   (11–13) inversely retouched points*

Broomhill, near Romsey) or individual horizontal concentrations of worked flint, where (1) there has been a non-selective retention of the various microlith shapes, (2) the standard of recovery is known to have been high, and (3) where survival of the material recovered has been most complete. It is failure to meet this last requirement that has meant the omission of excavated samples which one might otherwise have expected to have been included. The bulk of the previously unpublished material incorporated derives from sites investigated before the last war by R G V and L S V Venables and the late W F Rankine, and previously only passingly referred to in print (Clark and Rankine, 1939, 112–116; Rankine, 1948; 1949a; 1949b, 31–35). Half the assemblages included from Sussex, derive, it should be recalled from *surface* collection including those critical to the definition of the 'Horsham culture', and inclusion of this extra material from outside the county provides *excavated* samples of *known context* among which one might, or might not, find analogous assemblages.

To sort this combined information—microlith counts for each of the 49 assemblages—computer cluster analysis was used, a technique which compares each assemblage with every other assemblage, and also attempts to assign each to distinct groups or 'clusters'. The pattern of this grouping is displayed on a 'dendrogram' (Fig 7), where the vertical axis represents increasing dissimilarity as one ascends the diagram. Thus the higher a split occurs, or a new 'cluster' is formed, the more significant it is likely

to be archaeologically, while, as the number of groups or 'clusters' increases down the diagram, this significance decreases until in its lowest portion the differences monitored between them will have become ever more dependent on sampling errors, particularly where the original assemblages are small, and attribution may be disproportionately affected by the presence or absence of rare variables. The analysis performed would appear to show three main clusters at each of which it is important to look.

The first, or left-hand, 'cluster' incorporates all those sites which we would independently describe as 'Maglemosian', that is, sites whose microlithic component is dominated by simple obliquely blunted points (class 1) with a relatively low proportion of more elaborate shapes (classes 2a–4), of which only the relatively broad triangles could be described as 'geometric'. Over most of the area of its distribution this microlith assemblage is associated with transversely sharpened core-adzes, and with a bone/antler component represented in south-eastern Britain only by isolated finds of barbed points (Clark, 1932a, fig 2), and a small series of perforated bone 'picks' from the Thames, at Hammersmith, Putney, and Kew Bridge (Smith, 1934; Lacaille, 1961, fig 7, no 5), While this technology can be traced east to west from the western coast and islands of the Baltic to Cornwall and North Wales (Jacobi, 1977b), its southern boundary lies well north of the Somme and roughly on a level with Boulogne. If one compensates for a sea level close to —40 m OD (*c* 7000 bc) a westward extension of this

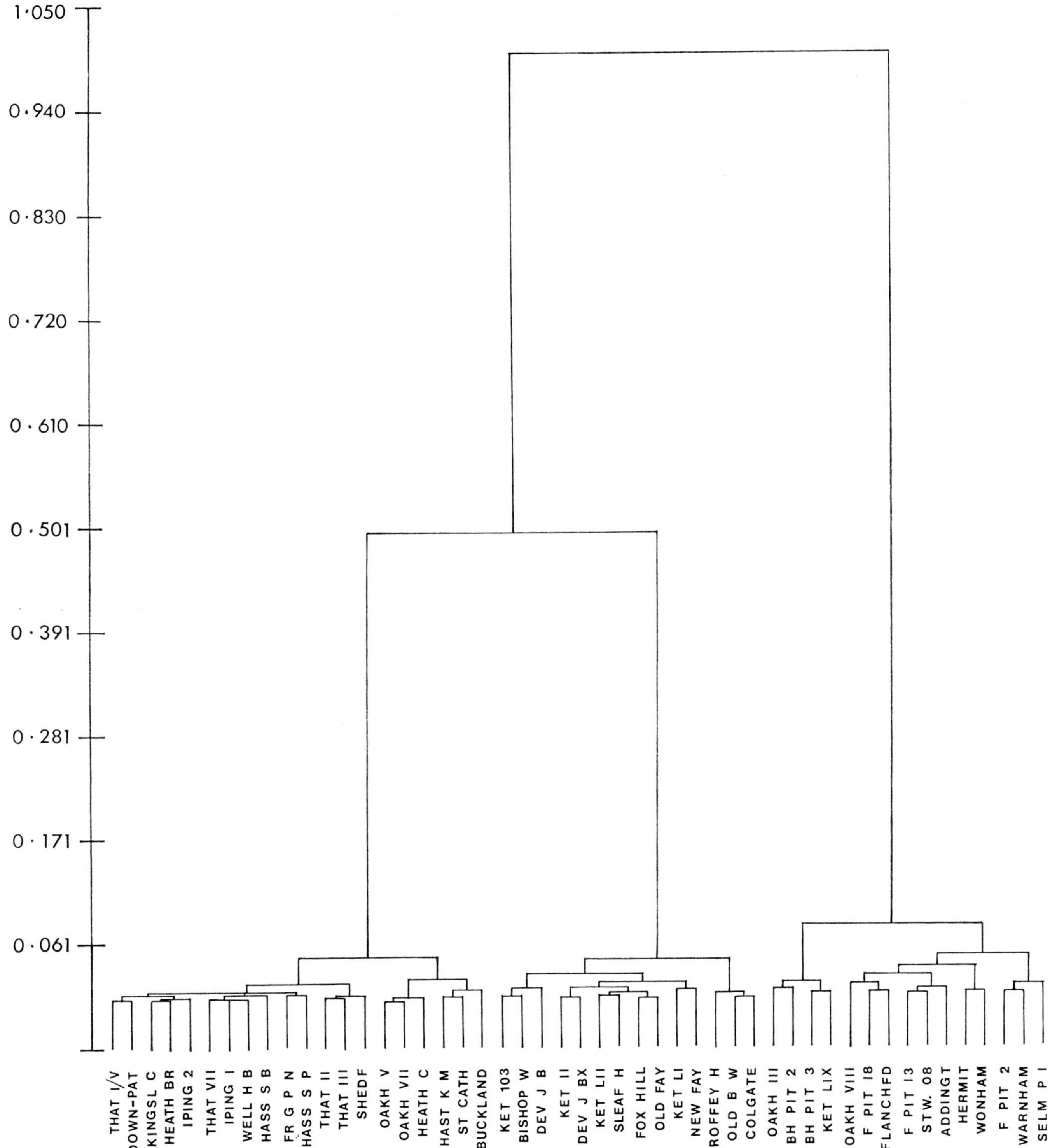

Fig 7 Wealden Mesolithic.   Cluster analysis of principal sites

line would coincide neatly with the northern coast of an expanding 'Channel Sea', with an average increase in width for the Sussex coastal plain of 15 miles (25 km).

Some eleven sites within the Weald and four just outside—Heath Brow, near Farnham (Rankine, in Oakley *et al*, 1939, 115), Shedfield (south Hants: Draper, 1968), Downton and Wellock's Hill, near Basingstoke—can be attributed to the Maglemosian, the Sussex find-spots clustering on the south-western arc of the Lower Greensand at Hassocks (South Bank), Heath Common, near Storrington, and Iping I and II (Fitzhall) near Midhurst. Of these assemblages that from Hassocks derives from surface collection, while a fifth Sussex site, West Heath, near West Harting, was omitted from the formal analysis since only a small proportion of the original finds survives in Chichester Museum and could be re-examined. Among the published illustrations, however, there is nothing (Clark, 1932b; Brailsford, 1937) which would not fit into a Maglemosian context.

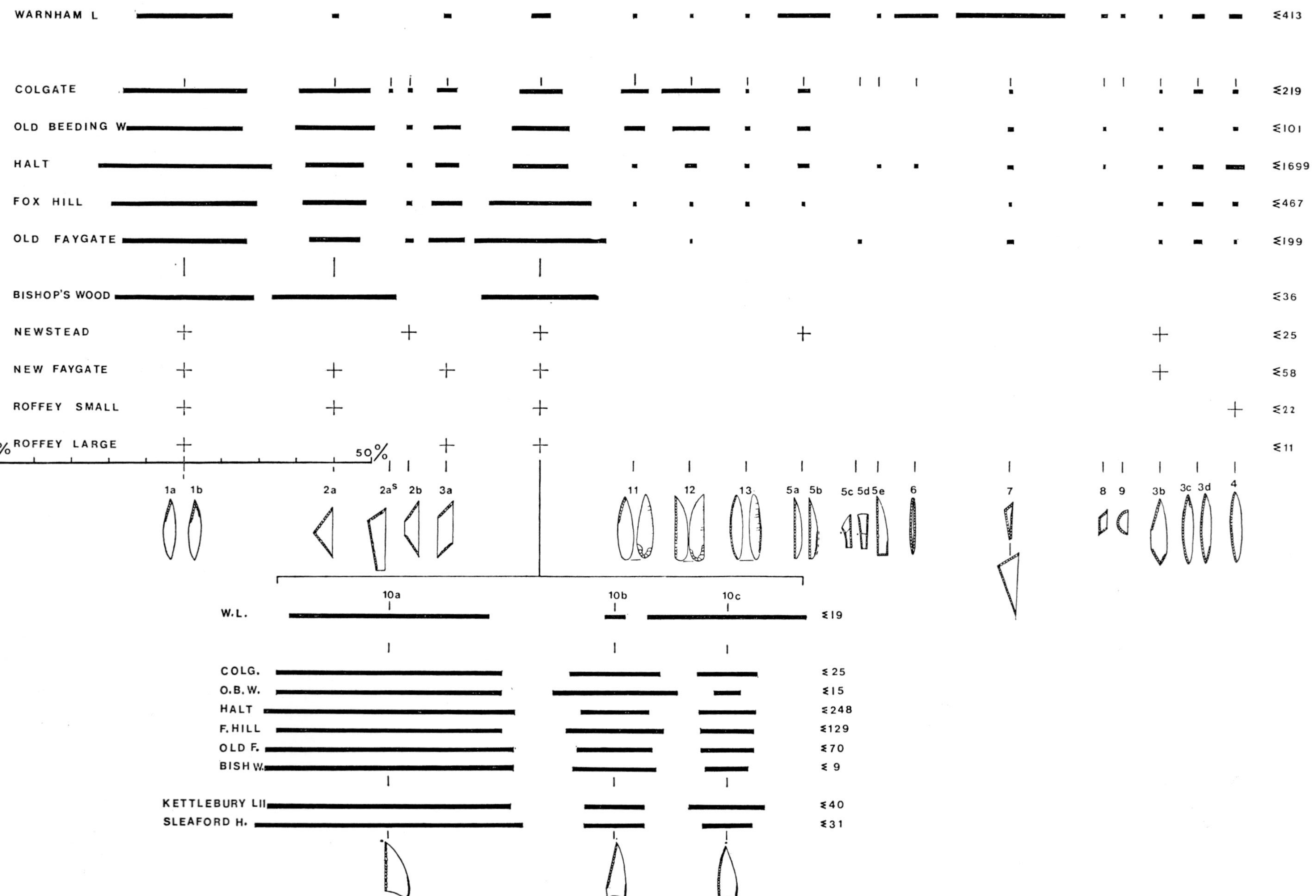

Fig 8   Content of microlithic sites near Horsham

Sadly, too, the material excavated from the summit of Blackdown Hill, near Haslemere (Swanton, 1904) has become confused with finds from other local sites (Clark, 1932a, fig 38, nos 18 and 24), and while the bulk would again fit an early context it cannot now be properly evaluated. The existence, however, of further possible early sites is suggested by the identification of at least five other concentrations of artefacts, all apparently associated with obliquely blunted points, on Iping and Minsted Commons, and also by the size of many of the obliquely blunted points from Selmeston, Hastings (see below), and the Honeywood collection from St Leonard's Forest.

In suggesting absolute ages for these early assemblages from Sussex we are dependent, at present, on making statistical comparisons with the most securely dated Maglemosian assemblages in south-eastern England: Oakhanger VII (phase 2) near Selborne with six determinations all close to 7000 bc, and Thatcham sites I/V and IIIA on the Kennet whose radiocarbon dates appear to fall into the first half of the 8th millennium bc (Churchill, 1962). Significantly within the cluster analysis, while the majority of early sites including both sites at Iping and Hassocks South Bank have joined with Thatcham, the assemblage from Heath Common has instead linked with Oakhanger sites V and VII to form a small subgroup low down the diagram, these sites standing apart in their possession of a markedly higher proportion of convex-backed points (classes 3c, 3d, and 4) and relatively fewer simple obliquely blunted points. If this separation is interpreted as being, locally at least, of chronological significance, it might be possible to argue that the assemblages from Iping and from Hassocks which clustered with Thatcham belong to the first part of the 8th millennium bc, ie to a moment before the local radiocarbon record opens, and to a stage earlier than the assemblage from Heath Common.

The absence of any *demonstrably* early site within the Ashdown Forest should probably be seen as a function of the state of present research, where while find-spots are being now rapidly identified, samples of microliths *sufficiently large* to indicate clearly the existence of such an early site are not yet available.

The analysis, as performed on this south-east English material, stands apart from that which would be achieved for any other area of Britain by breaking down into *three* rather than only *two* major clusters. While, as here, the first cluster would be made up of early (or 'Maglemosian') assemblages, the second cluster to be formed would be made up by assemblages whose principal microlithic components are narrow scalene microtriangles (class 7, Fig 6) and rod-like backed-bladelets (class 5), assemblages which would in the past have been termed as of 'Sauveterrian' affinities (Clark, 1955) and currently as 'later Mesolithic' (Jacobi, 1973; Mellars, 1974). Plotting of radiocarbon dates for these assemblages suggests that this 'micro-triangle' technology appeared earliest in the area south of the Massif Central (Jacobi, 1976, fig 7; Kozlowski, 1976, fig 2) and had reached northern England close to 6800 bc at a time when this portion of the island was still connected by a narrowing land-bridge to north Holland. For southern England, however, the earliest absolute age estimates for this technology of approximately 6500 bc derive from the lower filling of pit III at Broomhill, near Romsey (O'Malley and Jacobi, in press), while an estimate of just over 6000 bc is available for a hearth associated with later microlith shapes in front of the Stonewall Shelter (Kent).

A minimum of 80 find-spots within the Weald and a further 9 on the Sussex coastal plain can be related to this 'later' technology in which, as in the rest of Britain, when both are present, narrow *scalene triangles* sometimes highly elongated are many times more numerous than triangles of *isosceles* outline (GEEM: 1970), and of which the 15 most significant (surviving) assemblages from Hampshire (Broomhill pits II and III) and the Weald have combined to form the right-hand cluster of Fig 7, a cluster which by incorporating Warnham Lodge (Fig 8, top line) has separated it from the other 'classic' Horsham sites. The numbers of microliths from the individual sites at High Rocks were too few to allow inclusion into the analysis, although the small scalene triangles and rods from site F (Money, 1960, fig 19, nos 20–22) fit well with the radiocarbon dates obtained (see above).

While all these southern sites will cluster with 'later' assemblages with microtriangles from northern England, two features would tend to sort them into a separate *subgroup* within any such overall analysis: (1) the presence in some assemblages—most noticeably Selmeston, Farnham (pit II) and Warnham Lodge, all of which had clearly been large and complex sites—of a relatively large number of obliquely blunted and basally retouched (Horsham) points, quite possibly residual from earlier phases of activity at the same spots; and (2) a considerably higher ratio of rod-like microliths to scalene triangles with rods outnumbering triangles in the small subgroup formed in the present analysis by Oakhanger site III, Kettlebury LIX, and Broomhill.

As in northern England, however, these later industries divide into those which do or do not contain a range of specialized 'geometric' microliths—microlunates (class 9), microrhomboids (class 8), and micro'tranchets' (classes 5c and 5d) the two latter shapes not appearing in assemblages dated to before 5000 bc (Jacobi, in preparation) —ie close to the Boreal/Atlantic transition. It would be tempting, given that these novel shapes are recorded from only twelve of the 80 'later' find-spots identified within the Weald (cf The Hermitage, Stonewall, Warnham Lodge, and Selmeston) to suggest decreased exploitation after about 5000 bc, perhaps correlating with the high values for lime pollen recorded for nearly all Atlantic pollen diagrams from south-eastern England (Birks *et al*, 1975; Girling and Greig, 1977) including the Lower Greensand. In Denmark comparable pollen values have been interpreted as indicative of a lime woodland (Iversen, 1973) with a canopy sufficiently closed to sharply reduce the light reaching the forest floor, and hence in turn reduce potential browse. Thus ungulate yields within this environment may, it could be suggested, have been markedly less than those to have been expected below other woodland types. In short, south-eastern Britain may have been relatively less favourable to hunting groups than western (Jacobi, 1977b, in press) or northern Britain, for the latter part of the Mesolithic—hence the low apparent representation of find-spots demonstrably later than 5000 bc.

Attractive as this proposition may seem, it breaks down in two essential respects. Firstly while values for lime pollen can be shown to be higher in south-eastern England than elsewhere, the existence of a light-excluding canopy cannot be demonstrated (J Sheldon, *pers comm*). Indeed, for Denmark the suggestion was made at a moment when the real extent of inland Mesolithic settlement within this 'lime woodland' had not been fully grasped. Secondly, it is now apparent that even in south-eastern England, not all microlithic assemblages later than 5000 bc need contain these novel shapes. Thus, while their *presence* argues occupation after this date, it is not in fact possible to compare real totals of find-spots earlier or later than this threshold.

Having considered the qualities of the Sussex assemblages which have gone to make up the left- and right-hand clusters of Fig 7, and suggested that these corresponded to the early (Maglemosian) and later Mesolithic elsewhere in Britain, it remains to examine the centre cluster which renders this analysis distinct. This cluster has linked fourteen assemblages: six of them are surface sites east of Horsham, all except Fox Hill investigated by Attree and Piffard, while the seventh sample of Sussex material incorporated derives from a small site at Bishop's Wood near Warninglid excavated in the late 1940s (Newnham, 1958). Of the remainder, all are excavated samples, and all, except that from Sleaford Heath in East Hampshire, are from sites on the West Surrey Greensand east of Churt, that from Kettlebury 103 deriving from an excavation, using fine sieving techniques, still in progress.

In considering the material from the original Horsham sites it should be emphasized that not only are the collections surface ones, but that they derive from searching over very large areas of ground, sometimes, as in the case of Old Faygate, incorporating more than one flint concentration (Piffard Mss: Lewes Museum). Secondly, in the original publication of these sites (Clark, 1934b), only a part of the material was considered, the finds being unequally divided between the British and Lewes Museums with the implicit suggestion that that portion now at Lewes would represent, if considered in isolation, a biased sample of the whole. A small quantity of material has also passed to the Institute of Archaeology in London. In the present analysis, therefore, and in the data presented on Fig 8, these various collections have been recombined, but Honeywood's contribution, now at Lewes, omitted since the original publication a century ago (Honeywood, 1877), does not, despite comment in the subsequent literature, inspire confidence in either absolute provenance or the degree of selectivity involved.

The technological features which serve to link these sites, both excavated and surface, and also to define the cluster are the combination with obliquely blunted points, markedly shorter than those found in early Mesolithic contexts, of many hollow-based 'Horsham' points (class 10) and triangles (not microtriangles) of isosceles (class 2a) rather than scalene outline. Rarer, but consistently present are bitruncated 'rhombic' points (class 3a). So far significantly absent from all the excavated samples are narrow scalene triangles and other clearly later shapes, and it may be reasonable to suspect that their very rare presence among the surface samples with such forms (see above) as the microtranchet (Old Faygate) or microrhomboids (Halt and Old Beeding Wood) could, like the pressure flaked arrowheads recovered, represent later activity.

On three of the Horsham sites (Halt, Old Beeding Wood, and Colgate) this range of shapes is supplemented by symmetrical (class 11) and asymmetrical (class 12) microliths with their bases trimmed by inverse flaking to a pointed or rounded outline. The representation of these shapes, in part at least at the expense of the concave-based 'Horsham' points, is sufficiently strong to cause these three sites to form a distinct subgroup within the general cluster. Backed bladelets (class 5) broader than the narrow 'rods' characteristic of 'later' assemblages, can on these three sites perhaps be interpreted as unfinished points (class 12). While hollow-based points have been recognized from numerous sites in lowland England outside the Weald, and while isosceles triangles and obliquely blunted points

can occur in either early or later associations in most areas of Britain, the excavated samples within this cluster stand apart from assemblages elsewhere in Britain not only in the combination of these three shapes, together with bitruncated points, but also in an absence of distinctive later Mesolithic microlith shapes, most noticeably scalene 'microtriangles'. Similarly, while a mixture of equipment representing varying stages within the Mesolithic would scarcely be surprising for the six Horsham surface assemblages, and three of these sites appear to show a development of specialized inversely retouched points not found on the others (Fig 8), in each case isosceles triangles are many times more numerous than scalene forms, and the microlithic assemblages are dominated by the same, relatively small, range of shapes.

No absolute dating evidence is available from any of the sites within this cluster. However, at Oakhanger VII, where some half-dozen 'Horsham' points were recovered, those for which stratigraphic data could be recorded were found (Phase 3: Rankine, 1961, 2) several inches above the main artefact concentration (Phase 2) and hence apparently above the level of the radiocarbon determinations. Apart from a single obliquely blunted point, further associated microliths, if any, were not separately recorded, but the total microlith collection from the excavation includes no specimen which could not derive either from an early (Maglemosian) context, or from one of the excavated samples just considered. All one can strictly infer from these observations is the presence of Horsham points apparently higher in a mineral profile than charcoal dated close to 7000 bc, above a Maglemosian industry, and unaccompanied by any later form of microlith.

It must remain speculative, however, if sites with only isolated Horsham points and with assemblages dominated by obliquely blunted points, which have joined the left-hand cluster of the diagram (cf Hassocks (Stone Pound Pit: Toms, 1907; 1915), the Hastings Kitchen Midden, or St Catherine's Hill, near Guildford (Gabel, 1976)) could represent early stages in the local evolution of a Horsham technology, or the mixture of Horsham points with early assemblages which once had been 'stratified' as at Oakhanger. That no later microlithic shape is present among the 170 examples traced from Hastings would, if the argument presented below is accepted, suggest occupation within the early Boreal, when with a correspondingly *reduced sea-level* the home range of the 'kitchen midden' site will have incorporated only dry land.

In the absence, then, of independent dating evidence for this technology, it is necessary to look within mainland Europe for possible clues, precisely as did Clark some 40 years ago. Such a search suggests that the moment when one would be *most likely* to find a comparable technology (a predominance of isosceles forms among the triangles associated with basally retouched points) should be close to 7000 bc, while the area of its occurrence would have lain south of the Maglemosian technoterritory where such basally retouched points appear absent, that is, in Belgium, northern and central France, and south-western Germany. Over this large area recent work has defined three chronological stages within the Mesolithic (Rozoy, 1976) the early ('Stade Ancien') being distinguished most clearly from the middle stage by isosceles triangles as numerous as, or more numerous than, scalene forms. By the 'middle stage', taken (arbitrarily for most areas) as commencing close to 7000 bc, this ratio is reversed with, locally, scalene triangles the most common microlith category found, a sequence confirmed by stratigraphic successions at the Jägerhaus-Höhle bei Bronnen (Taute, 1972; 1973) and at Birsmatten (Bandi, 1963). The layers at Jägerhaus with only isosceles forms among the triangles are placed either side of 7000 bc, while layer 5 at Birsmatten, where they outnumber scalene forms and are similarly associated with obliquely blunted and basally retouched forms, is dated on the basis of pollen evidence to the end of the Pre-boreal, taken to end close to 6800 bc (Müller, in Bandi, 1963, 86).

While industries with many scalene triangles corresponding to the 'middle stage' were certainly present in southern Holland by 6700 bc (Jacobi, 1976, 72; Rozoy, 1976, fig 18) and northern Holland by 6600 bc and very possibly slightly earlier, if they indeed reached northern Britain via a land connexion from here (see above), absolute age estimates are, however, lacking for sites attributed to the 'Stade Ancien' in southern Holland, Belgium, the Ardennes, and the Paris Basin. Indeed, the only relevant determination would appear to derive from the Cave of Mannlefelsen (Oberlag: Haut-Rhin) where layer Q with an industry apparently dominated by isosceles triangles and containing basally retouched points is dated Gif 2387 = 7080 bc ± 160 (Thévenin and Sainty, 1974; Thévenin, 1976).

In short, the very sketchy evidence at our disposal suggests that in northern Europe industries with obliquely blunted points and triangles of isosceles outline (Early Maglemosian) precede those with many narrow scalene forms, the transition falling rather after 7000 bc, those scalene triangles in 8th millennium contexts being markedly large (Jacobi, 1977b for references). In western Europe, south of the Rhine, industries of this earlier stage (the 'Stade Ancien') also regularly include basally retouched points. Clark in his 1939 discussion of the Wealden Mesolithic stressed (98) that Britain had '. . . throughout history . . . stood at the corner of Europe benefiting by influences . . . from a variety of continental sources . . .'. While the remainder of Britain could be argued to show a two-fold chronological sequence—an 'Early Mesolithic' with the closest parallels in Denmark and northern Germany and a 'Later Mesolithic' deriving from northern Holland, it may be possible within the Weald to recognize a three-fold sequence in which, while industries conforming to the 'Early' and 'Later Mesolithic' elsewhere in the island can be readily distinguished, a third association of microlith shapes—at present confined to *within* the Weald—and with its closest analogues in the 'Mésolithique ancien' of France and Belgium appears also to be present. The limited continental data suggest that a technology with such a combination of shapes would most likely have been 'fashionable' close to 7000 bc, and it is suggested, albeit tentatively, that industries of this type, to which it is further proposed that the epithets 'Horsham' or 'Wealden' should be *restricted*, might slot in chronologically later than the local 'Maglemosian' but earlier than the appearance within the Weald, apparently at some point within the 7th millennium bc, of the more widely recognized 'Later' Mesolithic industries.

Particular combinations of microliths can be seen as individual 'solutions' to the problems of projectile construction, and their individual uptake must ultimately represent a choice on the part of any social group from among a number of possible 'solutions' current at any one time. Thus again the association of core-adzes, represented among the *excavated* material at Bishop's Wood and less certainly by surface finds on the Horsham sites, with a combination of microliths with which it is not elsewhere associated, and the use of core-adzes with 'Later' microlithic material right up until the end of the Mesolithic in south-eastern Britain, represents again a continued *selection*

by groups in a particular area for a piece of equipment which had been in use locally for a millennium. Elsewhere in Britain and northern Europe it was allowed simply to pass out of use.

For Sussex and indeed for the Weald as a whole there can be little doubt that the very sharp increase in the number of Mesolithic find-spots identified within the Ashdown Forest (Tebbutt, 1975) highlights this as the next logical area for research. Firstly, little early work (or rather collecting) has gone on in this region, and there is thus every probability of still being able to build up highly realistic distribution maps on ground less devastated by the recent human activity which has destroyed so many of the Lower Greensand heaths. Secondly, while it is still possible to investigate horizontally single-period occupation sites on the Greensand, the chances of dating these sites are by the physical qualities of the sites themselves minimal (see below: Oakhanger is an outstanding exception). Of 59 cave/rockshelter sites in England and Wales known to have been used in the Mesolithic, 17 (or 30%) are in the Sussex part of the Ashdown Forest, the first being identified as early as the 1930s (Hannah, 1932; Clark, 1934c). While their stratigraphies have proved complex (Money, 1960), the few investigated have nearly all yielded charcoal and their profiles have been shown to be relatively deep. Thus the possibility of building up an absolute chronology for the Sussex Mesolithic appears ultimately greater in the Ashdown Forest than on the Greensand.

Acknowledgements

I must thank Dr I H Longworth for permission to study the extensive Sussex collections, preserved in the British Museum, and the staffs of Barbican House, Brighton, Chichester, and Worthing Museums for allowing access to the material in their possession, and for help in very many ways. Mrs W M Rankine and Mr R G V Venables made available much unpublished material from their excavations, and without their help little start could have been made on interpreting the older Sussex finds. Mr C F Tebbutt and Mr E W Holden guided the research in many ways. Hazel Martingell prepared Figs 7 and 8, and helped organize all the data for computing and with the preparation of this text.

References

Abbott, W J L, 1896   'The Hastings Kitchen Midden', *J Anthrop Inst*, **25**, 122–45

Bandi, H G, 1963   'Birsmatten Basigrotte', *Acta Bernensia*, **1**, 271

Bell, M and Tatton-Brown, T, 1975   'A field survey of the Parish of Elsted and adjacent areas, West Sussex', *Bull Inst Archaeol*, **12**, 58–64

Birks, H J B, Deacon, J, and Peglar, S, 1975   'Pollen maps for the British Isles 5000 years ago', *Proc Roy Soc London*, Series B, **189**, 87–105

Brailsford, J W, 1937   'A new Microlithic site on West Heath', *Sussex Archaeol Collect*, **78**, 224–9

Churchill, D M, 1962   'The stratigraphy of the Mesolithic sites III and V at Thatcham, Berkshire, England', *Proc Prehist Soc*, **28**, 362–70

Clark, J G D, 1932a   *The Mesolithic Age in Britain*, Cambridge Univ Press

Clark, J G D, 1932b   'A Microlithic flaking site at West Heath, W Harting', *Sussex Archaeol Collect*, **73**, 145–55

Clark, J G D, 1934a   'A Late Mesolithic site at Selmeston, Sussex', *Antiq J*, **14**, 134–58

Clark, J G D, 1934b   'The classification of a microlithic culture: the Tardenoisian of Horsham', *Archaeol J*, **90** (1933), 52–77

Clark, J G D, 1934c   'Microliths from a rock shelter in central Sussex', *Proc Prehist Soc East Anglia*, **7**, 442–3

Clark, J G D, 1955   'A Microlithic industry from the Cambridgeshire fenland and other industries of Sauveterrian affinities from Britain', *Proc Prehist Soc*, **21**, 3–20

Clark, J G D, and Rankine, W F, 1939   'Excavations at Farnham, Surrey (1937–38): the Horsham Culture and the question of Mesolithic dwellings', *ibid*, **5**, 1, 61–118

Dimbleby, G W, 1960   'Report on pollen and charcoal', in Rankine, W F and W M and Dimbleby, G W, 1960   'Further excavations at a Mesolithic site at Oakhanger, Selborne, Hants', *ibid*, **26**, 246–62

Draper, J C, 1968   'Mesolithic distribution in south-east Hampshire', *Proc Hampshire Field Club*, **23**, Part 3, 110–19

Ellaby, R, 1976   'Reigate: Flanchford', *Surrey Archaeol Soc Bull*, **124**

Ellaby, R, 1977   'A Mesolithic site at Wonham', *Surrey Archaeol Collect*, **71**, 7–12

Gabel, G, 1976   'St Catherine's Hill: a Mesolithic site near Guildford', *Res Vol Surrey Archaeol Soc*, **3**, 77–101

GEEM (Cl Barrière, R Daniel, H Delporte, M Escalon de Fonton, R Parent, Abbé J Roche, Dr J G Rozoy, J Tixier, E Vignard), 1970   'Epipaléolithique. Mésolithique. Les microlithes géometriques', *BSPF* (1969), 355–66

Girling, M and Greig, J, 1977   'Palaeoecological investigations of a site at Hampstead Heath, London', *Nature*, **268**, 45–7

Hannah, I C, 1932   'Philpots Camp, West Hoathley', *Sussex Archaeol Collect*, **73**, 157–68

Honeywood, T, 1877   'Discovery of flint implements near Horsham, in St Leonard's Forest', *ibid*, **27**, 177–83

Iversen, J, 1973   'The development of Denmark's nature since the Last Glacial', *Danm Geol Unders V Raekke Nr* **7c**, 126, Copenhagen

Jacobi, R M, 1973   'Aspects of the Mesolithic Age in Great Britain', in *The Mesolithic in Europe* (ed S K Kozlowski)

Jacobi, R M, 1976   'Britain inside and outside Mesolithic Europe', *Proc Prehist Soc*, **42**, 67–84

Jacobi, R M, 1977a   'Population and landscape in Mesolithic Lowland Britain', CBA, *The effect of man on the landscape: the Lowland Zone* (in press)

Jacobi, R M, 1977b   'The Mesolithic in Wales', in *Before the Bluestones* (eds J A Taylor and D Q Bowen)

Keef, P A M, Wymer, J J, and Dimbleby, G W, 1965   'A Mesolithic site on Iping Common, Sussex, England', *Proc Prehist Soc*, **31**, 85–92

Kozlowski, S K, 1976   'Les courants interculturels dans le Mésolithique de l'Europe occidentale', *UISPP IXe Congrès Nice, Colloque* **19**, 135–60

Lacaille, A D, 1961   'Mesolithic facies in Middlesex and London', *Trans London and Middlesex Archaeol Soc*, **20**, Part 3, 101–50

Mellars, P A, 1974   'The Palaeolithic and Mesolithic', in *British Prehistory: a new outline* (ed C Renfrew), Duckworth, 41–99

Money, J H, 1960   'Excavations at High Rocks, Tunbridge Wells 1954–6', *Sussex Archaeol Collect*, **98**, 173–221

Money, J H, 1962   'Excavations at High Rocks, Tunbridge Wells 1954–6', *ibid*, **100**, 149–51

Newnham, W, 1958   'A Mesolithic site at Bishop's Wood, Warninglid', *Sussex Notes and Queries*, **15**, no 2, 63–4

Oakley, K P, Rankine, W F, and Lowther, A W G, 1939   *A survey of the prehistory of the Farnham district*, Surrey Archaeol Soc

Rankine, W F, 1936   'A Mesolithic site at Farnham', *Surrey Archaeol Collect*, **44**, 25–46

Rankine, W F, 1948   'Some remarkable flints from West Surrey Mesolithic sites', *ibid*, **49**, 1–14

Rankine, W F, 1949a   'Mesolithic chipping floors in the wind-blown deposits of West Surrey', *ibid*, **50**, 1–8

Rankine, W F, 1949b   'A Mesolithic survey of the West Surrey Greensand', *Res Papers Surrey Archaeol Soc*, **2**, 50

Rankine, W F, 1961   'A Mesolithic flaking floor at Oakhanger, Selborne, Hants: epitomised supplement to the abstract of the report published in the Proceedings of the Prehistoric Society 1960', 4 pp (privately printed)

Rozoy, J G, 1976   'Chronologie de l'Epipaléolithique de la Meuse à la Mediterranée'. *Extrait du Congrès Préhistorique de France*, XXe Session, Provence, 1974 (1976), 525–50

Seagrief, S C and Godwin, H, 1960   'Pollen diagrams from southern England: Elstead Surrey', *New Phytol*, **59**, 84–91

Smith, R A, 1934   'Examples of Mesolithic art', *Brit Mus Quart*, no 121, **8**, 144–5

Standing, S, 1964   *Flints from Millfields Farm, Rowhook*, 7

Swanton, E W, 1904   'Note upon some interesting Neolithic weapons recently found on Blackdown, near Haslemere', *South-Eastern Naturalist*

Taute, W, 1972   'Funde aus der Steinzeit in der Jägerhaus-Höhle bei Bronnen', Sonderdruck aus dem Thorbecke Bildbuch *Fridingen-Stadt an der oberen Donau*, 21–6

Taute, W, 1973   'Neue Forschungen zur Chronologie von Spätpaläolithikum und Mesolithikum in Süddeutschland', Neue paläolithische und mesolithische Ausgrabungen in der Bundesrepublik Deutschland, *IX INQUA Congress*, New Zealand, 59–66

Tebbutt, C F, 1975   'The prehistoric occupation of the Ashdown Forest area of the Weald', *Sussex Archaeol Collect*, **112** (1974), 34–43

Thévenin, A, 1976   'Paléo-Histoire de l'Est de la France du 7e au 5e millénaire avant JC', *UISPP IXe Congrès Nice, Colloque* **19**, 71–92

Thévenin, A and Sainty, J, 1974   'Une nouvelle stratigraphie de Post-glaciaire: l'abri du Mannlefelsen I à Oberlag (Haut-Rhin)', *BSPF*, **69**, 6–7

Thorley, A, 1971   'Vegetational history in the Vale of the Brooks', *Guide to Sussex excursions*, Inst Brit Geogr, 47–50

Toms, H S, 1907   'Pigmy flint implements found near Brighton', *Brighton and Hove Natural History and Philosophical Society*, 1–10

Toms, H S, 1915   'Notes on Pigmy flint implements found in Sussex', in *The Antiquary* (July 1915), 246–50

Wooldridge, S W and Goldring, F, 1953   *The Weald*, New Naturalist Series, Collins

Wymer, J J, 1962   'Excavations at the Maglemosian sites at Thatcham, Berkshire, England', *Proc Prehist Soc*, **28**, 329–61

Peter Drewett

The few radiocarbon dates from Sussex would suggest the presence of Neolithic elements by *c* 4300 BC and that they survived until *c* 2500 BC. There is strong evidence that during this period there existed in Sussex socially coherent and autonomous groups occupying discrete territories (Fig 9). The cycle of development from origins through to collapse of the social order appears, therefore, to span some 1800 years. The material culture, in so far as it reflects the social order, would suggest a rapid development of the social system which may have reached its point of climax as early as 4000 BC. By about 3500 BC the organization in Sussex may have begun to decline, although some elements survived until as late as 2500 BC. The late Neolithic in Sussex does not appear to have received the social boost, indicated by henges, apparent in Wessex and elsewhere.

The environmental background

Pollen analysis from the Vale of the Brooks south of Lewes indicated that the Downs around the Brooks were still wooded in the Neolithic, with primary clearance not beginning until the Middle Bronze Age (Thorley, 1971). However, molluscan analysis from three Neolithic sites, Alfriston, Offham, and Bishopstone, indicates an element of clearance in the Neolithic at all these sites. In addition, charcoal from Bishopstone (pit 357) indicated the presence of hawthorn, oak, hazel, ash, yew, and dogwood (Bell, 1977), while oak, hawthorn, and hazel were present in primary contexts at Offham (Drewett, 1977a), and hawthorn and birch at Alfriston (Drewett, 1975a). Hazel, hawthorn, and ash have also been found at New Barn Down, in pit X (Curwen, 1934a, 168). Molluscan analysis at Bishopstone (2510 bc) suggests that an anthropogenic woodland clearance may have taken place during the early part of the Neolithic. Samples from pit Fe 570 produced woodland fauna, while samples from the top of pit Fe 357 indicated a clear decrease in woodland intensity. However, analysis

of Neolithic levels under an adjacent lynchet showed an absence of woodland species with open-country species dominating at an early stage (Bell, 1977). Evidence from Offham and Alfriston indicates at least some clearance in the Neolithic. Mollusca from the old land surface under the oval barrow at Alfriston (2360 bc) suggest an environment, some time before the mound was built, of open grassland with a few shrubs (Thomas, in Drewett, 1975a). At Offham, molluscan analysis suggested that the cause-wayed enclosure was constructed within a small woodland clearing (Drewett, 1977a). More indirectly, the distribution of broken axes and arrowheads around the Neolithic settlement on Bullock Down (Drewett, 1977b) would indicate extensive use of the woodland resources around the settlement, with the presence of broken stone and flint axes suggesting some clearance.

The little evidence we have would, therefore, suggest that the Downs were lightly wooded in the Neolithic, with perhaps hawthorn, oak, and hazel occurring frequently, but with extensive, though local, clearance around settlement sites and perhaps smaller areas cleared for the construction of communal monuments. A similar picture is emerging from the Greensand areas (Holden, 1975) while, at present, evidence from other areas is absent. It is likely that the Ashdown Sands and the coastal plain may show similar localized clearance in the Neolithic, while it remains likely that the woods on the Wealden Clays remained only as an intermittently used woodland resource. The seventeen leaf-shaped arrowheads listed as early as 1936 from the Wealden Clays (Curwen, 1936a, 18) indicate some Neolithic presence in the Wealden Clay forest.

Settlements

The evidence for Neolithic settlement sites in Sussex is still very scanty, consisting of two sites where pits have been found during the excavation of sites of later date, a series of surface flint concentrations, thought to indicate

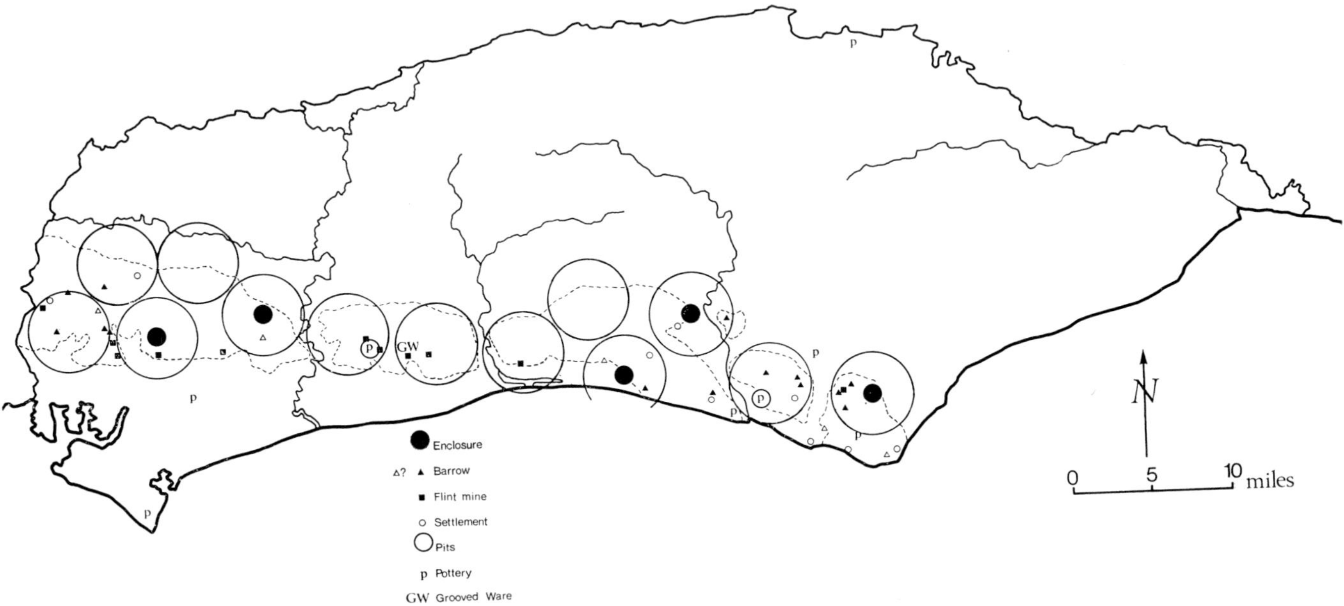

Fig 9   Neolithic Sussex.   Large circles represent possible territories (see Fig 13)

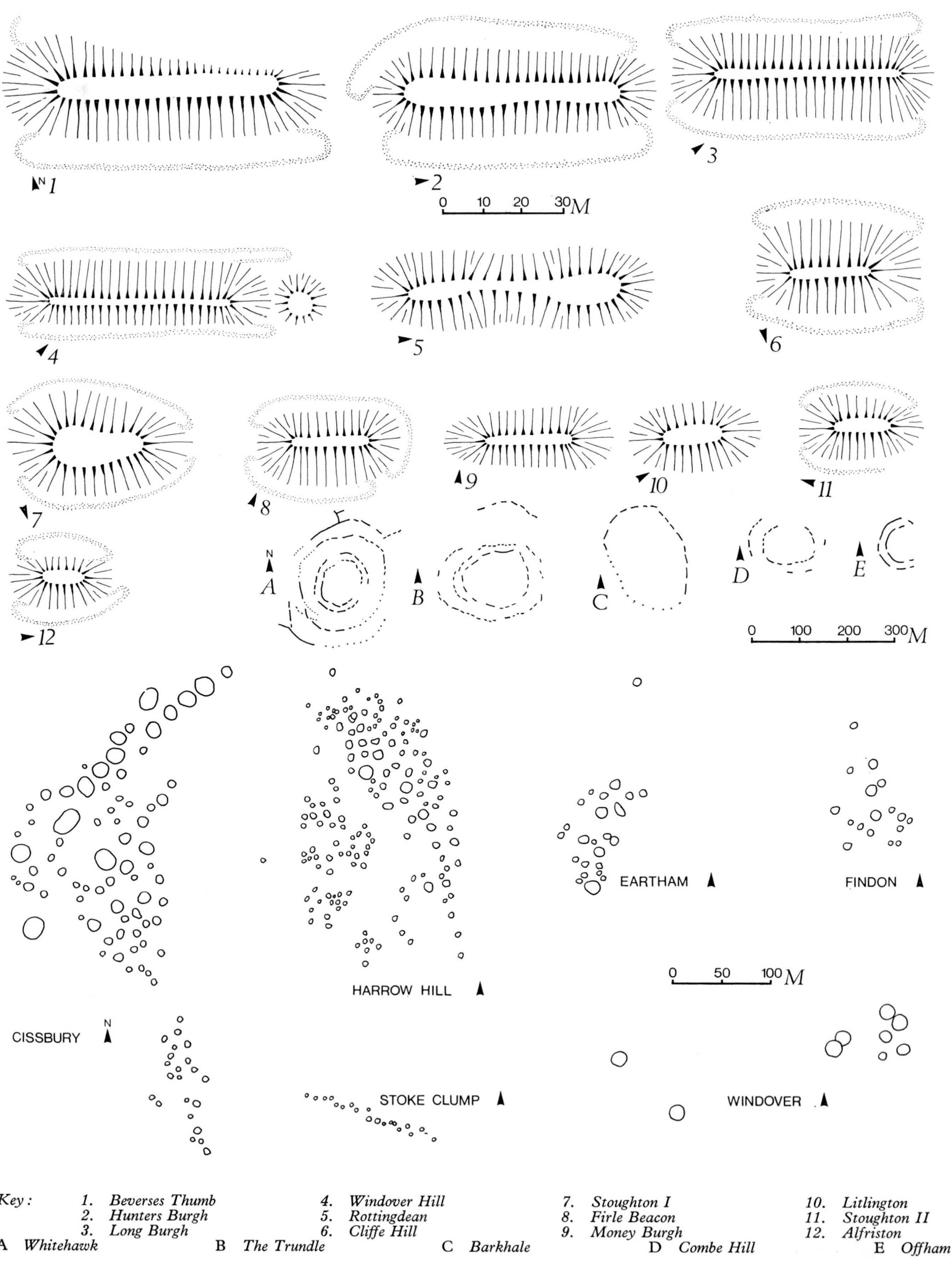

Key:
1. *Beverses Thumb*
2. *Hunters Burgh*
3. *Long Burgh*
4. *Windover Hill*
5. *Rottingdean*
6. *Cliffe Hill*
7. *Stoughton I*
8. *Firle Beacon*
9. *Money Burgh*
10. *Litlington*
11. *Stoughton II*
12. *Alfriston*

A *Whitehawk* B *The Trundle* C *Barkhale* D *Combe Hill* E *Offham*

Fig 10 *Neolithic communal works. Barrows 1–12. Causewayed enclosures A–E and flint mines below*

plough-spread occupation levels (eg Tebbutt, 1974) and some evidence for sporadic occupation of the Wealden rock shelters (eg Money, 1960). Pit X at New Barn Down, Clapham, contained round-based pottery of the early Neolithic ceramic tradition, a flint axe, scrapers, part of two sandstone rubbers, and 'a small quantity of animal bones' (Curwen, 1934a, 156). Several other pits at New Barn Down were excavated, but produced inconclusive dating evidence. A similar picture of pits and hollows, some with occupation material and some without, came from the recent excavations at Bishopstone. The two largest pits at Bishopstone were interpreted by the excavator, Martin Bell, as possibly storage pits. Both had near-vertical sides with pit Fe 357 being circular and 0·85 m deep and pit Fe 711 being oval and 1·54 m deep. In addition, six smaller pits with depths ranging from 0·20 to 0·50 m may well have also been storage pits. Two other irregular pits and two small scoops could have been dug to obtain flint or chalk. Four slight gullies, however, may represent the last traces of timber buildings.

In addition to these two almost certain settlement sites are a series of surface concentrations of Neolithic flint-work, and casual finds of Neolithic pottery, as at Selmeston (Drewett, 1975b) and Castle Hill, Newhaven (Field, 1939, 265). It is likely that the extensive concentrations of flintwork on the Downs (Fig 9) represent the last surviving traces of the settlement sites of the people constructing the causewayed enclosures and long barrows and digging the flint mines. The main problems with these sites are their size and the fact that most have been ploughed. Aerial photography and geophysical methods used on one such site at Bullock Down both produced disappointing results. At Bullock Down the broad extent of the site was defined by the distribution of earlier finds, together with a preliminary field survey. Two ploughed fields were available for intensive field survey over the winter of 1975–6. They were gridded using a 30 m grid and systematically walked. The surface collection revealed high concentrations of struck flakes, cores, axes, leaf-shaped arrowheads, scrapers, and serrated blades. It is proposed to continue this survey as more fields become available. In the light of this evidence, two small trenches (A and B) were excavated. The surface of the natural clay-with-flints was found some 0·27 m below the present surface. The modern ploughing reached a depth of some 0·20 m, although sherds of abraded pre-Roman Iron Age pottery suggest earlier ploughing disturbing lower layers. The two trenches were excavated on a 1 m grid, with the exact position of each flint and potsherd being recorded. The majority of the flintwork was found at the base of the modern plough-soil. The high concentration of flint flakes at the western end of trench B would suggest its close proximity to a flint-working floor. A general scatter of flints was found in trench A.

The evidence so far available from Bullock Down would indicate that this extensive site consists of a series of flint-working floors with blank areas between them. Future excavations may elucidate the many problems still surrounding these singularly unstudied sites.

Communal works

The most studied class of Neolithic site in Sussex is the causewayed enclosure (Fig 10). However, we still have no radiocarbon dates for them, although two carbon samples from Offham are currently at the British Museum. Five certain causewayed enclosures are known from Sussex. Two survive in West Sussex at The Trundle (Curwen, 1929a;

1931a) and Barkhale (Clipson, 1976), while three are known from East Sussex at Whitehawk (Williamson, 1930; Curwen, 1934b; 1936b), Combe Hill (Musson, 1950) and Offham Hill (Holden, 1973; Drewett, 1977a). All the enclosures consist of irregular circles of discontinuous ditches. Barkhale has one circle, Offham Hill and Combe Hill have two circles, while Whitehawk and The Trundle have four circles (Fig 10). It may be of significance that the three simpler enclosures (Barkhale, Offham, and Combe Hill) are all on the northern side of the Downs, while The Trundle and Whitehawk, being on a much larger scale, are on the southern side of the Downs. Also the southern pair enclose at least some of a hill top, whereas the northern three enclosures are on hill slopes. Figure 10 clearly illustrates the considerable variation in form and scale of the Sussex enclosures. However, the broadly similar scale of the inner enclosures at Whitehawk, The Trundle, Combe Hill, and Offham may indicate that originally they may have been more alike. Although it is uncertain whether all the circles at Whitehawk, The Trundle, and Combe Hill are contemporary, molluscan evidence from Offham (Thomas, in Drewett, 1977a) clearly indicates that the inner ditch is a primary feature with the outer ditch being added later.

None of the Sussex enclosures shows evidence for much activity in their interiors and, in common with causewayed enclosures elsewhere, the majority of the artefactual and faunal remains came from the ditches. Evidence from Offham, consisting of some 171 sherds (perhaps representing under 20 pots), only 23 flint implements, and a few animal bones (Drewett, 1977a) would suggest a very specialized function for at least that causewayed enclosure. A recent discussion on the function of these enclosures argued against their use for settlement, defence, as cattle compounds or trade centres (Drewett, 1977a). The currently accepted theory is that these enclosures represent communal meeting places (Smith, 1965), but with a far greater emphasis on ritual and burial than formerly suggested (Drewett, 1977a).

Unlike the causewayed enclosures, virtually no work has been done on the barrows of the Neolithic period in Sussex (Fig 10). Grinsell (1934) lists thirteen barrows: Alfriston, Stoughton I, Stoughton II, Litlington, Firle Beacon, Cliffe Hill, Money Burgh, Long Burgh, Rottingdean, Windover Hill, Hunter's Burgh, Beverses Thumb, and a doubtful example at Preston. Plans of two of these were published by the Curwens (1922), while five more plans were published by Toms (1924). By drawing all available plans to the same scale (Fig 10), a clear distinction between long barrows (1–5) and oval barrows (6–12) is apparent. A recent excavation of the oval barrow at Alfriston emphasizes the existence of oval barrows as a distinct class (Drewett, 1975a), probably appearing towards the end of the long barrow tradition. This oval barrow (Fig 11) was found to consist of a simple dump mound derived from material out of flanking ditches. It covered a single burial pit containing the crouched burial of a young female. The anomalous date for this burial (Drewett, 1975a, 151) is currently being reconsidered by the Radiocarbon Laboratory at Harwell. An antler pick from the ditch gave a radiocarbon date of 2360 ± 110 bc. Although this example was used for burial, evidence from elsewhere would suggest that some Neolithic barrows were not built primarily for burial, but were constructed to fulfil some ceremonial or religious function. Much more work is clearly needed on the long barrows in Sussex, both to date them more accurately, and to establish more detailed information about their function.

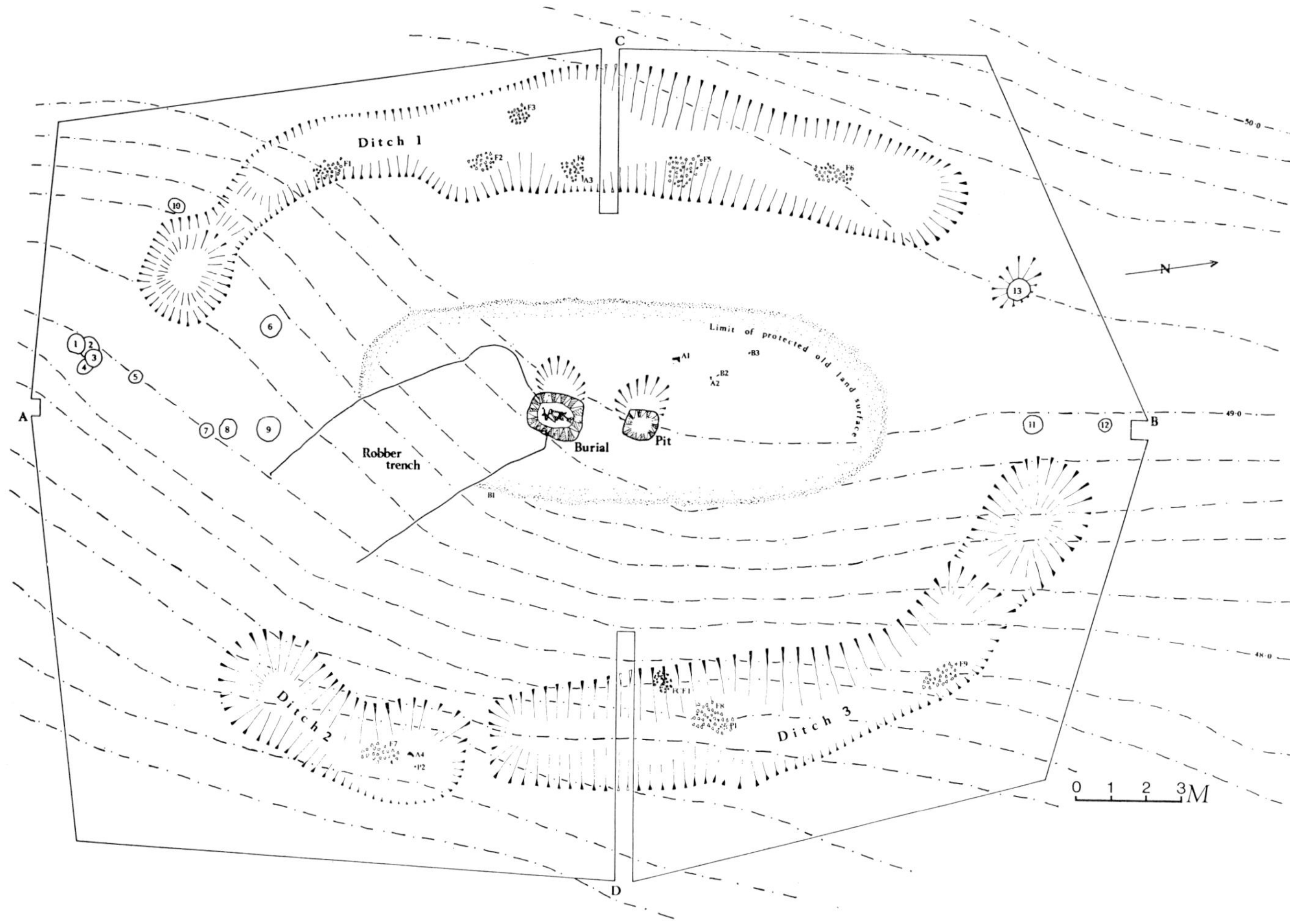

Fig 11   *Neolithic oval barrow excavated at Alfriston, 1974.   (After Drewett, 1975)*

Material culture

The surviving material culture from Neolithic Sussex falls into three distinct groups; flint and stone tools, pottery, and bone tools. This clearly represents only a fraction of the material culture actually in use, as organic materials like wood and leather clearly do not survive on most Sussex sites. Little systematic work has yet been undertaken on flintwork in Sussex, but three recent excavations illustrate the sharp contrast in the range of material from a settlement site (Bell, 1977), a barrow (Drewett, 1975a), and a causewayed enclosure (Drewett, 1977a).

Type *(mainly after Bell 1977)*	*Bishopstone:* *(settlement)*	*Alfriston:* *(barrow)*	*Offham:* *(enclosure)*
Flakes	5111	7998	6748
Rough waste	353	151	
Cores	140	47	66
Hammerstone	83	2	
Flake axes	1		
Polished axes	3		1
Chisels		1	
Axe roughouts	1		
Choppers	2		
Leaf arrowheads	7		8
Scrapers	98	16	2
Serrated flakes	67		7
Blade segments	14		
Backed knives	4	1	
Bifacial worked knives	1		
Fabricators	1		
'Rod'	1		
Notched pieces	60	10	
Awls	3		
Axe fragments	2		
Beaked pieces	2		
Burin	1		
Barbed and tanged arrowheads	1		
Other retouched pieces	158	84	5
Other utilized pieces	172		

Two main types of pottery frequently recur on Neolithic sites in Sussex. The most common type (87% at Bishopstone) is a coarse, calcined flint-tempered ware. This type dominated the assemblage at Whitehawk (Piggott's 'Ware a' in Curwen, 1934b, 114), Offham (Drewett, 1977a), and Bishopstone (Bell, 1977). It represents the classic simple, round-based forms of the early Neolithic ceramic tradition. Thin-sectioning of this fabric at Offham revealed a large quantity of large, angular, calcined flint inclusions, with some smaller, more rounded flint fragments. In addition, there were small, subrounded quartz grains and small, angular and splinter-like flint chips scattered throughout the clay matrix. Small iron-mineral inclusions and patches of iron staining occurred, and in one instance a large patch of 'grog' was present. The 'layered' texture of the sherd body was evident in thin-section. (Cartwright, in Drewett, 1977a). Thin-sectioning therefore clearly confirms the assumption that this ware is of local manufacture with the constituents probably derived from the Downland clay-with-flints.

The second most frequently recurring fabric, although much less so than the first type, is a finer ware, with regular-sized calcined flint filler. This fabric is associated

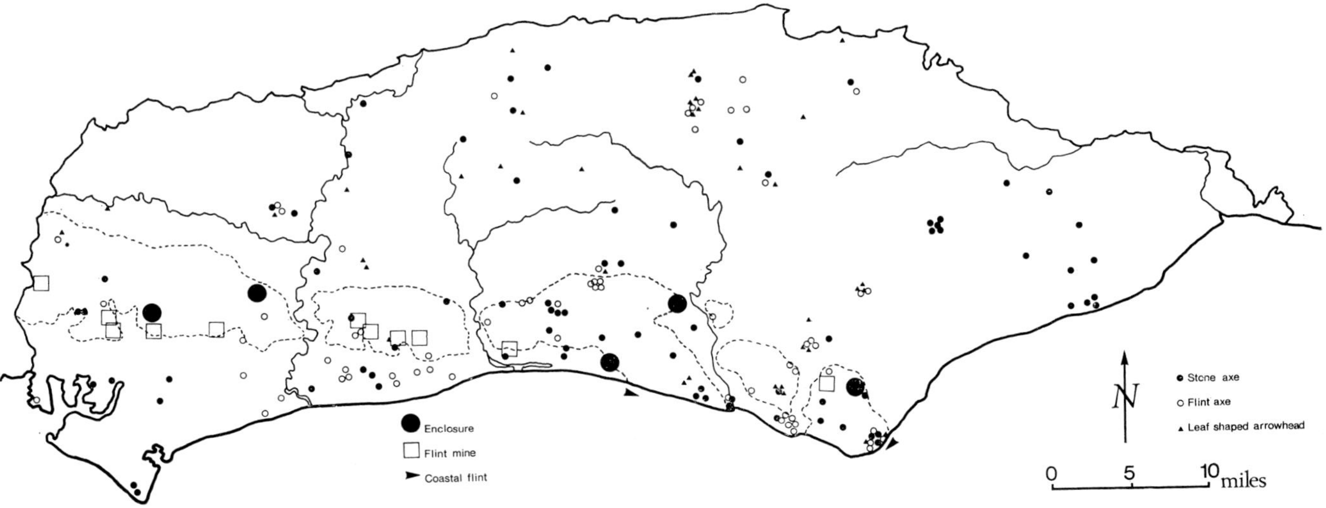

Fig 12 Neolithic Sussex. Distribution of published axes and arrowheads in relation to enclosures and sources of deep flint

with the distinctive carinated bowls at Whitehawk (Curwen, 1934b), Bishopstone (Bell, 1977), and Offham (Drewett, 1977a). By comparison with the first fabric, the thin-sectioning of this ware showed that the calcined flint inclusions were smaller and more numerous, although still mainly angular. Also more numerous were small to middle-sized flint inclusions, more regularly and evenly scattered throughout the denser clay matrix. Numerous subrounded to angular, small quartz grains, some iron-mineral inclusions, and patches of iron staining were also scattered throughout the body. Clearly, the constituents of this ware are the same as those of the first fabric, with a local source in the clay-with-flints. However, the far greater care with which these carinated bowls were made and fired would suggest either specialized but local potters, or, more likely, special care being taken to make pots of a particular type for a particular function.

The third most frequently recurring fabric clearly underlines the very localized nature of the pottery industry in Sussex. This ware, with a filler of marine origin, is found at Bishopstone and Whitehawk on the south side of the Downs, but not at Offham on the north side of the Downs. At Bishopstone 6·5% of the Neolithic pottery contained shell filler (Bell, 1977) while at Whitehawk a 'relatively small amount' contained shell fragments (Curwen, 1934b, 114). The presence of metamorphosed limestone in the thin-section of one shelly sherd from Bishopstone hinted at some external source, but a coastal origin for this appears likely.

The pottery industry in Sussex may therefore be seen primarily as very localized, but clearly influenced from outside with traits comparable with both the Hembury style and the Grimston/Lyles Hill series (Smith, 1974). At present little chronological division can be made in the pottery of Neolithic Sussex with both the fabrics and possibly the forms spanning virtually the whole period.

Bone tools are not common in Neolithic Sussex. The most frequently recurring type is the antler pick, as found at the flint mines at Harrow Hill (Curwen, 1926) and Blackpatch (Goodman, 1924) but also at the oval barrow at Alfriston (Drewett, 1975). Other types include bone points (Curwen, 1936a, 85), hammers (Curwen, 1926, 118), and combs (Curwen, 1936a, 84).

Commerce and trade

The mining of flint for both local use and probably extensive trading was clearly a major activity from the beginning of the Neolithic in Sussex (Fig 10). The six radiocarbon dates available would suggest their use for almost 1000 years from *c* 4300 to 3400 BC. There are now eleven known areas of flint mining in Sussex. These range from the massive mining complexes like that at Harrow Hill, with over 160 shafts (Curwen, 1926), down to the single shaft at Slonk Hill (R Hartridge, *pers comm*). Other flint mines are known from Long Down (Salisbury, 1961), Blackpatch (Goodman, 1924), Cissbury (Stevens, 1872; Curwen, 1931b), Windover Hill (Curwen, 1928; Holden, 1974), Church Hill, Lavant Down, Stoke Down, Bow Hill (Curwen, 1929b), and Compton Down. All of these flint mines, with the exception of Windover Hill, are to the west of Whitehawk. The absence of flint mines to the east of Whitehawk may be due to the fact that there are good flint outcrops in the cliff face, perhaps therefore removing the need to dig flint mines.

It is possible that most territorial groups in Sussex controlled a source of deep flint (see below). If this is so, a case could be made for the large mines in the west of the county producing excess for their local needs and therefore trading their surplus. If such an extensive trade network out of the county was in operation, one return product may well have been the polished stone axes imported from areas of igneous rock (Fig 12). The petrological survey of stone axes in Sussex is not yet complete, but there are already clear indications of nationwide contact (Evans, 1968). For example, three polished stone axes from Bullock Down, Beachy Head, have recently been thin-sectioned. One is of uralitized gabbro (Group I) from Cornwall, while the other two are of Greywacke, which can be matched with the older Palaeozoic rocks of Wales, the Lake District, or the south-west, but does not tally with any of the standard petrological groups.

The only other possible evidence for trade in Neolithic Sussex is the presence of metamorphosed limestone in some of the pottery from Bishopstone. The impression one gets from Sussex is of some external contact during the heyday of flint mining early in the Neolithic, but

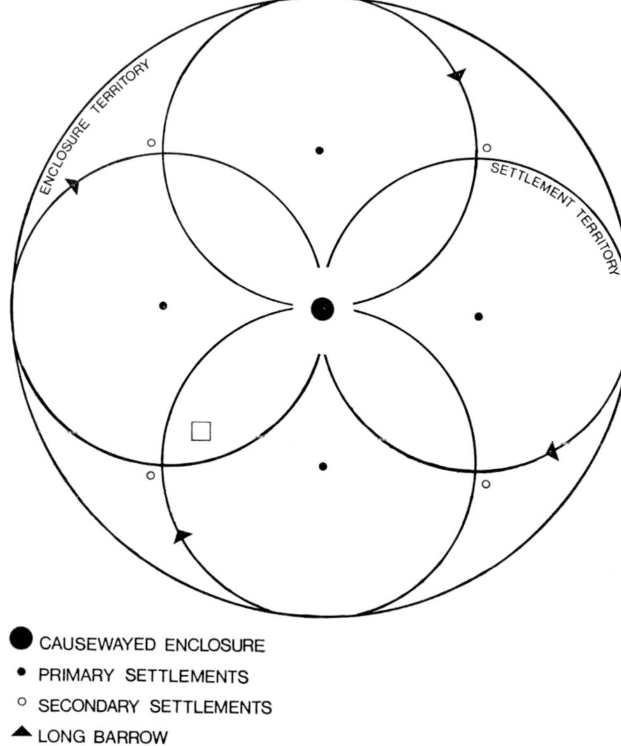

● CAUSEWAYED ENCLOSURE
• PRIMARY SETTLEMENTS
○ SECONDARY SETTLEMENTS
▲ LONG BARROW
□ FLINT MINE

Fig 13   Model of Neolithic territorial organization in Sussex

increasing insularity as the period progresses. The absence of henges, returned to below, perhaps underlines this isolation in the later Neolithic.

Economic basis

The evidence we have from Sussex would suggest a mixed farming strategy with a strong element of hunter/gathering. Animal bones from several sites show a recurrent picture of cattle, pigs, sheep/goat and deer:

	Whitehawk	Bishopstone	Alfriston	Offham
Cattle	+	+		+
Pig	+	+	+	+
Sheep/goat	+	+	+	+
Roe deer	+	+	+	+
Red deer	+		+	+
Dog	+		+	+
Beaver				+

Until the recent excavations at Bishopstone there was little direct evidence from Sussex for the growing of cereals, although this was always assumed from the presence of 'grain-rubbers' at sites like Whitehawk (Williamson, 1930, 80). However, flotation of the contents of pit Fe 357 at Bishopstone produced emmer wheat (*Triticum dicoccum*) and six-row barley (*Hordeum vulgare*). In addition, this pit produced wild plants, no doubt collected for food. These included fat hen, burdock, common orache, and chickweed (Bell, 1977).

Sea resources added significantly to the economy of Neolithic sites on the south side of the Downs. However, sites on the north side of the Downs, like Alfriston and Offham, did not produce a single marine shell. From both Bishopstone (Bell, 1977) and Whitehawk (Williamson, 1930, 85) have come shells of mussel, oyster, cockle, and *Scrophicularia plana*. Bishopstone also produced four limpet shells. At Bishopstone, pit Fe 357 produced no less than 2494 marine shells, suggesting that the gathering of shellfish was a significant, if only seasonal, part of Neolithic diet.

Territorial organization

In 1973, Renfrew put forward the suggestion that Neolithic Wessex was organized into a series of chiefdoms (Renfrew, 1973). He also suggested that long barrows may indicate the territories of individual settlements within a chieftain's territory. The concept of chiefdoms does, however, appear to rest on so many criteria which simply do not leave any trace in the archaeological record that a simpler model is suggested for Sussex. My aim here is to simply construct a model of territorial organization for use in future work in Sussex. It does appear possible in Sussex to define socially coherent groups occupying discrete territories. However, to establish whether these represent chiefdoms or stateless societies appears to me beyond the limitations of archaeological inference, given currently available data.

A tentative approach to the problem of Neolithic territorial organization was suggested for south-east Sussex in 1975 (Drewett, 1975a). Although the main purpose of that model still holds, ie to show the regular difference in situation between barrows and possible settlement sites, the inclusion of causewayed enclosures in that model perhaps masks the existence of a larger territorial division. The main problem in attempting to define the territory served by a causewayed enclosure is that if they are communal centres with a subsidiary burial function, they could be situated in the centre of a tribal area, whereas if burial was a primary function, it is possible that they were situated on the edge of territories (Drewett, 1975a, 139-40). The situation of the Sussex enclosures towards the northern or southern limits of the Downs may suggest they are on the limits of territories. However, increasing evidence for occupation off the Downs, eg on the Greensand at Selmeston (Drewett, 1975b), may indicate that the margins of the Downs could actually be in the centre of territories similar to the medieval parishes spanning upland and lowland. The answers clearly lie in further fieldwork. However, if we assume that the five known causewayed enclosures in Sussex are contemporary, as present information would suggest, it is likely that they represent non-overlapping territorial areas made up of several smaller settlement territories. If 4 km radius circles are drawn around the known enclosures it will be seen that no overlap occurs (Fig 9). This would suggest the possibility that this is approximately the area served by such enclosures. By filling in the gaps between such areas on the Downs with similar-sized circles it is possible to suggest thirteen such areas on the South Downs (Fig 9). Naturally, such a working hypothesis requires testing through intensive fieldwork. Each causewayed enclosure could contain about four settlement territories of the 2 km size suggested earlier (Drewett, 1975a, 137–42), together with four secondary settlements (Fig 13).

It is possible to relate the known flint mines to this suggested model (Fig 9). However, here we clearly have the additional factor of availability of raw material, which may well override territorial organization. It is noticeable, however, that seven of the proposed causewayed enclosure territories have access to known flint mines, while two more would have had access to cliff exposures of flint in East Sussex. Only four proposed territories have no known access to good, deep flint.

In Sussex it is, therefore, possible to demonstrate the existence of settlement sites perhaps occupied by extended family or clan groups, each maintaining its own clan long barrow, but grouping together to pool resources to construct a causewayed enclosure and dig a flint mine. This would indicate the existence of a socially coherent and autonomous group occupying a particular territory, which is as convenient a definition as any of a tribe.

The late Neolithic in Sussex remains a greater problem. With the exception of a few sherds of Grooved Ware (Fig 9) from the flint mines at Findon (Smith, 1956, 187) very little else demonstrably late Neolithic is known from Sussex until the Beaker period (eg Holden, 1975). No henges are known from Sussex which, if taken to indicate a continuation of territorial organization from the causewayed enclosures, would suggest a change in, or collapse of, the social order in Sussex during the late 3rd millennium BC.

Appendix: Radiocarbon dates for the Neolithic in Sussex

Settlements

	Radiocarbon date	Suess Calibration
Bishopstone	2510±70 bc (HAR 1662)	3390–3260 BC
Rackham (Beaker?)	2000±140 bc (HAR 360)	2500 BC

Barrows

Alfriston	2360±110 bc (HAR 940)	3350–2970 BC

Flint Mines

Church Hill, Findon	3390±150 bc (BM 181)	4340–4270 BC
Blackpatch, Worthing	3140±130 bc (BM 290)	4210–3970 BC
Harrow Hill	2980±150 bc (BM 182)	3710 BC
Cissbury	2780±150 bc (BM 185)	3650–3540 BC
	2770±150 bc (BM 183)	3650–3540 BC
	2700±150 bc (BM 184)	3500–3410 BC

References

Bell, M, 1977　'Excavations on Rookery Hill, Bishopstone, East Sussex', *Sussex Archaeol Collect*, **115** (forthcoming)

Clipson, J, 1976　*Excavations at the Neolithic causewayed enclosure at Barkhale (by Dr Seton-Williams)*, unpublished dissertation, Inst Archaeol, Univ London

Curwen, E and Curwen, E C, 1922　'Two unrecorded Long Barrows', *Sussex Archaeol Collect*, **63**, 172–5

Curwen, E and Curwen, E C, 1926　'Harrow Hill flint-mine excavation, 1924–5', *ibid*, **67**, 103–38

Curwen, E C, 1928　'The antiquities on Windover Hill', *ibid*, **69**, 94–101

Curwen, E C, 1929a　'Excavations in the Trundle', *ibid*, **70**, 32–85

Curwen, E C, 1929b　*Prehistoric Sussex*, London

Curwen, E C, 1931a　'Excavations in the Trundle. Second season, 1930', *Sussex Archaeol Collect*, **72**, 100–49

Curwen, E C, 1931b　'The date of Cissbury Camp', *Antiq J*, **11**, 14–36

Curwen, E C, 1934a　'A Late Bronze Age farm and a Neolithic pit-dwelling on New Barn Down, Clapham, near Worthing', *Sussex Archaeol Collect*, **74**, 153–7

Curwen, E C, 1934b　'Excavations in Whitehawk Neolithic Camp, Brighton, 1932–3', *Antiq J*, **14**, no 2, 99–133

Curwen, E C, 1936a　'On Sussex flint arrowheads', *Sussex Archaeol Collect*, **77**, 15–25

Curwen, E C, 1936b　'Excavations in Whitehawk Camp, Brighton. Third season, 1935', *ibid*, **77**, 60–92

Drewett, P L, 1975a　'The excavation of an oval burial mound of the third millennium bc at Alfriston, East Sussex, 1974', *Proc Prehist Soc*, **41**, 119–52

Drewett, P L, 1975b　'A Neolithic pot from Selmeston, East Sussex', *Sussex Archaeol Collect*, **113**, 193–4

Drewett, P L, 1977a　'The excavation of a Neolithic causewayed enclosure on Offham Hill, East Sussex, 1976', *Proc Prehist Soc*, **43**, 201–42

Drewett, P L, 1977b　'Preliminary excavations of a Neolithic open settlement on Bullock Down, Beachy Head, East Sussex', in 'Rescue Archaeology in Sussex, 1976', *Bull Inst Archaeol*, **14**, 1–61

Evans, K J, 1968　'Stone implements in Sussex', *Sussex Notes and Queries*, 1968, no 1, 15–21

Field, L F, 1939　'Castle Hill, Newhaven', *Sussex Archaeol Collect*, **80**, 263–73

Goodman, C H, 1924　'Blackpatch flint-mine excavation, 1922', *ibid*, **65**, 69–111

Grinsell, L, 1934　'Sussex barrows', *ibid*, **75**, 220

Holden, E, 1973　'The possible remains of a Neolithic causewayed camp on Offham Hill, Hamsey', *ibid*, **111**, 109–10

Holden, E H, 1974　'Flint mines on Windover Hill, Wilmington', *ibid*, **112**, 154

Holden, E H, 1975　'A Late Neolithic site at Rackham', *ibid*, **113**, 85–103

Money, J H, 1960　'Excavations at High Rocks, Tunbridge Wells, 1954–61', *ibid*, **98**, 173–221

Musson, R, 1950　'An excavation at Combe Hill Camp near Eastbourne', *ibid*, **89**, 105–16

Renfrew, C, 1973　'Monuments, mobilization and social organization in Neolithic Wessex', in *The explanation of culture change: models in prehistory* (ed C Renfrew), Duckworth, London, 540–57

Salisbury, E F, 1961　'Prehistoric flint mines on Long Down, Eartham, 1955–1958', *Sussex Archaeol Collect*, **99**, 66–73

Smith, I F, 1956　*The decorative art of Neolithic ceramics in south-eastern England and its relations*, unpublished PhD thesis, Univ London

Smith, I F, 1965　*Windmill Hill and Avebury, excavations by Alexander Keiller 1925-1939*, Oxford

Smith, I F, 1974　'The Neolithic', in *British Prehistory* (ed C Renfrew), Duckworth, London

Stevens, J, 1872　'The flintworks at Cissbury', *Sussex Archaeol Collect*, **24**, 145–65

Tebbutt, C F, 1974　'The prehistoric occupation of the Ashdown Forest area of the Weald', *ibid*, **112**, 34–43

Thorley, A, 1971　'Vegetational history in the Vale of the Brooks', *Guide to Sussex excursions*, Inst Brit Geogr, 47–50

Toms, H S, 1924　'Long Barrows in Sussex', *Sussex Archaeol Collect*, **65**, 157–65

Williamson, R P R, 1930　'Excavations in Whitehawk Neolithic Camp, near Brighton', *ibid*, **71**, 57–96

Ann Ellison

The Beaker Period (*c* 2000–1500 BC)

The beginning of the Beaker Period in Britain is marked by the arrival of new pottery types from the continent and a new burial rite involving the single inhumation of individuals in a crouched position under small round barrows with interrupted ditches. The Beaker phenomenon provides the first firm evidence of an influx of people into this country from Europe since the initial Neolithic phase, and the whole pottery series has been reassessed by Clarke (1970). The earliest imports are All Over Cord and European bell beakers followed by a series of types with distinct Dutch and German prototypes: the Wessex/Middle Rhine, Northern/Middle Rhine, Northern/North Rhine, and Barbed Wire beakers. Developing from these there were two main series of indigenous beaker styles which are found substantially in northern and southern Britain respectively (N1 to N4 and S1 to S4), and a third series in East Anglia which developed primarily from the Northern/North Rhine and Barbed Wire beakers. There have been 28 finds of Beaker vessels and fragments in Sussex. Early imported types are represented by one European bell beaker from Whitehawk Camp, four Wessex/Middle Rhine vessels from Beggars Haven, Hassocks Sand Pit, Rodmell, and Selsey, and two Barbed Wire beakers from Falmer and Findon. The indigenous northern series is, as to be suspected, represented by only one vessel (from Burpham) but the southern and East Anglian series account for the remaining nine examples.

The most informative advance to Beaker studies in Sussex has been the partial area excavation of the Beaker settlement discovered in 1909 by H S Toms at Belle Tout near Beachy Head (Bradley, 1970). Careful plotting of intrusive flints, possible post settings, and the distribution of finds of flint and pottery led to the definition of a series of seven post structures of varying size and shape, some shallow pits, and a midden enclosed by minor and major banks and ditches. The existence of some of the structures was confirmed by the use of trend analysis on the finds distributions, and further sophisticated analysis of the distributions led to the identification of several knapping areas and working sites within the settlement. The site could best be dated by the pottery assemblage which falls into two main groups: a cord-decorated domestic assemblage of the primary British Beaker group, the All Over Cord series, dating from the 18th century BC, and a later group of beakers in the East Anglian style decorated with comb, finger-nail, and finger pinched motifs and dating possibly from the 17th century BC. Other major advances to knowledge arising from this excavation include the publication of a large Beaker flint assemblage and the identification of grain and other seed impressions embodied within many of the pottery sherds. The excavation and analysis of a large Beaker flint assemblage from Rackham has allowed the definition of a new class of Neolithic and Bronze Age site associated with tanning and leather-working (Holden and Bradley, 1976).

The Early Bronze Age (*c* 1500–1200 BC)

Recent work on the 'Wessex culture' has concentrated on the rich burial goods and fancy barrows of the central Wessex region (eg Coles and Taylor, 1971; Fleming, 1971),

and the virtual lack of rich grave goods of this period on the South Downs remains an unexplained problem. Field survey has failed to identify any fancy barrows apart from the few listed by Grinsell in 1931, which are situated in the borders of central Wessex itself. Several round barrows of turf construction have recently been excavated on the Lower Greensand in West Sussex, but they had all been robbed and produced no Early Bronze Age grave goods (Drewett, 1975). However, the Minsted barrow contained an interesting pollen assemblage and radiocarbon dates placed the West Heath Common barrows within the Early Bronze Age period. There are only two rich Early Bronze Age burial assemblages: the complex jet, amber, and faience necklace and the bronze finger ring found with a Collared Urn at Ox Teddle Bottom near Lewes (Curwen, 1954, fig 42), and the fine handled amber cup associated with an igneous stone axe-hammer, rivetted bronze dagger, and a whetstone in the Hove barrow (Curwen, 1954, pl XIII). This battle axe falls into Roe's Snowshill Group Stage V (Roe, 1966) and other Sussex battle axes are listed in her corpus. Early Bronze Age daggers have been exhaustively catalogued by Gerloff (1974). The common pottery type of the Early Bronze Age is the Collared Urn and these are well represented in Sussex, which has produced at least 25 complete or near-complete examples. In his study of Collared Urns from England and Wales, Longworth defined a primary series of urns that carry demonstrably early traits which could be linked to a derivation from late Neolithic Peterborough Ware (Longworth, 1961). The primary series lasts from the initial phase of the Wessex culture into the later phase, with the secondary series taking over from about 1400 BC. Traits defining vessels of the primary series include internal moulding, a disproportionately narrow base, internal decoration other than on the rim bevel, and decoration extending below the shoulder. In Sussex such urns have been recovered from Cliff Hill (Lewes), Hassocks Sandpit, Westbourne, and Lewes Golf Course, while the remaining 21 known Collared Urns belong to Longworth's secondary series.

In 1956 Butler and Smith examined the grave goods, mainly bronze razors and beads of various kinds, associated with certain biconical urns and concluded that the ceramic group probably dated from the period during or immediately after the Wessex culture. These Wessex Biconical Urns are divisible into clear regional groups and can be derived from late Neolithic Grooved Ware (Wainwright and Longworth, 1971, 249; Ellison, unpublished). This class of pottery is, however, extremely rare in Sussex and this may reflect the almost total absence of Grooved Ware finds in the county. The only two well known examples of biconical urns are from Charmandean and South Heighton, while two more have recently been rediscovered in Hastings Museum and identified as coming from an urn cemetery near Alfriston (*Sussex Archaeol Collect*, 37 (1890), 193–4; Holden, 1972, 117, note 2).

Middle and Late Bronze Age (*c* 1200–700 BC)

During the 1920s and 1930s a series of Bronze Age settlements were tested by excavation on a small scale, the main Bronze Age ones being Park Brow, Sompting

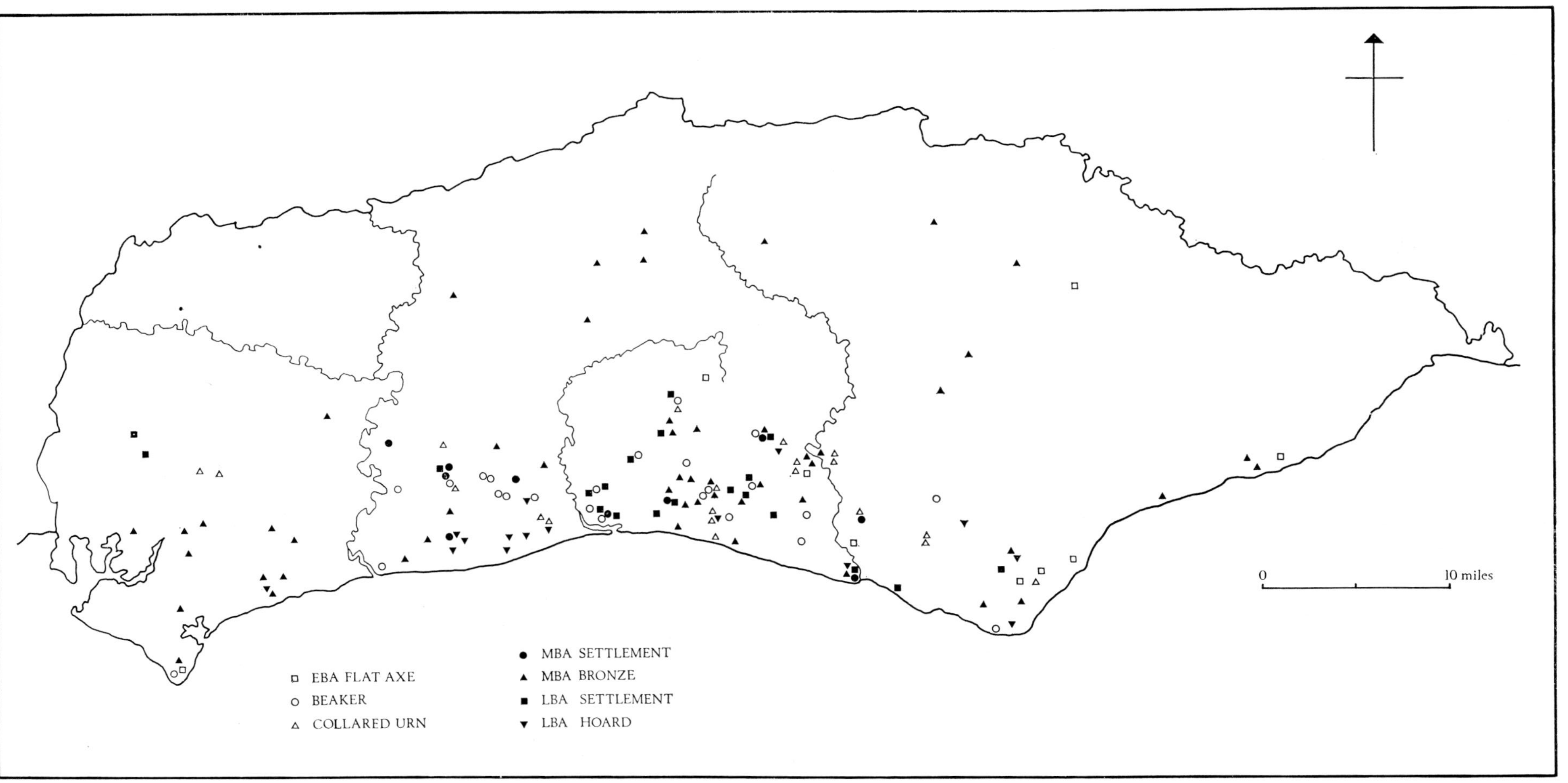

Fig 14 Bronze Age Sussex

(Wolseley, Smith, and Hawley, 1927), Plumpton Plain (Holleyman and Curwen, 1935), and New Barn Down (Curwen, 1934). The general nature of these small banked enclosures surrounding round wooden structures was thus established, and the finding of coherent series of pottery sometimes associated with fragments of bronze implements confirmed their Bronze Age date. The detailed reports on the pottery from these and other settlements in Sussex by the notable British Museum prehistorians Reginald Smith and Christopher Hawkes provided a firm foundation for a type of series of Sussex pottery for the late Bronze Age and the whole of the Iron Age which was neatly summarized by Wilson and Burstow (1948) and illustrated by a display board in the Sussex Archaeological Society's Museum at Lewes. Musson's illustrated catalogue of Bronze Age pottery (Musson, 1954) included drawings of all the available complete vessels and also, for the first time, catalogued the Beakers and Early Bronze Age pottery from Sussex.

The near-total excavation of a settlement on Itford Hill (Burstow and Holleyman, 1957) and an urnfield barrow on Steyning Round Hill (Burstow, 1958) provided even more information on socio-economic aspects of the later Bronze Age which complemented the earlier concentration on pottery typology. Since then Dr Radcliffe-Densham has sampled several small settlement sites (Radcliffe-Densham, 1953; 1961; 1966), but the most important discovery of recent years has been the Itford Hill cemetery barrow, excavated in 1971 (Holden, 1972). The importance of the site lay not only in the total dissection of an interesting burial monument but also in the discovery of an almost complete handled, decorated jar to which sherds from the excavated settlement site nearby could be fitted (Ellison, in Holden, 1972, 110). This therefore provided the first firm link between a contemporary settlement and burial place in the whole British Bronze Age.

Pottery

Hawkes' original typological scheme, based on the pottery from Plumpton Plain sites A and B (Hawkes, 1935) was a scheme founded on form rather than fabric. This was the scheme adopted and adapted by Wilson and Burstow (1948) and in the Itford Hill pottery report (Burstow and Holleyman, 1957). However, the use of this scheme has caused some confusion, owing to the equation of Hawkes' Types A1–A3 and B1–B3. There is definitely no direct continuity from the A1 finger-printed buckets to the B1 vessels with rounded profile and heavy cordons (B1B) or those with neck cordon and out-flaring rim (B1A). Nor can the B3 bag-shaped vessels with marked protruding foot be equated with the rough shapeless examples of A3. It was decided, therefore, to devise a completely new series of types for this area, working from first principles (the forms are illustrated in Fig 15):

Type	Form	Previous category
1	Shapeless baggy jar, sometimes with turned-over simple rim	A3
2	Ovoid or straight-sided jar with plain unperforated applied lugs at maximum diameter	A3
3	Ovoid jar with plain, unperforated applied lugs and out-flaring rim	A3
4	Straight-sided small pot with perforated applied lugs	A3
5	Small ovoid pot with perforated lugs	A3
6	Plain large urn with slack biconical profile and slightly emphasized carination	A1/A3
7	Globular jar with bar-handles and incised geometric decoration	A4
8	Plain bucket-shaped urn	A1
9	Bucket urn with line of finger-tipping applied directly on the body	A1
10	Bucket urn with finger-tipped cordon	None
11	Squat ovoid jar with protruding base and applied finger-tipped cordon at maximum diameter	B1B
12	Large shouldered jar with out-flaring rim and applied finger-tipped cordon in hollow of neck	B1A
13	Large shouldered jar with finger-tipped cordon round carination	None
14	Plain large shouldered jar with slack profile	B5
15	Small rounded pot with incised geometric decoration	B4
16	Urnfield imports	B4
17	Plain ovoid jar with protruding foot	B2?
18	Plain straight-sided jar with protruding foot	None
19	Plain low bowl with incipient foot-ring	B6

All the later Bronze Age pottery in Sussex has calcined flint filler. This includes the finer decorated forms (Types 7 and 15) and the probable imports (Type 16). The imports only have fine flint, but all the other types tend to have a dense filler of medium and large flint fragments. In the absence of the variety of fillers that is found, for instance, in Wessex, it has not been possible in this case to use fabric as an important criterion for defining pottery types. The Type 7 handled jars do tend to have medium rather than large dense flint filler, but the main difference is one of surface treatment. The surfaces of these pots have been carefully smoothed, while the other classes tend to be finger-smeared or finger-tip-dimpled. Types 2, 3, and 6 tend to have smoother surface finishes than the other general-purpose jar forms.

When the pottery is sorted according to the typology set out above and the occurrences of each type in each site assemblage are listed, it is possible to divide the pottery into two main groups, Types 1–10 and Types 11–19. The types belonging to each of these groups regularly recur together on a series of sites. These two groups conform roughly to the Plumpton Plain A and B assemblages originally defined by Hawkes (1935). At Plumpton Plain the B assemblage was associated with an Urnfield imported pot and a fragment of winged bronze axe and, on this basis, Hawkes dated the two assemblages to his LBA I and LBA II respectively (Hawkes, 1935, 57–9; 1960). However, in the light of the earlier dating of the metal types associated with such settlements in southern England, it was realized that much of the pottery previously assigned to the Late Bronze Age must have been already in circulation during the Middle Bronze Age. The radiocarbon date for the grain from the Itford Hill settlement site of 1000 $\pm$ 35 BC (GrU–6167) confirmed that this should be true for the earlier cluster of pottery types discussed above. The two clusters can therefore be taken to represent Middle Bronze Age and Late Bronze Age assemblages respectively. Apart from the associated bronze axe fragment and Urnfield pottery at Plumpton Plain site B, a Late Bronze Age dating for the second grouping is further confirmed by the occurrence of a Late Bronze Age hoard of palstaves and winged and socketed axes in a pot from Forty Acre Brickfield, Worthing. The pot is plain with a rounded shoulder and slightly outward flaring rim, thus conforming to Type 14 of the later grouping.

Four settlement sites have produced examples of pottery types belonging to both chronological groupings: Kingston Buci, West Blatchington, Castle Hill (Newhaven), and Highdown Hill. Unfortunately most of these assemblages were retrieved in rescue operations and no detailed stratigraphic relationships have been recorded. The pottery evidence does, however, firmly suggest that there were Middle and Late Bronze Age occupations on these four sites.

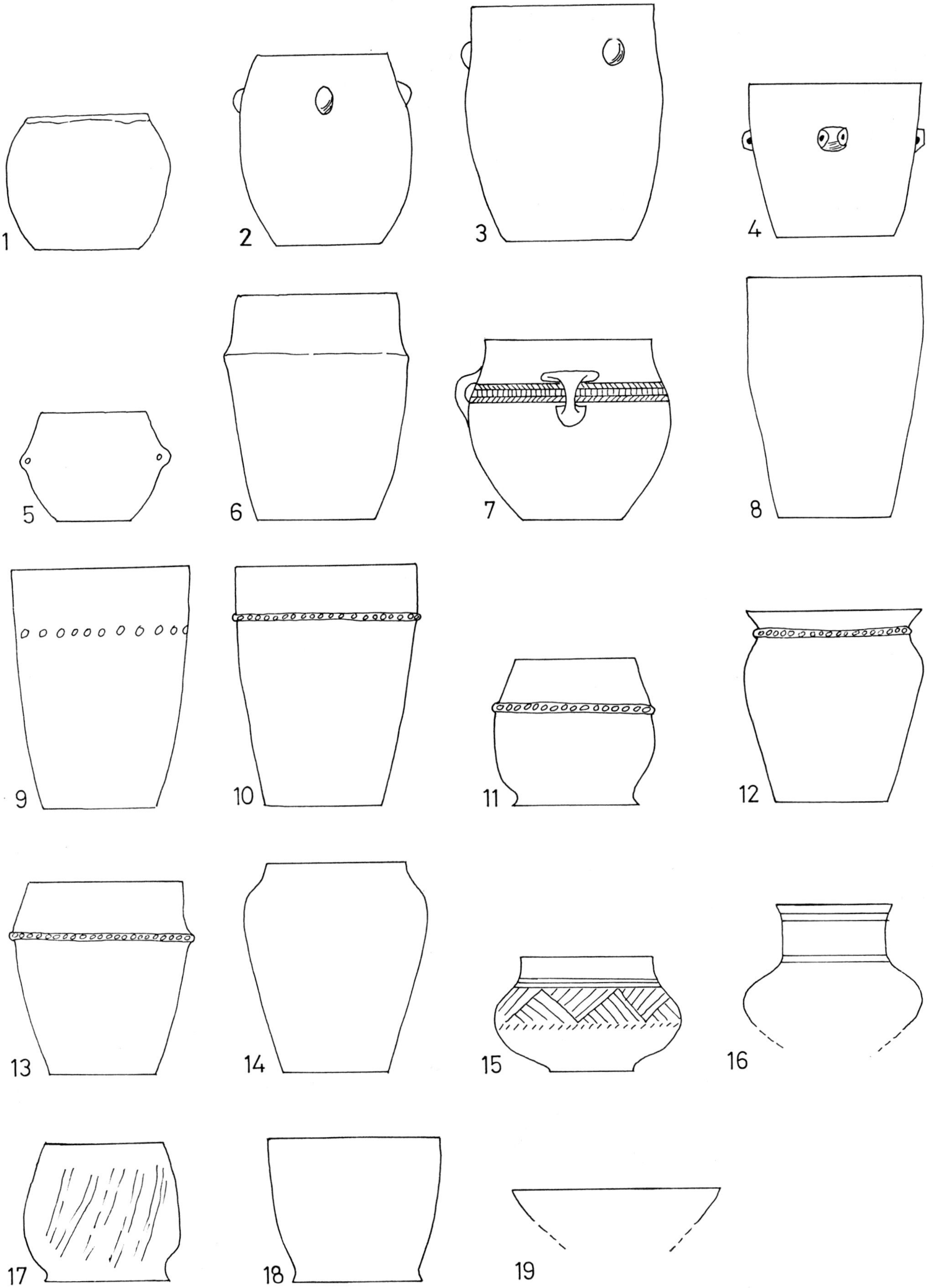

Fig 15   Later Bronze Age pottery types

Having established these two typological-chronological pottery groupings, it is possible to sort the pottery from the cemeteries, single burials, and stray finds into their chronological groups. The three known cemetery sites (Steyning Round Hill, Alfriston, and the Itford Hill barrow) all have pottery assemblages that fall within the Middle Bronze Age groupings, and, rather surprisingly, so do all the pots from single burials and unknown contexts except for two examples: Lancing and Broadwater.

The Middle Bronze Age assemblage

This assemblage forms a very distinctive local group. There are a fair number of plain vessels among the collared urns known from Sussex (eg Musson, 1954, nos 230, 240, 260, 300, 310, 320, 330), and the tradition of simple, plain slightly carinated vessels seems to have carried through to the Middle Bronze Age. The very slightly biconical profile is found on Type 6 of the Middle Bronze Age assemblage. This form never occurs in the Wessex or East Anglian Middle Bronze Age pottery groups. The ovoid lugged jar (Type 2) forms a very common component of the Sussex group. Similar vessels occur in the Thames Valley assemblage, and smaller straight-sided examples also occur in Wessex, but the Sussex assemblage also includes a purely local version of this type: the lugged ovoid jar with outward-flaring rim (Type 3). The plain bag-shaped jars (Types 1 and 5) are another purely local type, although the simple buckets, with or without finger decorations (Types 8, 9 and 10), are ubiquitous throughout southern England. The site assemblage that best exemplifies this chronological group is that from the Itford Hill cemetery barrow and the settlement assemblage to which it is linked by the matching sherd of a Type 7 jar, and this group has been described in detail elsewhere (Ellison, in Holden, 1972, 204–11).

The Type 7 globular jars with bar handles have been found on five settlements associated with other Middle Bronze Age ceramic types. They differ very much from the three main types of Globular Urn in Wessex, in respect of their fabric, form, decorative motifs, and the presence of bar handles rather than lugs. The filler is usually dense medium calcined flint and the form is much more squat than any of the Wessex globulars. In size this Sussex group match best the Type IIa Dorset globulars, but the Sussex ones have a more bulbous profile and the decoration and fabric types are at opposite extremes (dense flint in Sussex, varying flint with grog in Dorset; incised geometric motifs in Sussex, wide finger-grooving on IIa urns in Dorset). The Sussex globular jar motifs form a very restricted repertoire, although they have been combined ingeniously to give varying effects on different vessels. The uniformity of size, fabric, form, and decorative motif might suggest that the vessels of this group may have been made by a certain individual or school of craftsmen. That such specialized activity was existent in the area during the Middle Bronze Age is demonstrated by the tight distribution of the idiosyncratic 'Sussex Loops' in the Brighton area (see below).

Hawkes originally suggested that his A4 vessels (Type 7) derived from northern France, as there were good parallels for them at Fort Harrouard (Hawkes, 1935, 44). However, none of the pottery illustrated by Phillippe (1936) or Sandars (1957) resembles this group at all closely. Nor are there any good parallels from other French sites. The Type 7 geometric motifs can easily be matched on local Beakers and, in particular, the Sussex Collared Urns (eg 'fern' motif appears on Musson, 1958, nos 350, 362,

and 363), but the globular form and the handles do seem to be an innovation.

The Type 7 handled jars occur throughout central Sussex, but within the coarse-ware types it is possible to detect a regional division. Plastic applied cordons with finger-tipping only occur west of the River Adur (Steyning Round Hill, Cock Hill, New Barn Down, Amberley Mount, and Blackpatch), and in this area there are more bucket forms represented. In contrast to this, the assemblages east of the River Adur (Plumpton Plain A, Itford Hill settlement and barrow) are characterized by large numbers of small bag-shaped vessels which are often lugged (Types 2, 3, and 5). There does therefore seem to be evidence for two regional coarse-ware styles, although this is not demonstrated conclusively by a disparity in the fabrics. There is a tendency for there to be smaller flint filler in the pots of the eastern group, but they may merely be a reflection of the preponderance of smaller vessels in this area. The fact that the very uniform Type 7 vessels have a wider distribution than the two coarse-ware groups lends further weight to the theory of their having been the result of specialist craftsmanship.

The Late Bronze Age assemblage

The same range of forms is present as in the Middle Bronze Age assemblage: small baggy pots (now with protruding bases) and large storage vessels. However, the only vessel with incised geometric ornament, apart from the suspected imports, is one small pot from Plumpton Plain site B (Hawkes, 1935, fig 11, Type 15). There are many more pots carrying finger-tipped cordons (Types 11, 12, 13, and 16) and profiles tend to be sharper. Characteristic angular vessels are the storage jar with out-flaring rim and an applied cabled cordon in the neck angle (Type 12) and the plain high-shouldered jar (Type 14). No regional variations are apparent, but this may be due to the fact that there is less material available for study than in the Middle Bronze Age.

The various vessel forms could easily have developed stylistically from the Middle Bronze Age forms. The development of protruding bases would have improved the stability of the bag-shaped vessels, and the development of narrower-necked jars and the flaring rims may have aided the fastening of covers for the storage vessels. A similar typological development seems to have occurred in other parts of Britain.

Metalwork

Middle and Late Bronze Age bronze types and their distributions in Sussex were fully illustrated by Curwen (1954). More recent research has concentrated on the publication of corpuses of material and the compilation of more detailed typologies in England as a whole. The best summaries available in print are provided by Burgess (1968) and Rowlands (1976). Following the backdating of the 'Ornament Horizon' bronzes to the Middle Bronze Age period (Smith, 1959) it was recognized that the Deverel-Rimbury settlements (and some of these in Sussex) could also be dated to this earlier period. Rowlands has described the Sussex Middle Bronze Age industry which is characterized by local palstave types and a distinctive style in ornaments which include the specialized 'Sussex Loops' and a Sussex variant of the quoit-headed pin (Rowlands, 1976, 128–31). His Brighton palstave subgroup shows one of the clearest subgroupings of metalwork in this period. Late Bronze Age Sussex is dominated by the coastal concentration of material

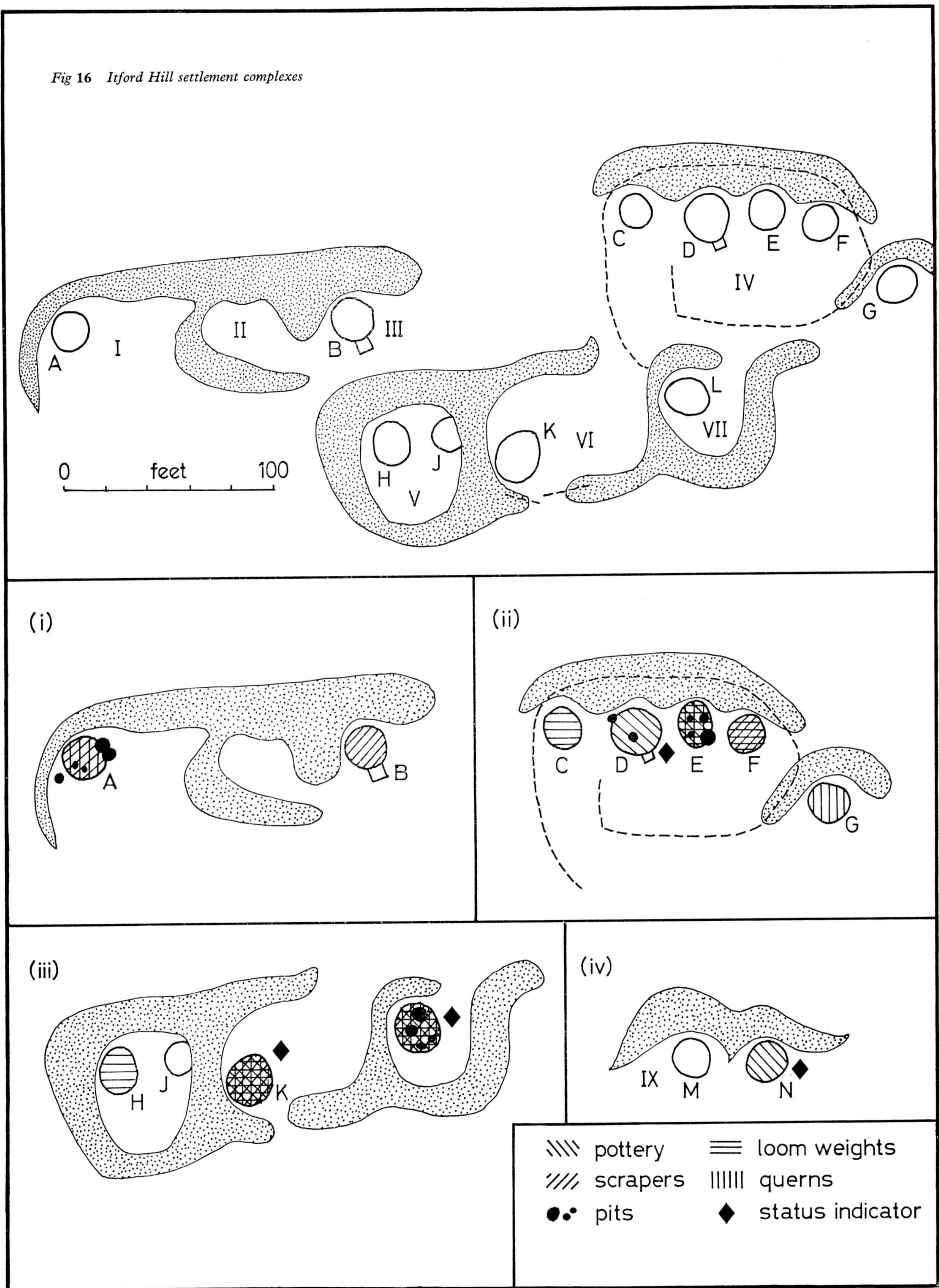

Fig 16   Itford Hill settlement complexes
A
I
II
B
III
C
D
E
F
IV
G
H
J
K
L
VI
VII
V
0   feet   100
(i)
A
B
(ii)
C
D
E
F
G
(iii)
H
J
K
(iv)
IX
M
N
pottery
loom weights
scrapers
querns
pits
status indicator

belonging to the 'Carp's Tongue Complex' and has been examined in detail by Coombes (1972).

Settlements

Later Bronze Age settlements in southern England as a whole can be divided into two groups on the basis of both size and shape. All but one of the Sussex examples fall into the category of small sites, which tend to be circular or square in shape and form the standard agricultural units of the later Bronze Age landscape. Only Highdown Hill fits into a much smaller group of distinctly larger sites which are characterized by ovoid or rectangular plans. Throughout southern England these sites have produced significant quantities of later Bronze Age metalwork, including gold at Highdown Hill, and are situated at the junctions of the distributions of various regional pottery groups. A higher-ranking function possibly linked to a developing system of redistribution of goods seems to be indicated. As well as the distinct regional grouping of later Bronze Age pottery types in southern England, regional variation in the morphology of settlement types can be detected. Thus the small Sussex settlements with their low banks and ditches (New Barn Down, Plumpton Plain A), evidence of hedges (Blackpatch), and interrupted palisades (Cock Hill, Itford Hill) contrast strongly with the more massive continuously palisaded enclosures of central Wessex. In southern England as a whole, site catchment analysis (Ellison and Harriss, 1972) shows that a very large proportion of later Bronze Age settlements are located adjacent to good-quality arable zones as well as lighter soils, and this confirms a hypothesis of general mixed farming economy during the period. In Sussex many of the Middle Bronze Age settlements are situated on or adjacent to the rich Brickearth of the coastal plain, and it is these sites with the highest quality arable soil which survive into the Late Bronze Age period.

Spatial analysis of the settlement sites throughout southern England indicates that there was a standard domestic unit in use. This unit comprised one large circular living hut, one or two subsidiary huts, and storage structures, either in the form of small pits or four- and six-post structures. It is probable that each such unit was occupied by a small kin group practising mixed agriculture in the area around the settlement site, and owing to the lack of evidence for the replacement of posts in most cases, that each unit was occupied for a fairly short length of time. In Sussex the individual units are sometimes enclosed separately, as at Plumpton Plain site A, while at Cock Hill two such units which were probably contemporary can be detected within a single enclosure. However, the most convincing evidence comes from the Itford Hill settlement where a detailed reassessment indicates the existence of four successive settlement units. The complex of earthwork enclosures, which was fairly fully excavated, can be divided into four distinct elements as follows:

i	enclosures	I, II, III
ii		IV, VIII
iii		V, VI, VII
iv		IX

No section drawings or any record of the stratigraphical relationships between the various enclosures were made by the excavators, but from the published plans it is possible to deduce that iii was later than i and ii and that there was a sequence of development within each complex. For instance, hut J was partly covered by the earthwork

bank of enclosure V. Using the bag list kindly supplied by Mr Burstow, all the categories of finds were related to the structures within which they were found and the densities were plotted on to the site plan (Fig 16). From a consideration of the resulting patterns it is possible to postulate the following conclusions concerning the functional content of each complex:

i   A porched living hut (B) plus a food-storage and food-preparation hut (A) containing scrapers, small pits, and querns.

ii   A porched living hut (D), a food-preparation hut (G) with querns only, a work-hut (F) with scrapers and loom-weights, a hut for food-preparation and weaving (E), and a small subsidiary hut (C) possibly used for animals or as sleeping quarters.

iii   Two huts with occupation evidence (K and L), both with querns, but only one of them with internal pits (L). Huts H and J may have been used for animals or for sleeping. H apparently replaced J.

iv   Two huts, one of which produced some pottery and the shale armlet fragment.

It has been possible to postulate the former existence of four independent and successive units of roughly uniform size and similar composition in terms of structures and their functions. It can further be postulated that each complex formed the occupation area of a similar social unit and, in this respect, it is interesting to note that one status indicator was found in each of the three complexes: ii—chalk phallus, iii—decorated pottery, and iv—shale armlet.

Further evidence for the social interpretation of the complexes is provided by the fact that the A4 rim sherd in complex iii fits one of the almost complete urns recovered from the adjacent Itford Hill cemetery barrow. The age and sex pattern of the individuals buried in this barrow, which indicates that a single family group might be represented, is not appropriate to the population of the total Itford Hill settlement as interpreted by Burstow and Holleyman (1957, fig 31), which would have comprised twelve separate huts. However, this population structure might fit the inhabitants of one of the smaller settlement complexes defined above, and the pottery evidence discussed above suggests that the cemetery barrow was in fact the burial place of the inhabitants of complex iii.

Current and future excavations at Blackpatch, Alciston, may provide an opportunity to examine further settlement units and to assess their chronological relationships and economic setting.

References

Bradley, R J, 1970   'The excavation of a Beaker settlement at Belle Tout, East Sussex, England', *Proc Prehist Soc*, 36, 312–379

Burgess, C B, 1968   'The Later Bronze Age in the British Isles and North-Western France,' *Archaeol J*, 125, 1–45

Burstow, G P, 1958   'A Late Bronze Age urnfield on Steyning Round Hill, Sussex', *ibid*, 24, 158

Burstow, G P and Holleyman, G A, 1957   'Late Bronze Age settlement on Itford Hill, Sussex', *ibid*, 23, 167–212

Butler, J J, and Smith, I F, 1956   'Razors, urns and the British Middle Bronze Age', *Univ London, Institute of Archaeology Annual Report*, 12, 20–52

Clarke, D L, 1970   *Beaker pottery of Great Britain and Ireland*, Cambridge

Coles, J M and Taylor, J J, 1971   'The Wessex culture: a minimal view', *Antiquity*, 45, 13

Coombes, D, 1972   *The Late Bronze Age in south-eastern England*, unpublished PhD thesis, Univ Cambridge

Curwen, E C, 1934   'A Late Bronze Age farm and a Neolithic pit dwelling on New Barn Down, near Worthing', *Sussex Archaeol Collect*, 75, 137–70

Curwen, E C, 1954   *The archaeology of Sussex*, 2 edn, Methuen

Drewett, P L, 1975   'Rescue archaeology in Sussex, 1974', *Bull Inst Archaeol*, no **12**, 13–70

Ellison, A and Harriss, J, 1972   'Settlement and land use in the prehistory and early history of southern England; a study based on locational models', in *Models in archaeology* (ed D L Clarke), Methuen

Fleming, A, 1971   'Territorial patterns in Bronze Age Wessex', *Proc Prehist Soc*, **37**, 164

Gerloff, S, 1974   'The Early Bronze Age daggers in Great Britain and a reconsideration of the Wessex culture', *Prähistorische Bronzefunde*, Abt VI, Band **2**, Beck, Munich

Grinsell, L V, 1931   'Sussex in the Bronze Age', *Sussex Archaeol Collect*, **72**, 30–68

Hawkes, C F C, 1935   'The pottery from the sites on Plumpton Plain' *Proc Prehist Soc*, **1**, 39–59

Hawkes, C F C, 1960   'A scheme for the British Bronze Age' (address to the CBA Bronze Age conference, London, December 1960)

Holden, E W, 1972   'A Bronze Age cemetery-barrow on Itford Hill, Beddingham, Sussex', *Sussex Archaeol Collect*, **110**, 70–117

Holden, E W and Bradley, R J, 1976   'A Late Neolithic site at Rackham', *ibid*, **113**, 85–103

Holleyman, G A and Curwen, E C, 1935   'Late Bronze Age lynchet-settlements on Plumpton Plain, Sussex', *Proc Prehist Soc*, **1**, 16–38

Longworth, I H, 1961   'The origins and development of the primary series in the Collared Urn tradition in England and Wales', *ibid*, **27**, 263–306

Musson, R C, 1954   'An illustrated catalogue of Sussex Beaker and Bronze Age pottery', *Sussex Archaeol Collect*, **92**, 106

Phillippe, J, 1936   'Le Fort-Harrouard', *L'Anthropologie*, **46**, 257–301 and 541–612

Ratcliffe-Densham, H B A and M M, 1953   'A Celtic farm on Blackpatch', *Sussex Archaeol Collect*, **91**, 69

Ratcliffe-Densham, H B A and M M, 1961   'An anomalous earthwork of the Late Bronze Age, on Cock Hill, Sussex', *ibid*, **99**, 78–101

Ratcliffe-Densham, H B A and M M, 1966   'Amberley Mount: its agricultural story from the Late Bronze Age', *ibid*, **104**, 6–25

Roe, F, 1966   'The battle-axe series in Britain', *Proc Prehist Soc*, **32**, 199–245

Rowlands, M J, 1976   *The organisation of Middle Bronze Age metalworking*, Brit Archaeol Rep **31**

Sandars, N, 1957   *Bronze Age cultures in France*, Cambridge

Smith, M A, 1959 'Some Somerset hoards and their place in the Bronze Age of southern Britain', *Proc Prehist Soc*, **25**, 144–87

Wainwright, G J and Longworth, I H, 1971   *Durrington Walls*, Soc Antiquaries Res Rep no **29**

Wilson, A E and Burstow, G P, 1948   'The evolution of Sussex Iron Age pottery', *Sussex Archaeol Collect*, **87**, 77

Wolseley, G R, Smith, R A, and Hawley, W, 1927   'Prehistoric and Roman settlements on Park Brow', *Archaeologia*, **76**, 1–40

James Money

This account covers both the Sussex Weald and those parts of the High Weald which lie in the south-eastern corner of Surrey and the south-western corner of Kent, because they are geographically and archaeologically indivisible. The environmental background to the Weald is discussed in Joan Sheldon's paper, so need not be reconsidered here. For the purpose of this paper, the pre-Roman Iron Age is divided into early (up to 150 BC) and late (150 BC to AD 43) phases.

Unfortunately, virtually no field work has been undertaken in the High Weald with the specific intention of discovering Iron Age sites. Our knowledge is therefore restricted almost entirely to the obvious sites like hill-forts and ironworking sites with their slag heaps.

The only site that can be attributed to the early pre-Roman Iron Age is Castle Hill, where there are two enclosures with radiocarbon dates in the 4th and 3rd centuries BC (Money, 1976). The two forts are situated on a spur of high ground controlling a natural north-west, south-east route which the A21 follows today. Castle Hill also exercised indirect control over the crossing of the River Medway at Tonbridge on the important north-south route across the Weald (Margary, 1949; Fig 1). Around the 4th century BC a bivallate fortification enclosing 1·8 ha was built on the brow of the spur. However, after a brief occupation, the revetment of the inner rampart (beside the east entrance at least) was destroyed by fire and collapsed into the ditch. This destruction may have been followed by a peaceful phase during which farming took place. During the 3rd century BC a univallate fortification enclosing 1·01 ha was built to the south-west of the first fort. This second fort appears to have been occupied for only a very short period and then it fell into disuse.

There are six hill-forts, four in the High Weald (High Rocks, Saxonbury, Garden Hill and Philpots) and two on the Lower Greensand (Hammer Wood and Henfield) which, on varying grounds of probability and possibility, can be assigned to the late pre-Roman Iron Age. It seems likely that these forts were built against some actual or potential threat, assuming that some of the smaller ones were not simply for enclosing stock. Possible threats could have been Belgic settlers in areas around the Weald, the Romans, or unfriendly neighbours at any time.

According to Caesar the maritime areas of south-eastern Britain were raided and then settled by Belgae from Gaul, who for the main part retained their tribal names (*BG* V, 12; *BG* II, 4, 5, 14), and maintained their links with Gaul. Caesar's statements make it clear that the Belgae were installed in south-eastern Britain by the second quarter of the 1st century BC and possibly earlier. Of the many find-spots of Gallo-Belgic A, B, C, D, E and F coins, British L coins, and the coins of Tasciovanus, Tincommius and Cunobelin, only eleven are known from the Weald. This probably reflects a general lack of Belgic presence.

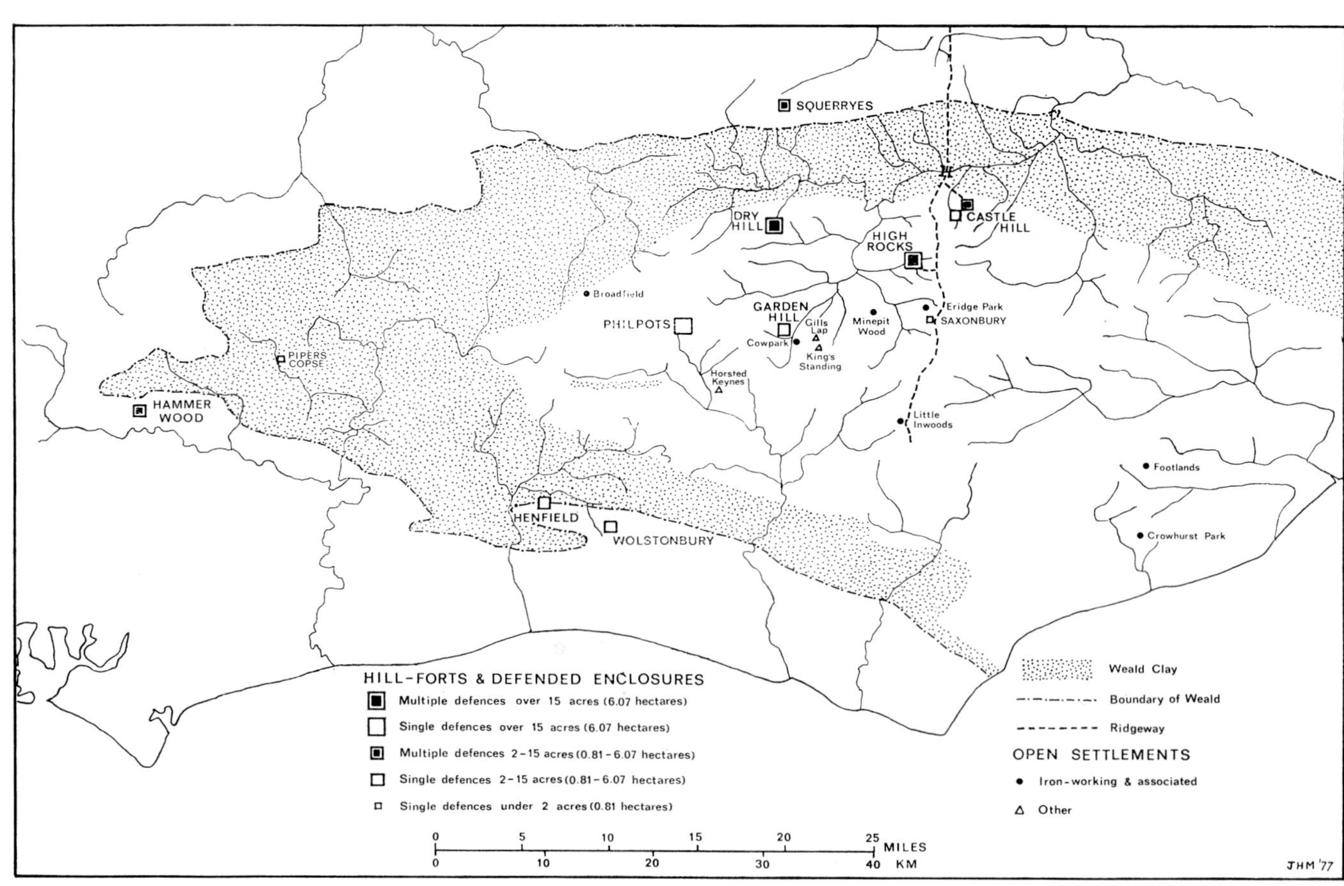

Fig 17   *Iron Age sites in the Weald*

They may not have wished to live in the Weald, or they may have been prevented from doing so by the inhabitants. Nevertheless, the threat of Belgic pressure at one time or another may have prompted some hill-fort building.

There is no evidence that Caesar had designs on or entered the Weald, or that his incursions into south-eastern Britain affected the Weald in any way. However, the Claudian invasion soon overran the area, to be followed by a rapid occupation and development of the Weald. Although there is no evidence, the possibility that the threat of invasion by Gaius (Caligula) in AD 41, and the actual invasion by Claudius in AD 43, stimulated some hill-fort building in the Weald should be considered.

Considering the third possibility, that of unfriendly neighbours, perhaps these promontory forts were strong points where the inhabitants of local open settlements could gather when threatened. They may also have been used regularly as secure winter quarters when agriculture and iron production were in abeyance.

The hill-fort at High Rocks (Money, 1941; 1968) lies one mile south-west of Tunbridge Wells at the end of a promontory. It has strong natural defences with the precipitous sandstone escarpment of the High Rocks on its north and west sides and a steep hillslope on the southern side. Only from the east is the approach level. Excavations by the author indicated that parts of the area were occupied and arable farming was practised at some time before the first fort was built. The first hill-fort consisted of a single bank and ditch enclosing 9·71 ha. These defences were soon abandoned, with evidence for cultivation and possibly ironworking indicating peaceful activities in the area. The hill-fort was then refortified with double banks and ditches. The site was perhaps occupied into the Romano-British period (Money, 1968).

Saxonbury, some 4·4 km to the south-east of High Rocks, also controls a sector of the north-south ridgeway (Margary, 1949). A single bank and ditch, with one entrance, enclose about 0·6 ha. Within this enclosure Winbolt found the stone foundations of an oval enclosure which appeared to predate the rampart (Winbolt, 1930). It is similar in shape to, but about half the size of the earlier enclosure at Wolstonbury, where the outer (later) enclosure is not unlike Saxonbury, but about twice as large (Curwen, 1930). Winbolt found iron slag, pottery which included S-shaped profiles and foot-rings, and a coin of Vespasian or Titus (AD 69–81). Close to Saxonbury is an open settlement in Eridge Park (Money, 1977a) which appears to have been occupied at about the same time.

The fort at Garden Hill lies at the end of a north-east pointing spur in the north-west corner of Ashdown Forest (Tebbutt, 1970; Money, 1973; 1977b). It encloses about 2·7 ha and has a certain inturned entrance at the north-east corner, with another possible entrance at the north-west corner. The inturned entrance had stone-revetted and palisaded banks, through which ran a metalled road. There were two sets of stone-packed gate-posts. Late pre-Roman Iron Age occupation within the enclosure is represented by two round houses (Building D in square H-9 and another in K-10) both built on artificially levelled ground (Money, 1977b; fig 3). Both ironmaking (ore roasting and smelting) and ironworking (forging) were conducted at Garden Hill at an early stage.

The hill-fort at Philpots, West Hoathly (Curwen, 1925; Holgate, 1926; Hannah, 1932) is situated on a promontory of Tunbridge Wells sand in a similar situation to High Rocks. It encloses some 7 ha and has two entrances. It appears to be mainly univallate, but at one point the banks could be double. Although there is no direct dating evidence, a late pre-Roman Iron Age date seems likely.

The promontory fort at Hammer Wood, Iping (Boyden, 1958) encloses 3·6 ha. There are double and partly triple ramparts across the neck of the promontory, the inner rampart having a stone revetment. A slightly larger enclosure (4·85 ha) was made by constructing a single bank and ditch across a promontory at Henfield (Curwen, 1925).

The enclosures at Dry Hill, Lingfield (Winbolt and Margary, 1933) and Piper's Copse, Kirdford (Winbolt, 1936) have produced no dating evidence at all, but are likely to be roughly contemporary with those already described.

The second group of pre-Roman Iron Age sites in Sussex relates to the iron industry. The Weald contained an abundance of all the basic materials required for early ironworking. The best ore came from the bottom of the Wadhurst Clay, which conveniently lay immediately above the stone of the Ashdown Sand (used for furnace construction). There was also plenty of timber, particularly oak, for fuel and building.

Caesar and Strabo mention Britain as a source of iron. Caesar stated that 'in the midland districts of Britain, tin is produced, in the maritime, iron, but there is only a small supply' (*BG* V, 12). Strabo, writing between 7 BC and AD 19, says of Britain that 'it bears grain, cattle, gold, silver and iron, these things accordingly are exported from the island' (*Geog* 4, 5, 3). Caesar's remark can be taken to indicate that in the middle of the 1st century BC iron production in south-western Britain was on a small scale. However, if by Strabo's time, 50 years later, Britain was able to export iron, there must have been a considerable expansion of the industry in the meantime.

We are at a disadvantage in interpreting the scanty archaeological evidence, first because so little excavation has been done, secondly because pre-Roman workings have been overlaid or swept away by production on the same sites under the Romans, and thirdly because the coarse pottery of the Weald retains many pre-Roman features into the 2nd century (Cleere, 1974, 173) and must, therefore, be treated with reserve as dating evidence.

In the 'maritime region' Henry Cleere considers that only Footlands, Sedlescombe (Straker, 1931; Chown, 1946–7) and Crowhurst Park (Straker, 1931; Straker and Lucas, 1938) have any claim to be pre-Roman. All other sites in this area seem to be Roman foundations (Cleere, 1974, 173). Further north and inland, there may have been pre-Roman production at Saxonbury, and there is rather stronger evidence from Eridge Park (Money, 1977a). Pottery from this site includes saucepan pots of Wealden type, Wealden copies of Belgic forms, and decorated sherds of Eastern Atrebatic ware. At Little Inwoods, Hadlow Down (Cattell, 1970; 1971) charcoal from the slag heap gave a radiocarbon date of 30 ± 100 bc (HV–2985). Other early radiocarbon dates include one of ad 1 ± 43 (BM–365) from Minepit Wood (Money, 1974) and two from Broadfields, Crawley (Gibson-Hill, 1976) of 190 ± 80 bc (HAR–971) and 60 ± 60 bc (HAR–970).

Both ironmaking and ironworking took place at Garden Hill either in the lifetime of the hill-fort or soon afterwards (Money, 1977b). Although the nearby Pippingford Park furnace excavated in 1977 is considered on pottery evidence to be just post-Conquest (Tebbutt and Cleere, 1973), pottery associated with the furnaces at Cowpark, Pipping-ford, which Tebbutt investigated in 1977, is so far all of

Iron Age type. It is difficult to avoid the conclusion that, though it might not itself be pre-Conquest, the iron production at Garden Hill and nearby furnaces was based on tradition and practice that was.

This evidence suggests that before the Conquest iron was produced in various suitable parts of the Weald, beginning perhaps as early as the 3rd century BC. Production was still on a small scale in the middle of the 1st century BC, but was expanding in the years immediately before the Conquest. By AD 43 the industry was sufficiently developed to allow rapid and widespread expansion under Roman influence.

With our limited knowledge of the Iron Age in the Weald, only three other occupation sites have been located: at Gillslap (Margary, 1930) and Kings Standing (Margary, 1930) on Ashdown Forest, and at Horsted Keynes (Hardy and Curwen, 1937). Most of the pottery from Horsted Keynes was decorated Eastern Atrebatic (Cunliffe, 1974, 89; 91; 344).

From the very scanty and scattered evidence noted above, certain tentative conclusions may be drawn about the Iron Age occupation of the Weald.

Until the late pre-Roman Iron Age occupation of the High Weald, which was heavily forested, was on a very small scale, perhaps limited to its northern edge. There was a settlement at Castle Hill, which was cleared of forest and suitable for farming. It controlled important communications and was defensible when threatened. The Weald's potential as a source of iron attracted communities to suitable points, perhaps as early as the 3rd century BC. During the late pre-Roman Iron Age (150 BC–AD 43) Wealden people, who settled and farmed suitable areas and continued to develop the production of iron, tended to congregate in the central part of the High Weald, where they established themselves at sites like High Rocks, Saxonbury, Garden Hill and Philpots, which were habitable, defensible, dominated the surrounding countryside and local communications and, in times of danger or in the winter (when agriculture and iron production were in abeyance), could provide refuge to neighbouring open sites. The promontory forts of Hammer Wood and Henfield on the northern edge of the Lower Greensand may also belong to this period.

There is no evidence that the Weald was affected by the incursions of Julius Caesar in 55–54 BC, and in the mid 1st century BC iron production was still on a small scale, but by the end of the century was large enough to allow iron to be exported. By the time of the Roman Conquest iron production was sufficiently developed to allow rapid and widespread expansion under Roman influences.

References

Boyden, J R, 1958   'Excavations at Hammer Wood, Iping, 1957', *Sussex Archaeol Collect*, **96**, 149–63

Cattell, C S, 1970   'Preliminary research findings relating to the bloomery period of the iron industry in the upper basin of the eastern Rother (East Sussex)', *Bull Historical Metall Group* **4**, no 1, 18–20

Cattell, C S, 1971   'A note on the dating of bloomeries in the upper basin of the eastern Rother', *Bull Historical Metall Group* **5**, no 2, 76

Chown, E, 1946–7   'Painted Iron Age pottery at Sedlescombe', *Sussex Notes and Queries*, **11**, 148–51

Cleere, H, 1974   'The Roman iron industry of the Weald and its connexions with the *Classis Britannica*', *Archaeol J*, **131**, 171–99

Cunliffe, B W, 1974   *Iron Age communities in Britain*, London

Curwen, E and E C, 1925   'Two Wealden promontory forts', *Sussex Archaeol Collect*, **66**, 176–80

Curwen, E C, 1930   'Wolstonbury', *ibid*, **71**, 237–45

Gibson-Hill, J, 1976   'Further excavations at the Romano-British ironworking site at Broadfields, Crawley', *Bull Inst Archaeol*, **13**, 79–88

Hannah, I C, 1932   'Philpots Camp, West Hoathly', *Sussex Archaeol Collect*, **73**, 156–67

Hardy, H R and Curwen, E C, 1937   'An Iron Age pottery site near Horsted Keynes', *ibid*, **78**, 252–65

Holgate, M S, 1926   'The surroundings of Philpots Camp', *ibid*, **67**, 222–4

Margary, I D, 1930   'A Celtic enclosure in Ashdown Forest and Kings Standing, Ashdown Forest', *Sussex Notes and Queries*, **3**, 71–6

Margary, I D, 1949   *Roman ways in the Weald*, 2 impr, London, 258–9; 264–5

Money, J H, 1941   'An interim report on excavations at High Rocks, Tunbridge Wells, 1940', *Sussex Archaeol Collect*, **82**, 104–9

Money, J H, 1968   'Excavations in the Iron Age hill-fort at High Rocks, Tunbridge Wells, 1957–61', *ibid*, **106**, 158–205

Money, J H, 1973   'Garden Hill', *Curr Archaeol*, **41**, 185–8

Money, J H, 1974   'Iron Age and Romano-British ironworking site in Minepit Wood, Rotherfield, Sussex', *Bull Historical Metall Group* **8**, no 1, 1–20

Money, J H, 1976   'Excavations in the two Iron Age hill-forts on Castle Hill, Capel, near Tonbridge, 1965 and 1969–71', *Archaeol Cantiana*, **91**, 61–85; *ibid*, **94** (forthcoming)

Money, J H, 1977a   'Iron Age and Romano-British settlement in Eridge Park', *Sussex Archaeol Collect* (forthcoming)

Money, J H, 1977b   'The Iron Age hill-fort and Romano-British ironworking settlement at Garden Hill, Sussex: interim report on excavations, 1968–76', *Britannia*, **8**, 339–50

Straker, E, 1931   *Wealden iron*, London

Straker, E and Lucas, B H, 1938   'A Romano-British bloomery in East Sussex', *Sussex Archaeol Collect*, **79**, 224–32

Tebbutt, C F, 1970   'Garden Hill Camp, Hartfield', *ibid*, **108**, 39–49

Tebbutt, C F and Cleere, H F, 1973   'A Romano-British bloomery at Pippingford, Hartfield', *ibid*, **111**, 27–40

Winbolt, S E, 1930   'Excavations at Saxonbury Camp', *ibid*, **71**, 222–36

Winbolt, S E and Margary, I D, 1933   'Dry Hill Camp, Lingfield', *Surrey Archaeol Collect*, **41**, 79–92

Winbolt, S E, 1936   'An early Iron Age camp in Piper's Copse, Kirdford', *Sussex Archaeol Collect*, **77**, 244–9

This article will be mainly concerned with settlement patterns and the economy of the Iron Age. No radiocarbon dates are yet available for any Iron Age site on the Downs or the Coastal Plain, and thus the backbone of the chronology is the pottery sequence. Since this has been comprehensively described elsewhere (Cunliffe, 1974), no discussion of Iron Age pottery is included here.

The Downs

At least 50 Iron Age sites are known on the Sussex Downs (Fig 18). Although the most conspicuous and well known of these are the hill-forts, the basic social and economic unit of the Iron Age is the small agricultural settlement, which carries on the Bronze Age tradition of mixed farming, exemplified by Itford Hill.

These agricultural settlements, or farmsteads, are found throughout the Iron Age, from early ones such as Muntham Court and Findon Park, to later ones such as Charleston Brow and Shepherds Garden, Arundel. Many settlements are located on south-facing spurs, though not necessarily on the highest point, and are often surrounded by, or adjacent to, contemporary field systems. In several cases there is considerable continuity of occupation; at Park Brow, for example, three separate settlement sites of different periods, from Middle Bronze Age to Romano-British, are known on the same chalk spur, and the field system is equally accessible from each one (Fig 19).

Sites with continuity of occupation often demonstrate a pattern in the location of the domestic area relative to the field system. Where a trackway survives, the settlement may be at one end (eg Bullock Down, Fig 19), or adjacent to it (eg Charleston Brow, Fig 19), and the same pattern holds for Romano-British settlement.

The settlements of the Iron Age are more numerous, more varied, and frequently larger than those of the Bronze Age (Fig 20). Some have an enclosing earthwork which may be substantial enough to be regarded as defensive, as was probably the case at Bury Hill, or it may simply serve to demarcate the domestic area, as at Bishopstone. Alternatively, enclosure may be effected by means of a wooden palisade; Muntham Court (Burstow and Holleyman 1957) and the early Iron Age site at Park Brow are good examples of this. (The palisade is a well known feature on Bronze Age sites, and it is therefore not surprising that it is so far known only on early Iron Age sites.) Finally, there are open settlements such as Slonk Hill (R Hartridge, *pers comm*). Even in the absence of an earthwork or palisade, the domestic area may effectively be defined by the edge of a trackway and the inner boundary of a field system, and there is always the possibility of the existence of a thick hedge having served the same purpose.

Several settlements have been excavated, but only three on a large scale, namely Bishopstone, Slonk Hill, and Muntham Court. The results of these excavations provide a coherent picture of the economy, based on mixed farming. The arable contribution is indicated by the presence of fields contemporary with the settlement, and by the discovery of grain, often charred, in pits and other features. At Bishopstone by far the most predominant cereal remains were those of spelt, followed by barley (Bell, 1977a). Artefacts such as iron ploughshares, sickles for reaping, and quernstones for grinding grain have also been found. Cross-plough marks cut into the chalk subsoil were found at Bishopstone, sealed by a late Iron Age context (Bell, 1977a). The pastoral element in the economy is well attested by the presence of animal bones, those of cattle and sheep occurring most frequently. Sheep may also have been kept for wool; certainly, spindle whorls and loom weights of baked clay or chalk are among the most ubiquitous of finds on Iron Age sites, indicating the importance of spinning and weaving. Bone weaving combs are also known.

The diet was sometimes supplemented by marine shellfish, the remains of which have been found on several sites (eg Bishopstone). Hunting and fowling seem to have been little practised (Bell, 1977a).

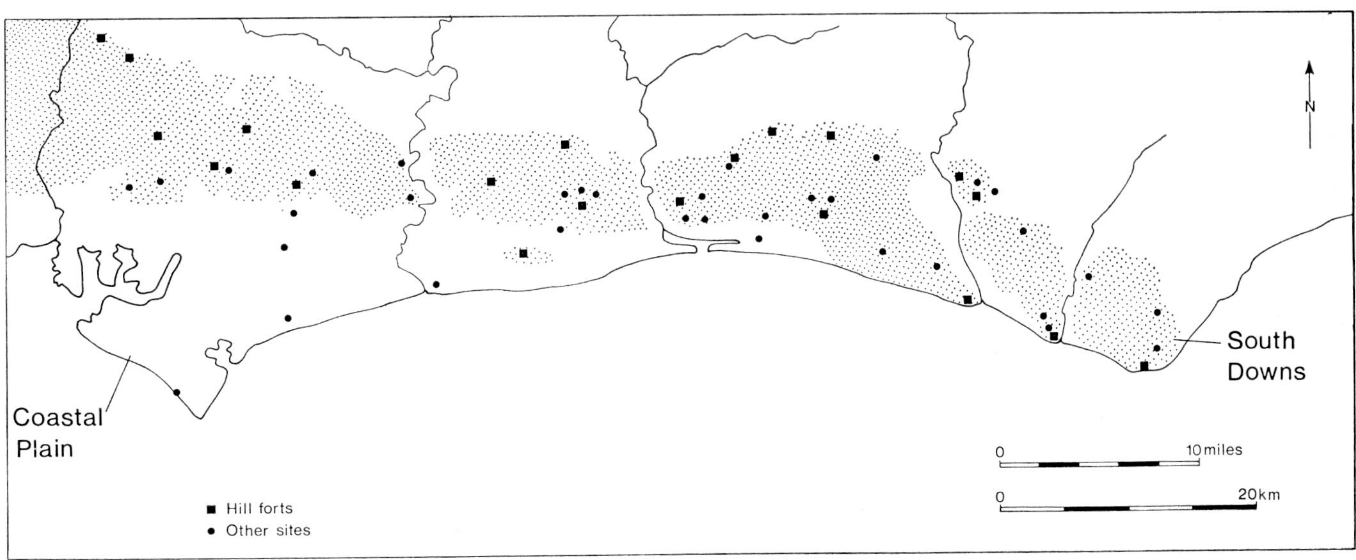

Fig 18 Distribution map of Iron Age sites on the Downs and Coastal Plain

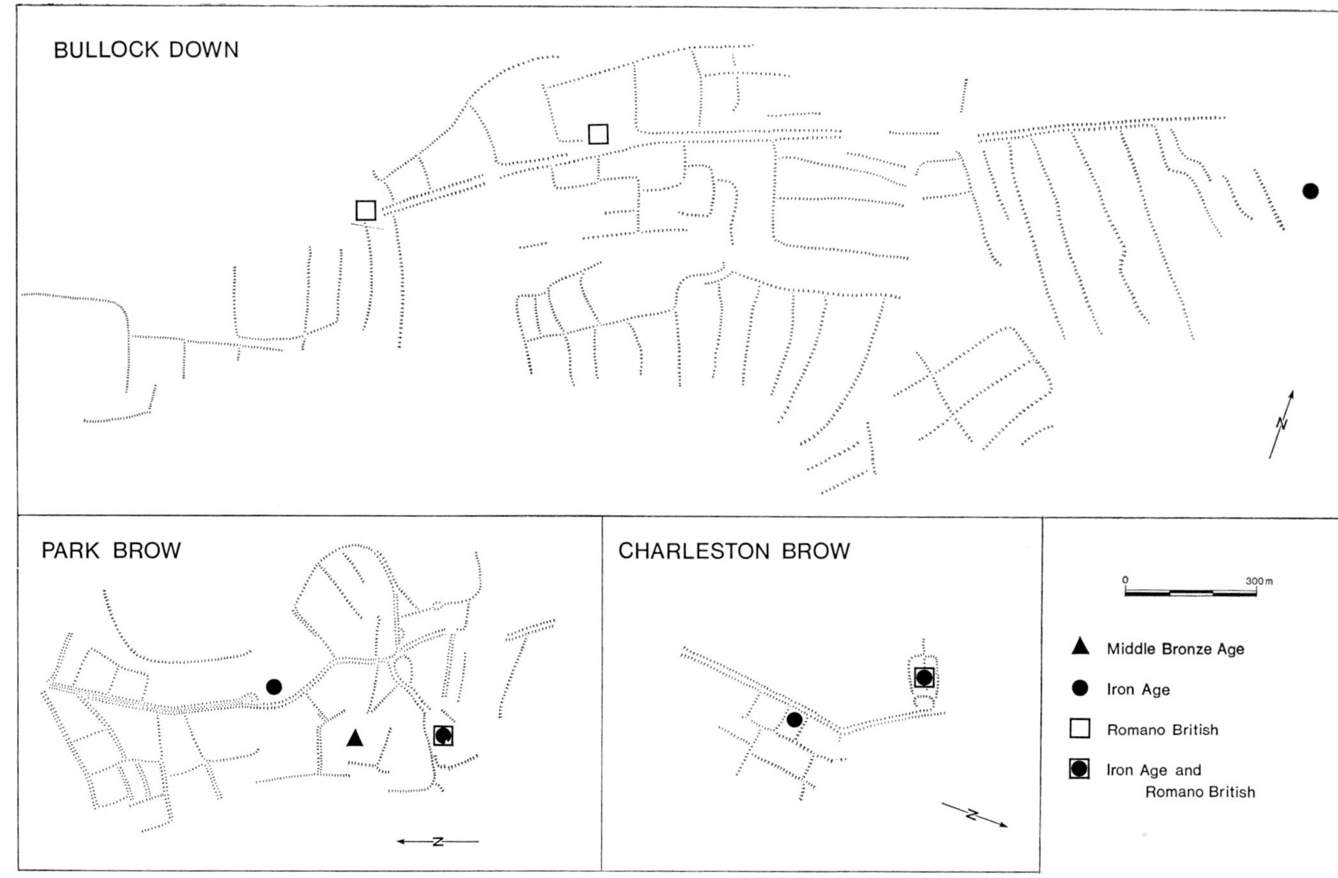

Fig **19**   *Location of settlements in relation to trackways and field systems*

The size of the social group occupying an Iron Age farmstead is not easy to establish; here the lack of a totally excavated settlement and the elusiveness of Iron Age houses (see below) are crucial. It is thus necessary to look outside Sussex for relevant evidence; for example, the complete excavation of a 0·4 ha enclosure at Tollard Royal (Wilts) revealed one circular hut, suggesting a single family unit (Wainwright, 1968). Larger enclosures may have been inhabited by several family units, and could perhaps be thought of as small hamlets.

Hill-forts

Superimposed on this continuum of agricultural communities are the twenty hill-forts. Any attempt to integrate the role of hill-forts with the pattern of farmsteads already discussed faces several problems. The first is that although most of the hill-forts have been dated, little work has been done on hill-fort interiors in Sussex. Again we are obliged to look outside Sussex; Cunliffe's work at Danebury (Hants) is obviously of great relevance. The second difficulty is that the Sussex hill-forts are an extremely heterogeneous group of earthworks (Figs 21 and 22). The largest is Belle Tout where, even after $2\frac{1}{2}$ millennia of coastal erosion, a feeble univallate earthwork encloses 25 ha; the smallest, the rectangular earthwork on Harrow Hill, encloses 0·4 ha. It is thus inherently unlikely that all these hill-forts share a common function, or functions. Finally, a few of the smaller hill-forts seem to be little more than defended farmsteads. The Caburn is a good example: excavation has shown that the site began

as a palisaded farm, but was later fortified (Wilson, 1938). Perhaps it should be regarded as an unusually importatn farmstead. Highdown is probably another. (It is also worth bearing in mind the possibility that hill-forts situated on the northern edge of the Downs might be more satisfactorily considered in relating to Iron Age communities in the Weald, exploiting both Downland and Wealden resources.)

Excavation has clarified some of these problems. In particular, two phases of hill-fort construction have been identified, giving rise, successively, to what Cunliffe (1976a) has described as *early hill-forts* and *developed hill-forts.*

The first of these phases, the early hill-forts, is dated by its pottery to the earliest part of the Iron Age, centring on the 6th and 5th centuries BC; examples of this phase are Harting Beacon, Hollingbury, Chanctonbury, Ranscombe Camp, and Belle Tout, and probably also Harrow Hill, Thundersbarrow, and Wolstonbury. In the case of the last three, the pottery evidence is not conclusive. Wolstonbury is also exceptional in having its ditch inside the rampart (Curwen, 1930); whether it should be regarded as a hill-fort of an aberrant type, or a totally different kind of site, is not clear. None of these forts possesses strong defences and none appears to have been in use for a long period. In addition, several early hill-forts develop from smaller, feebler enclosures on the same site. At Thundersbarrow, a small, square enclosure was encircled by a later, more rounded earthwork (Curwen, 1933); at Hollingbury, a ditched enclosure was enlarged along one side and fortified (Curwen, 1932); at Wolstonbury, an oval enclosure

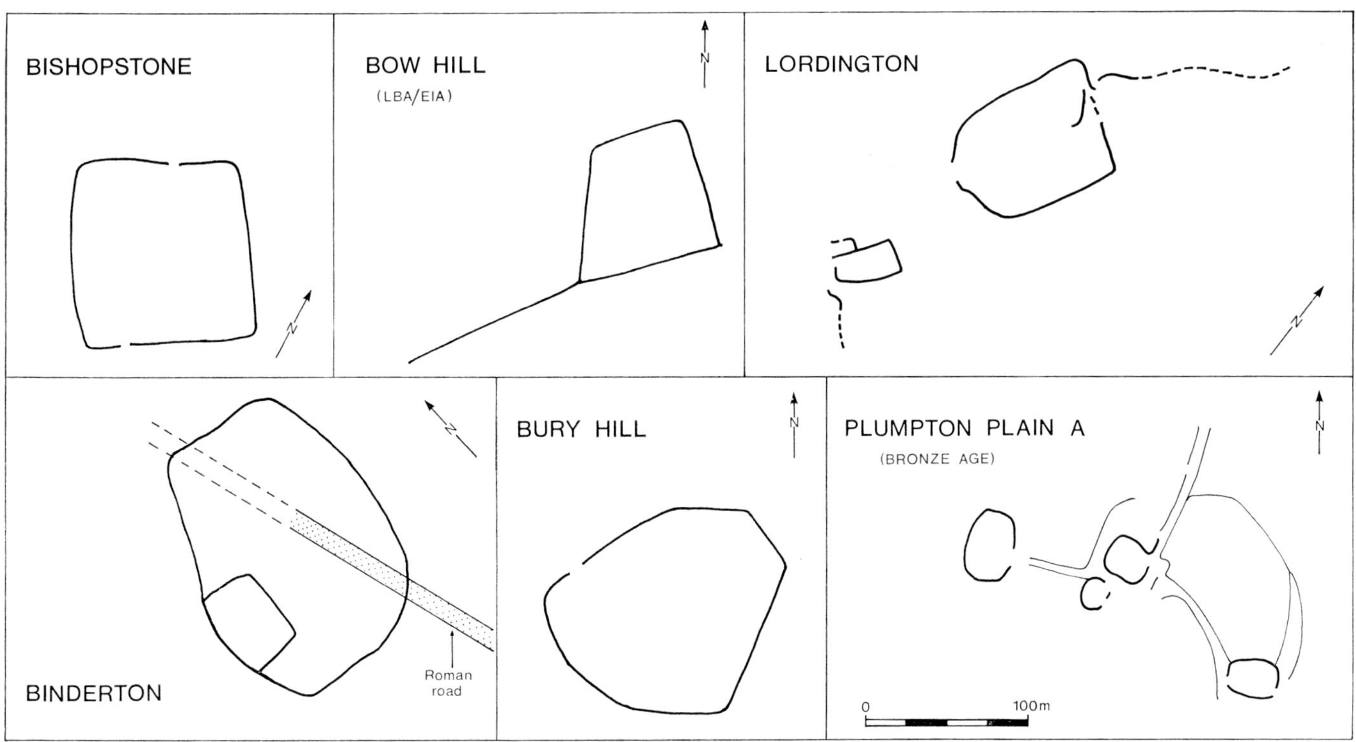

Fig 20   Comparative plans of Iron Age enclosures on the Downs (with the Bronze Age settlement at Plumpton Plain for comparison)

was enlarged (Curwen, 1930). Hollingbury was also found to contain a 50 m length of palisade, but how this related to the rest of the hill-fort is not known. Harrow Hill shows a slightly different pattern of development; it does not develop out of an earlier earthwork, but an irregular line of shallow postholes was found beneath the rampart, and this has been interpreted as evidence of a palisaded enclosure preceding the earthwork (Holleyman, 1937).

Despite the differences in size, the hill-forts of this early group do have certain similarities, sufficient perhaps for them to be regarded as having a common function, namely, the enclosure of stock. While this is extremely plausible, it is obviously difficult to prove incontrovertibly. Harrow Hill is the only site where there is direct evidence of activities relating to stock; during the 1936 excavation small parts of the interior were investigated, and well over 50 ox skulls were found, with hardly any limb bones. The excavator calculated that if these findings were representative, then at least 1000 ox skulls must be present (Holleyman, 1937). The large number of skulls may simply indicate butchering, but may also have ritual overtones (see below). If the stock enclosure interpretation is correct, these hill-forts may only have been used seasonally, or intermittently, the animals being collected for slaughtering, or buying and selling, or simply to keep them safe from marauders.

The variation in size among early hill-forts no doubt reflects the interaction of many local factors, such as the density of population, the number of animals needing to be corralled, and the extent of cooperation between communities. Larger examples, such as Harting Beacon, are surely communal works, whereas smaller ones, such as Harrow Hill, were probably constructed by comparatively few people.

There remains the problem of whether the early hill-forts were inhabited. None of the hill-forts shows signs of intensive occupation, but at Hollingbury several round houses were found in the southern half of the hill-fort (Fig 23), though large areas were empty of houses or other structures (J Holmes, *pers comm*). At Harting Beacon, the distribution of potsherds within the ploughed interior suggests a focus of domestic activity in the south-east corner of the hill-fort, though excavation has revealed only four-post structures and a few pits (Bedwin, 1977a).

The developed hill-fort phase begins as the early phase is coming to an end. Whereas the early hill-forts are distributed all along the Sussex Downs, regional differences appear in this second phase (Fig 24). The characteristic developed hill-forts, Cissbury, Torberry, and the Trundle, are all west of the Adur. Each has strong defences, although Torberry has suffered badly from ploughing; the Trundle and Torberry also have inturned entrances typical of the later Iron Age. At Torberry, the entrance took the form of two parallel flanking walls, 26 m long and built of chalk blocks (Cunliffe, 1976b). The inturned entrance excavated at the Trundle was 18 m long; judging by the amount of flint rubble found in the gateway, there had existed flanking walls of flint (Curwen, 1931). Very large holes for gateposts were found on both these sites.

Curwen was in no doubt as to the nature of these developed hill-forts; as early as the 1930s he was describing them as 'walled towns' (Curwen, 1937). The use of the word 'town' carries considerable implications as to the internal organization and functioning of such a hill-fort. Although there is no direct evidence from Sussex sites, it is clear from Cunliffe's work at Danebury that a high degree of order was maintained in the layout of houses and other structures throughout a long period of intensive occupation (Cunliffe, 1976a); Danebury is thus a site of essentially urban character, and the developed hill-forts in Sussex may well be similar.

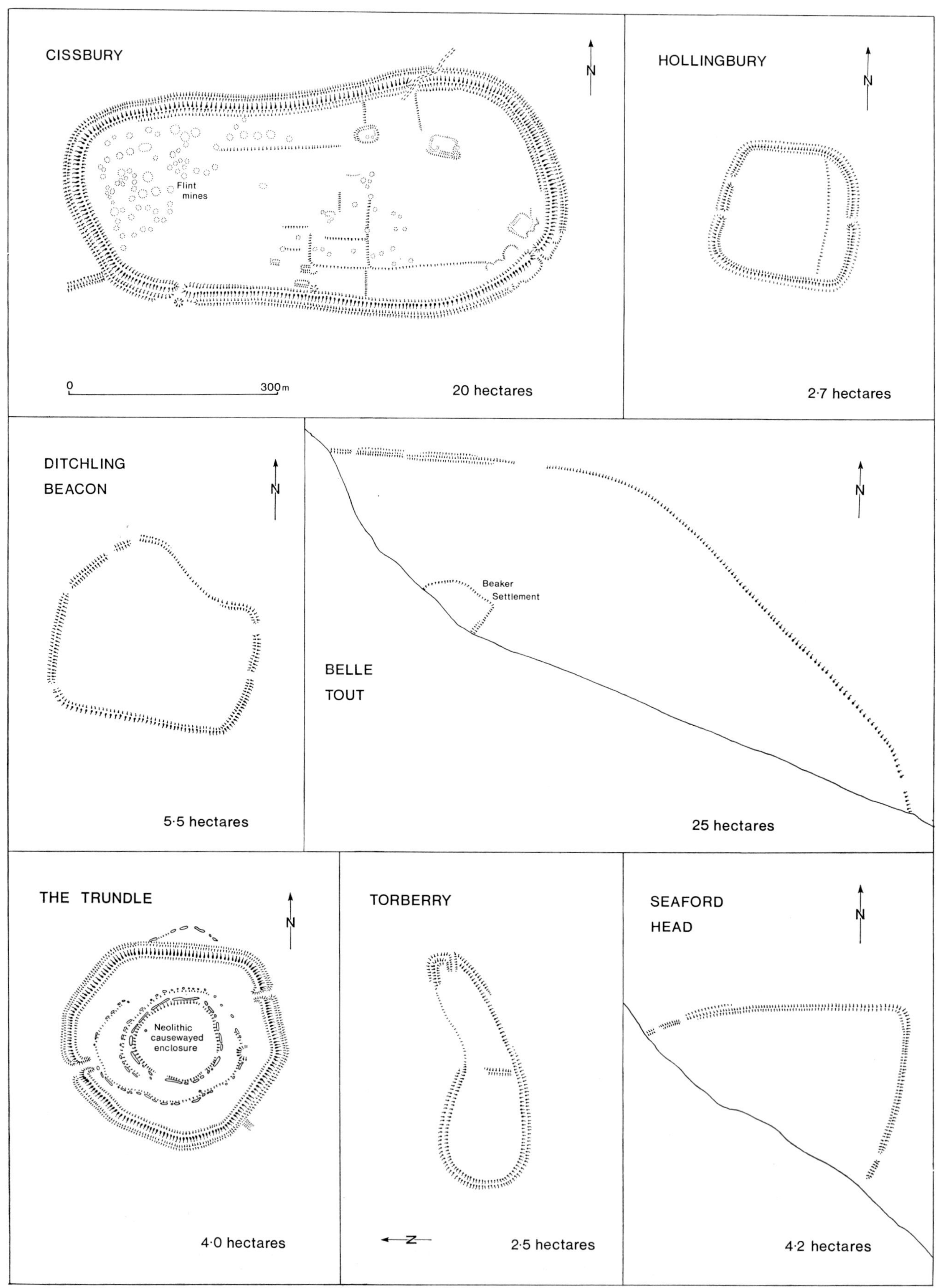

Fig **21** *Comparative plans of Sussex hill-forts—I*

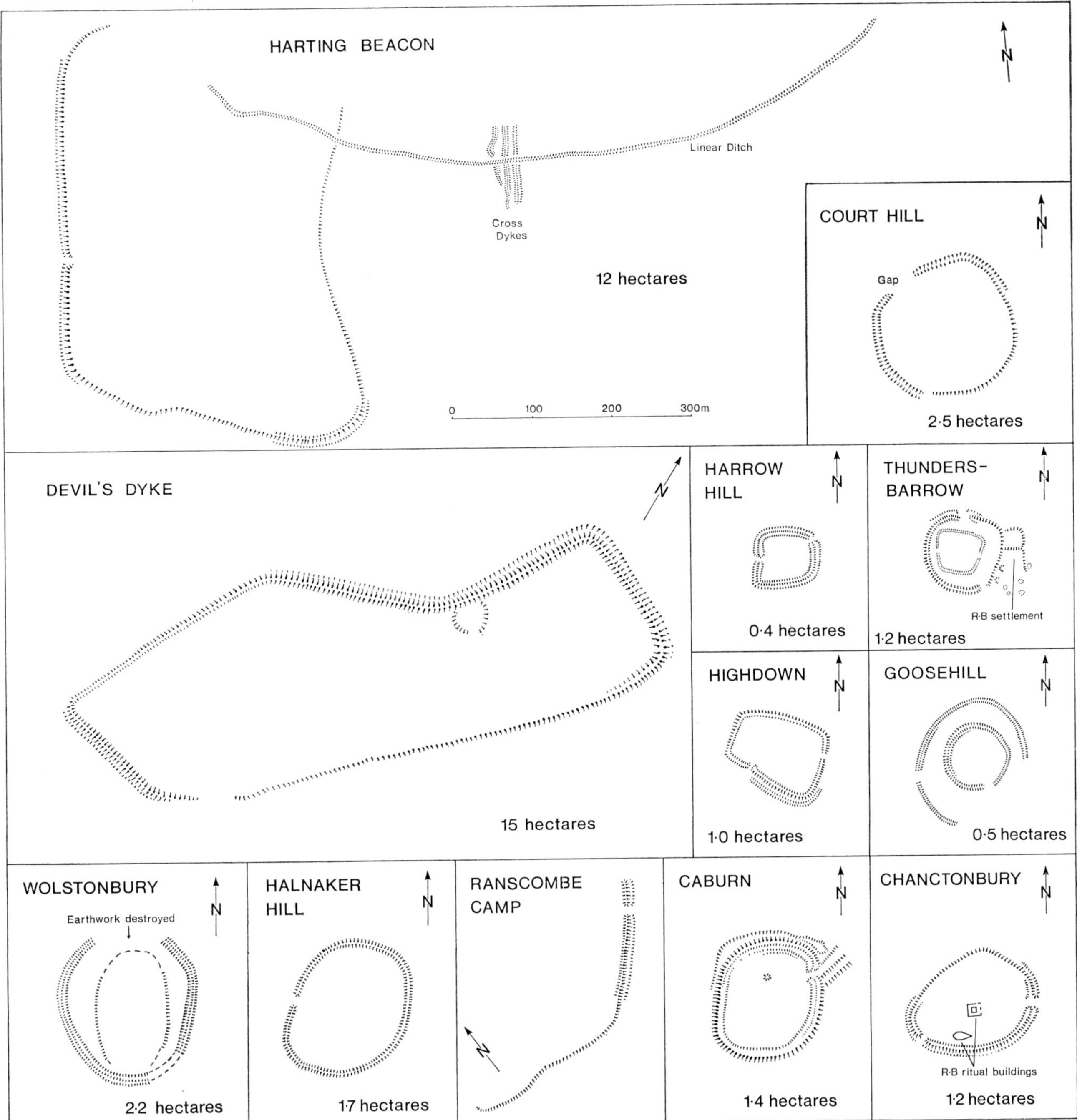

Fig 22   Comparative plans of Sussex hill-forts—II

It is difficult to avoid the conclusion that these hill-forts became the political and economic centres of a given area. In Sussex this is particularly evident because, to the west of the Adur, there is one developed hill-fort on each block of Downland between the main rivers, a pattern which is continued into the eastern part of Hampshire. Such hill-forts would be at the top of an economic pyramid, the base of which consists of many outlying farmsteads. They would inevitably become natural foci for trade and specialist activities in the same way as a small market town serves local farms today.

The evidence from excavation dates the origins of the developed hill-forts to the 5th and 4th centuries BC.

What is remarkable is that occupation of each one ends *c* 100 BC, ie no hill-fort in Sussex west of the Adur is occupied or in use for about 150 years before the Roman invasion. Indeed, the context of their abandonment is uncertain. The gate at Torberry was thought to have been slighted deliberately, but no intrusive pottery was identified with this event (Cunliffe, 1976b). Given the date of the abandonment, it seems likely that it is associated with Belgic incursion, for which there is far more evidence in West Sussex than in East Sussex.

On the Downs, east of the Adur, no strictly comparable series of developed hill-forts exists. Admittedly, on each block of Downland, there is a hill-fort which is

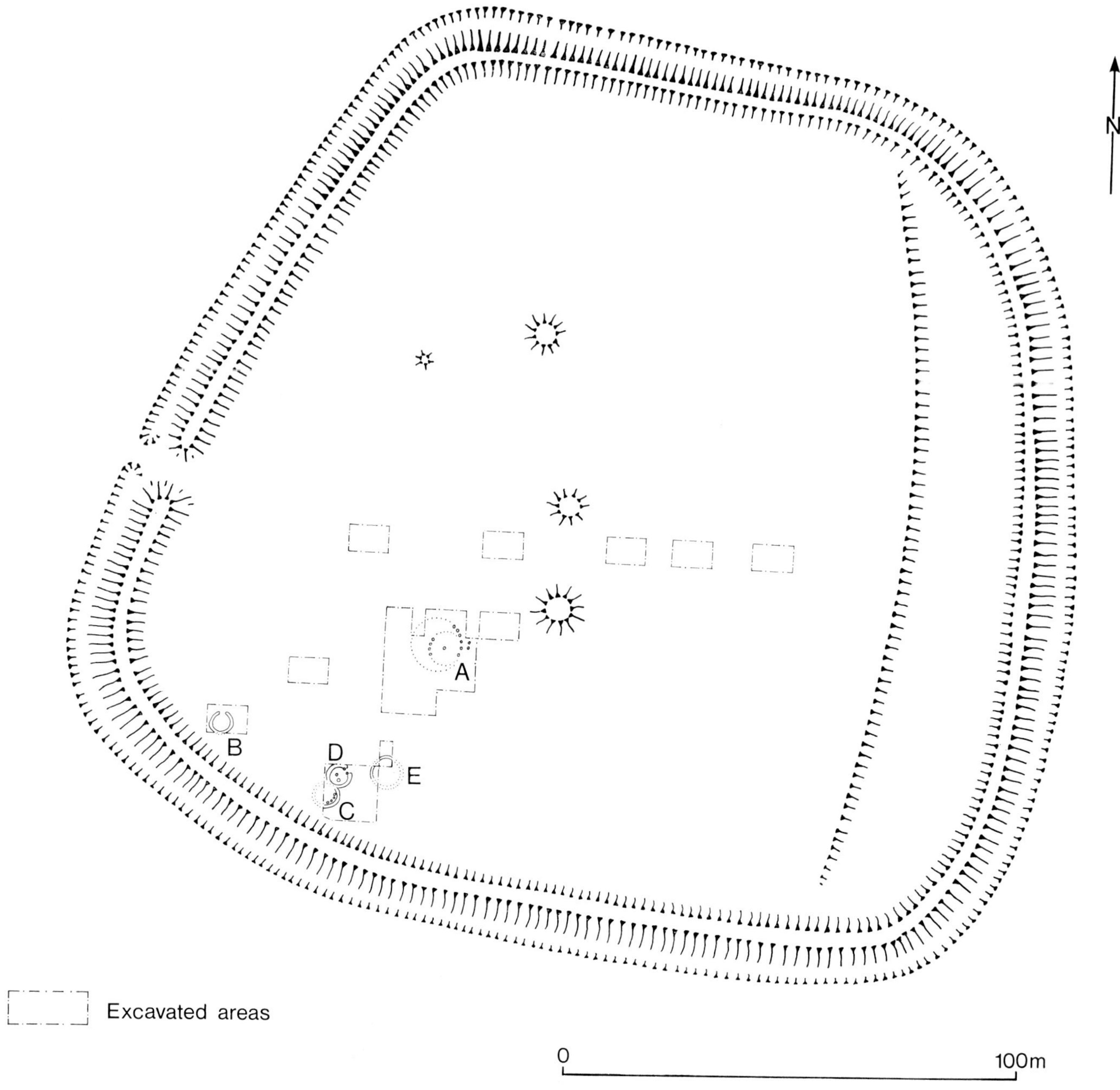

Fig 23   Plan of excavations at Hollingbury, showing round houses

occupied in the later part of the Iron Age, namely Devil's Dyke, the Caburn, and perhaps Castle Hill, Newhaven. As a group, these will be referred to as *late hill-forts*, though there is so little uniformity among them that this is only a label of convenience. The single factor linking these hill-forts is that each appears to have been occupied in the last century before the Roman invasion, in contrast to the developed hill-forts.

The sequence at the Caburn is the best understood. The site was initially a simple farmstead, dated to the 6th and 5th centuries BC (Wilson, 1938). Fortification took place later, with a simple dump rampart consisting of up-cast from the ditch. The site was re-fortified in the middle of the first century AD, probably as a response to the Roman invasion, but no evidence of a battle has been found.

Devil's Dyke is morphologically quite different. It is a much larger hill-fort than the Caburn, with an irregular outline and feeble defences. From physical appearance it might seem to belong to the category of early hill-forts, but a very limited excavation inside the fort revealed a shallow gully in the topsoil, a feature which was interpreted as the foundations of a circular hut (Burstow and Wilson, 1936). The associated pottery was dated 50 BC–AD 50, but it should be pointed out that the excavation corresponded to only 0·0001% of the hill-fort interior and may therefore be quite unrepresentative.

Finally, there is the former earthwork on Castle Hill, Newhaven. This is now completely obliterated, but if 18th and 19th century maps are reliable, the area enclosed was up to 15 ha. A great deal of pottery has been recovered from the hill top (Field, 1939), dating from the Neolithic

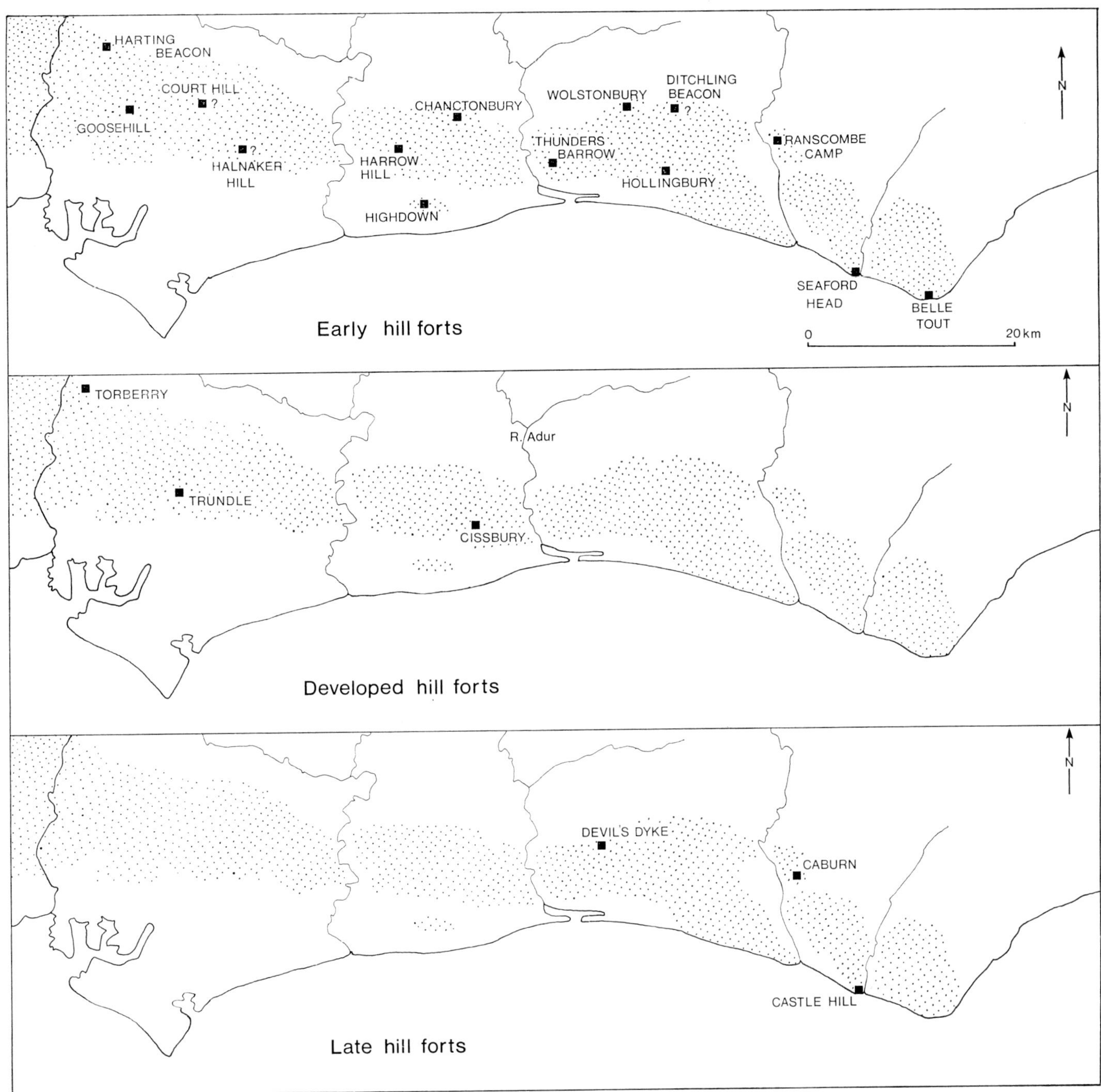

Fig **24** *Early, developed, and late hill-forts in Sussex*

to the Roman period, with much of it belonging to various stages of the Iron Age. Unfortunately it is impossible to associate any of these groups of pottery with the earthwork. To understand the different pattern of hill-fort development east and west of the Adur, it is necessary first to ask the question, why build hill-forts at all? Hill-forts appear all over southern Britain during the Iron Age, and the construction of these defended sites clearly reflects the unsettled nature of society, Early writers were ready to see the Iron Age in terms of a series of Continental invasions, with hill-forts as a dramatic manifestation of a rather warlike period. However, more critical examination of the evidence from excavation (eg Harding, 1974)

provides little support for invasion before the arrival of the Belgae in the late Iron Age.

A more plausible model is the economic one, in which population pressure is seen as the major factor responsible for social unrest (Bradley, 1971). The increased number of Iron Age sites compared with those of the Bronze Age may be reasonably considered as evidence of higher population. Eventually, it is suggested, there will come a time when all available land will have been settled, and unrest will inevitably have followed. Furthermore, it has been pointed out that many of the linear earthworks known as cross dykes probably functioned as territorial boundaries in the early Iron Age, or even late Bronze Age; an analysis of the relation of cross dykes and Iron Age sites on the

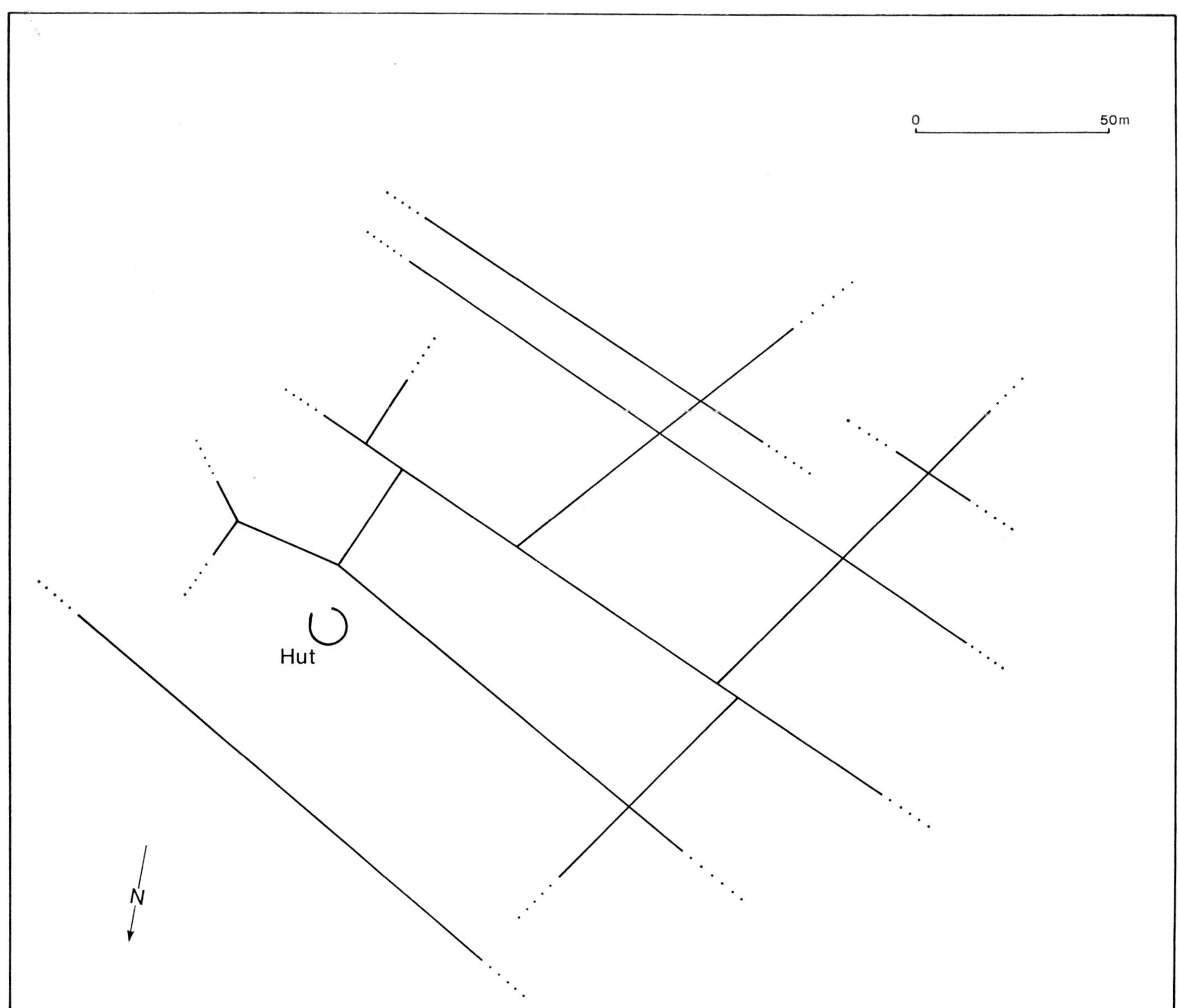

Fig 25   Plan of the Iron Age field system at North Bersted

narrow Ebble-Nadder ridge in Wiltshire has shown this convincingly (Fowler, 1964).

Thus, the appearance on the Downs of the first defended sites (the early hill-forts) and the first land boundaries (the cross dykes) can be regarded as responses to population pressure. By the time of the developed hill-forts, the pattern has crystallized in the form of large, heavily defended sites like the Trundle and Cissbury. These hill-forts are the centres of much larger territories, in which the boundaries are the main rivers; it is possible that early Iron Age cross dykes have become obsolete by this time.

Given this model of events, the lack of a series of developed hill-forts east of the Adur could have many causes. Population pressure may have been less intense, or may have been manifest rather later in this area; the well-defined group of early hill-forts perhaps makes this unlikely. Alternatively, lack of social cohesiveness may have prevented the channelling of communal effort into the building of developed hill-forts.

The Coastal Plain

There are four different subsoils on the Coastal Plain: brick earth (which accounts for 60%), gravel, alluvium, and clay. Few Iron Age sites are known, and little excavation has been carried out; only one settlement has been investigated (Bedwin and Pitts, 1977).

The potential of the Coastal Plain is considerable; its soils are fertile, though heavy, and there is good access from the sea, with several sheltered harbours. In addition, Roman settlement in this area is known to have been extensive. Why is there so little sign of Iron Age occupation? Almost certainly this is not due to the lack of sites, but rather to the difficulty of finding them. No Iron Age sites on the Coastal Plain are defined by earthworks, nor do known sites show up from the air; moreover, ploughing rarely reveals them. Although Roman pottery is brought to the surface by the plough, prehistoric sherds in general are not; where they do appear they are so abraded as to be recognizable only by fabric. This

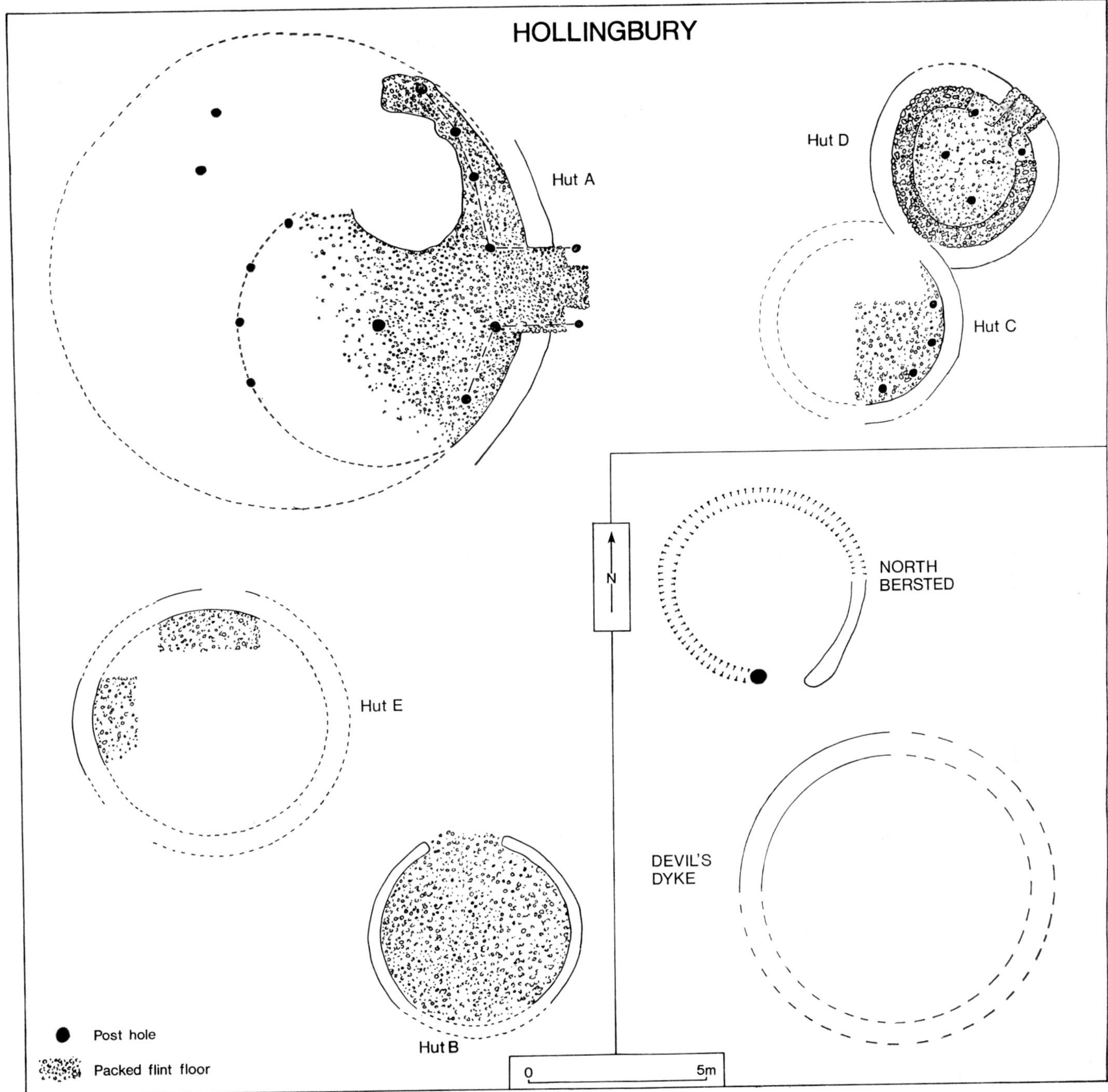

Fig 26 Comparative plans of Iron Age houses in Sussex

is no doubt a result of the acidity of the soils, especially the brick earth (Pitts, 1975). Thus, until very recently, no Iron Age site had been found by fieldwalking ploughed areas.

The single excavated site, at North Bersted, Bognor Regis, is situated on low-lying brick earth (Bedwin and Pitts, 1977). The main feature of this site is its network of drainage ditches, which act as field boundaries (Fig 25). It was not possible to determine the full extent of the ditch system because of modern urban build-up, but at least 5 ha were traced, and the total area could have been much greater. The remains of one small, circular hut were also found. The construction, and perhaps also the maintenance, of such an extensive ditch system would have

involved a considerable amount of work, perhaps requiring communal effort. Since only one hut was found, it is possible that the North Bersted settlement is of a 'dispersed' type, with individual huts located at intervals within the system of fields.

The economic basis of this settlement cannot be fully assessed. Large numbers of animal bones were recovered, among which cattle were numerically the most important, followed by sheep and pig. However, flotation of soil samples from various features produced no plant remains, probably because of poor preservation. What the diet consisted of, apart from meat, is thus unknown.

Iron Age occupation at North Bersted is dated by its pottery from the 4th century BC to shortly before the

Roman invasion; considerable quantities of saucepan pottery and Belgic wares were found.

Part of a similar ditch system was found at Worthing, where trial trenches revealed approximately rectangular fields, 72 m by 18 m, also on brick earth (Lewis, 1960). The pottery from the ditch silts was largely Roman, but a little Iron Age material was also found, and the excavator suggested that the field system was laid down in the later part of the Iron Age and continued in use until the 3rd century AD.

Much of the remainder of the evidence for Iron Age occupation on the Coastal Plain is incomplete and unsatisfactory. For example, there are several find-spots of early Iron Age pottery in the Littlehampton area, centred on the villa (Bedwin, 1977b). The villa itself was excavated in 1949, and has not been published, but it is clear from the material surviving in Littlehampton Museum that considerable evidence of early Iron Age occupation was found, including a large pit, 2 m wide and 1·5 m deep. Within the pit were two separate layers of charred grain, about 0·5 m apart. The grain was very well preserved, and consisted largely of spelt, though rye and barley were also present (Arthur, 1954).

One important activity about which little is known is the production of salt from sea water. Bradley (1975) has located several salt-working sites along the coast, dating to the late Iron Age and Roman periods. Excavation of one of these sites would be extremely useful.

Finally, there is the question of the large numbers of Iron Age coins, potsherds and features such as 'hut floors', uncovered by coastal erosion to the west of Selsey Bill (eg Heron-Allen, 1910). These findings have been interpreted as evidence for the existence of an oppidum, now largely or completely destroyed; the Chichester Dykes are thus seen as protective outworks of a type known from other oppida (Cunliffe, 1976a).

If there was an oppidum at Selsey, it would have been the focus of late Iron Age occupation on the Coastal Plain. Whether this occupation took the form of settlements of the North Bersted type can only be decided by further excavation. Despite the difficulty of finding sites, it does seem likely that there was considerable settlement in the area, particularly during the later Iron Age, and that in the century of so before the Roman invasion the political and mercantile centre was an oppidum at Selsey.

In West Sussex, therefore, the abandonment of the three developed hill-forts and the growth of Selsey would seem to be connected. (The possibility of other oppida, as yet undiscovered, should be kept in mind). Whether we should suppose violent overthrow of the political power centred on developed hill-forts, or simply economic outflanking of Downland sites by an oppidum better suited to deal with cross-channel trade is not clear.

Iron Age houses

The limited number of Iron Age house plans from Sussex sites is all the more remarkable when compared with the characteristic small round houses known from many Bronze Age sites. Since this lack of Iron Age houses does not reflect lack of excavation, it may be that many of them are of a form that survives poorly in the archaeological record. Admittedly, some small round houses are known on the Downs and Coastal Plain, but they do not by any means exhibit the uniformity of the Bronze Age type.

The best defined series of houses comes from Hollingbury, where excavation has uncovered several round houses from 5·5 m to 13 m in diameter, all of early Iron Age date (Fig 26; Huts A–E). These houses were recognized by the presence of ring gullies of various sizes, and also, in some cases, by postholes. A porch was present on the largest hut (Hut A); the smallest, Hut D, had the most substantial wall and several fragments of triangular loom weights were found nearby (J Holmes, *pers comm*).

Just inside the Caburn, an arc of four postholes which, if continued, would imply a circular structure of 9 m diameter, was interpreted as a hut (Wilson, 1938). Large-scale excavation within the Caburn would probably reveal many more.

A different type of round house was partially excavated inside Devil's Dyke; this took the form of a shallow circular ring gully, 9 m in diameter, dug entirely within the topsoil. The survival of such a feature is extremely fortunate, and if round houses of this kind were common in the Iron Age, it is hardly surprising that only one has been found; a single ploughing would remove all traces of such a gully (Burstow and Wilson, 1936).

At North Bersted, a small circular hut, also consisting of a ring gully, was found (Bedwin and Pitts, 1977); this is the only hut so far identified on the Coastal Plain. At 6 m the diameter is smaller than most of the houses known on the Downs. The ring gully was quite substantial, however, surviving to a depth of up to 40 cm below the base of the ploughsoil.

The possibility of square or rectangular huts should not be overlooked. On several settlements rectangular surface depressions or platforms have been excavated, revealing them to be especially rich in domestic debris; these have been plausibly interpreted as hut sites, even though no pattern of postholes has been detected (eg at Charleston Brow; Parsons and Curwen, 1933). One such depression at Park Brow did yield a rectangular structure, 10 m by 3 m, consisting of two parallel rows of postholes (Wolseley and Smith, 1924). A structure of similar dimensions, though with a quite different arrangement of postholes was excavated at Bishopstone (Bell, 1977a). The question of whether these structures really were huts or represent some other constantly recurring type of building, such as a granary, is still an open one.

During the 1939 excavation at Highdown, part of a square structure was uncovered, just inside the rampart, and was described by the excavator as an Iron Age hut (Wilson, 1940). The one wall exposed consisted of a row of postholes in a continuous trench, a type of construction which is more familiar on some pagan Anglo-Saxon sites (Bell, 1977b). Furthermore, a re-examination of pottery from the Highdown excavation has revealed the presence of small, abraded Anglo-Saxon sherds, more likely to derive from a settlement than from a cemetery. The dating of this square structure to the Iron Age is thus doubtful.

Burial rites and evidence of other ritual

If it is true that Iron Age house plans are difficult to identify, then the methods of disposal of the dead are equally elusive, and few Iron Age burials are known. At Bishopstone two inhumations were found; one was in a rubbish pit and the other, the contracted skeleton of a young woman, was cut into the fill of the enclosure ditch. Associated with this latter burial were several bones of a young infant, and also part of an animal long bone with a perforation, and half a chalk spindle whorl (Bell, 1977a). Other inhumations are known, from Northwick, Eastbourne, where a skeleton was accompanied by a whole pot of La Tène III date, (Budgen, 1930), and also from

Glynde, where the burial of a female and infant was found in the ditch of an Iron Age enclosure (Burstow, 1961–2). This burial was discovered by workmen, however, and no associated pottery was recorded; consequently, some doubt surrounds the dating of this find. Finally, a single inhumation was found 'in a cairn of chalk blocks' in the ditch of Highdown hill-fort; there were no grave goods, and the burial was dated by context (Wilson, 1940).

Two cremations in early Iron Age vessels are known, one from Park Brow, and the other from the Caburn. The latter burial was in the bottom of a low barrow (Wilson, 1938). If any tendency can be discerned among this meagre evidence, it is that cremation was more likely in the early Iron Age, but inhumation became more common later; at no stage, however, is there complete uniformity of burial rite.

Clearly, this restricted number of burials cannot account for more than a very small proportion of the population. The only indication of the treatment received by the remainder of the population comes from the disarticulated fragments of human bones found on many Iron Age sites, eg the Caburn, Harting Beacon, the Trundle, and North Bersted. This would imply either some form of exposure rite, or shallow burials in or near the domestic area, as at Bishopstone. On sites with lengthy occupation, later activities might well disturb earlier burials, and result in the scattering of bones.

There is little evidence in the archaeological record for other types of Iron Age ritual. Although three Romano-British temples are known on the Downs (Chanctonbury, Bow Hill, and Lancing Ring), no Iron Age ritual structures have yet been identified. Since the Romano-British temple at Chanctonbury is situated within an early Iron Age hill-fort (Mitchell, 1910), it is possible that an Iron Age precursor existed (Bedwin, 1978).

The only Iron Age site at which some form of ritual activity can be inferred is Findon Park (Fox and Wolseley, 1928). The skull of an ox, in the centre of a closely set ring of flints, was found on the floor of one of the pits. The nearest parallel to this is the discovery, in a Romano-British ritual context, of three pits each with the skull of an ox laid on other bones of the skeleton, at Muntham Court (Burstow and Holleyman, 1957). This underlines the continuity of some religious beliefs, from the Iron Age into the Roman period.

Acknowledgements

I should like to thank Mr John Holmes for giving me a great deal of information about his excavations at Hollingbury (especially Figs 23 and 26). I am also grateful to F G Aldsworth and P L Drewett for their assistance with some of the other illustrations.

References

Arthur, J R B, 1954   'Prehistoric wheats in Sussex', *Sussex Archaeol Collect*, **92**, 37–47

Bedwin, O, 1977a   'Excavations in Harting Beacon Hill Fort, West Sussex 1976', *ibid*, **116** (forthcoming)

Bedwin, O, 1977b   'Early Iron Age pottery at Littlehampton', *ibid*, **116** (forthcoming)

Bedwin, O, 1978   'Excavations at Chanctonbury Ring, Wiston, West Sussex 1977', *ibid*, **117** (forthcoming)

Bedwin, O and Pitts, M W, 1977   'The excavation of an Iron Age settlement at North Bersted, Bognor Regis, West Sussex 1975–76', *ibid*, **117** (forthcoming)

Bell, M G, 1977a   'Excavations on Rookery Hill, Bishopstone, East Sussex', *ibid*, **115**

Bell, M G, 1977b   'Saxon settlements and buildings in Sussex', in *Ælla and after* (ed P Brandon)

Bradley, R J, 1971   'Stock raising and the origin of hill-forts on the South Downs', *Antiq J*, **51**, 8–29

Bradley, R J, 1975   *Salt: the study of an ancient industry* (eds K de Brisay and K A Evans), Colchester Archaeological Group, Colchester

Burstow, G P, 1961–2   'Typewritten notes on two seasons excavations of an Iron Age enclosure at Balcombe Pit, Glynde Quarry 1961–2', Sussex Archaeol Soc Library, Barbican House, Lewes

Burstow, G P and Holleyman, G A, 1957   'Muntham Court', *Archaeol Newsletter*, **6**, no 4, 101–2

Burstow, G P and Wilson, A E, 1936   'Excavation of a Celtic village on the Ladies Golf Course, The Dyke, Brighton', *Sussex Archaeol Collect*, **77**, 195–201

Cunliffe, B W, 1974   *Iron Age communities in Britain*

Cunliffe, B W, 1976a   'The origins of urbanisation in Britain', in *Oppida in barbarian Europe* (eds B W Cunliffe and T Rowley)

Cunliffe, B W, 1976b   'Iron Age sites in central southern England', *CBA Res Rep* **16**

Curwen, E C, 1930   'Wolstonbury', *Sussex Archaeol Collect*, **71**, 237–45

Curwen, E C, 1931   'Excavations in the Trundle, 2nd season, 1930', *ibid*, **72**, 100–49

Curwen, E C, 1932   'Excavations at Hollingbury Camp, Sussex', *Antiq J*, **12**, 1–16

Curwen, E C, 1933   'Excavations on Thundersbarrow Hill, Sussex', *ibid*, **13**, 109–33

Curwen, E C, 1937   *The archaeology of Sussex*, 1 edn

Field, L F, 1939   'Castle Hill, Newhaven', *Sussex Archaeol Collect*, **80**, 263–8

Fowler, P J, 1964   'Cross dykes on the Ebble-Nadder Ridge', *Wiltshire Archaeol Mag*, **59**, 46–67

Fox, C and Wolseley, G R, 1928   'The Early Iron Age site at Findon Park, Findon, Sussex', *Antiq J*, **8**, 449–60

Harding, D W, 1974   *The Iron Age in Lowland Britain*

Heron-Allen, E, 1910   *Selsey Bill: historic and prehistoric*

Holleyman, G A, 1937   'Harrow Hill excavations, 1936', *Sussex Archaeol Collect*, **78**, 230–54

Lewis, G D, 1960   'Some recent discoveries in West Sussex', *ibid*, **98**, 21

Mitchell, G S, 1910   'Excavations at Chanctonbury Ring 1909', *ibid*, **53**, 131–7

Parsons, W J and Curwen, E C, 1933   'An agricultural settlement on Charleston Brow, near Firle Beacon', *ibid*, **74**, 164–80

Pitts, M W, 1975   'A field survey of Oving and district with a trial excavation of an Iron Age site at North Bersted, West Sussex', *Bull Inst Archaeol*, **13**, 19–20

Wainwright, G J, 1968   'The excavation of a Durotrigian farmstead near Tollard Royal in Cranbourne Chase, southern England', *Proc Prehist Soc*, **34**, 102–47

Wilson, A E, 1938   'Excavations in the ramparts and the gateway of the Caburn, August–October 1937', *Sussex Archaeol Collect*, **79**, 168–94

Wilson, A E, 1940   'Report on the excavations at Highdown Hill, Sussex', *ibid*, **81**, 173–203

Wolseley, G R and Smith, R A, 1924   'Discoveries near Cissbury', *Antiq J*, **4**, 347–59

Chichester (*Noviomagus Regnensium*) lies just east of the most easterly of the inlets which make up the Chichester harbour (Fig 27), and the origins of the Roman town stem from the invasion of AD 43. From what little is known of the political situation in the south-east of Britain just prior to the invasion, it seems likely that the pro-Roman kingdom of Verica was considerably reduced in size as a result of the aggressive policies pursued by the Catuvellauni. The main oppidum of this shrunken kingdom was probably at Selsey, but there may well have been other oppida within the area of the Chichester Dykes; and there is now some evidence which might point to a settlement below the north-west area of the later town, or slightly outside the western limits, between Fishbourne and Chichester. Recent large-scale excavations in the north-west quadrant of the city (*Chichester* **3**, 43) show that Arretine and Gallo-Belgic wares, some dating to 25–30 years before the invasion, together with a number of Iron Age coins, have been found in the earliest levels. There is so far an absence of large amounts of identifiable Atrebatic pottery and structures, and since the evidence as it stands is capable of more than one interpretation, it is perhaps best to reserve judgement for the time being.

The first features in the earliest layers, both at Chichester and the harbour area of Fishbourne, are clearly military (Cunliffe, 1971, **1**, 38–46; *Chichester* **2**, 104; *Chichester* **3**, 43, 179), and are likely to belong to the base camp of the II Legion. This legion, under its commander Vespasian, is known to have campaigned from the Isle of Wight to Devon, subduing two hostile tribes and taking twenty native oppida (Suetonius, Vesp 4).

Large amounts of military equipment and house plans resembling military barracks and stores have been found below Chapel Street, and military finds have occurred in the centre of the town below the central car park. The full extent of the camp is not known, but the military style ditch found outside the Eastgate (*Chichester* **1**, 56–67) may belong to this period, although it appeared to be facing towards the later town and may have delimited a camp east of the city. Alternatively, the ditch could be part of a defensive enceinte belonging to the early town, for which, as yet, no defences can be firmly postulated.

The military occupation at legionary strength is unlikely to have lasted for more than two years at the outside, but it is possible that a small depot may have remained on the site for some years afterwards.

Civil development (Fig 28)

The intensive excavations in the north-west quadrant show that the military phase was followed soon after by a period of industrial activity, when fine Gallo-Belgic style pottery was made and the enamelling of small bronze jewellery items was carried out. This was succeeded between the years *c* AD 60 –70 by the erection of a series of substantial timber framed houses on masonry cills and conforming to the alignment of the early barrack buildings. This period may represent the development of the native town of the client king Tiberius Claudius Cogidubnus. Some of the public buildings, including the Temple of Neptune and Minerva with its famous inscription (*VCH Sussex* **3**, 13) and the *thermae* (*Chichester* **3**, 145), may have been planned at this time, although it may have

been well on into the 80s before the baths were finished. There is a striking similarity between some of the finer masonry details from the palace at Fishbourne and those from the *thermae* at Chichester, and it may well be that construction of the palace was followed without a break by the erection of some of the public buildings in Chichester, with the same masons being employed. Cogidubnus is unlikely to have lived on much after the mid 80s; after his death the new tribal capital of the Regni became the civitas capital of the region with all the lands previously governed by the old king being brought under Roman jurisdiction.

Late in the 1st century there was a change in the character of the town. Some at least of the main streets were laid out on the original alignment of the military camp, and considerable landscaping of the central area of the town was undertaken, with a large spread of gravel laid across the demolished buildings of the native town. The landscaping was not completed until well on into the 2nd century; Antonine samian has been found below the gravel spread in three areas in the north-west quadrant and it seems that this period of replanning and rebuilding may have been of an ad hoc nature, being extended as and when buildings were replaced. A study of the pottery from a series of sections through the Roman streets in the same area suggests that the street grid, or most of it, was slightly earlier than the central gravel layout.

The position of the Forum has not yet been demonstrated beyond all reasonable doubt, but it is most likely to lie below the Dolphin and Anchor and the properties to the north of it and along the west side of North Street. Recent street works have shown there to be at least one and, possibly, two large buildings below North Street with their western limits below the west pavement. The most southerly building extends almost as far as the City Cross, and this range of buildings, which includes a hypocaust, sets the eastern limit to the Forum area.

The same street works (early 1977) showed a series of massive masonry walls at the north end of South Street, running east–west, and it is evident that a large building occupies the area immediately south of the City Cross; however, it is not yet clear whether it is aligned north–south along the course of Roman South Street or whether it forms the southern boundary of the large gravel spread. Further west, below the Cathedral, is another large building with a very fine polychrome mosaic (*Chichester* **1**, 130–3). This is immediately south of the *thermae*, bounding the west side of the gravel spread (*Chichester* **3**, fig 4.2), and it seems that the central gravel area was surrounded on the west, east and, possibly, the south sides by large buildings, which may have been public ones, with the Forum being situated at some point within. During the period when the town was developing, first under Cogidubnus and later as a cantonal capital, it may have been without defences. It is possible that an earlier defensive system existed, as it did at Silchester (Boon, 1974, 44–5), but no trace of one has been found to date if the 'military' ditch outside the Eastgate (see above) is excluded as a possibility. Boon ascribes the inner earthwork at Silchester to Cogidubnus and suggests that it may well have been intended as a defence against Caratacus. The argument assumes that Cogidubnus as a client king would have been permitted to erect defensive works within his

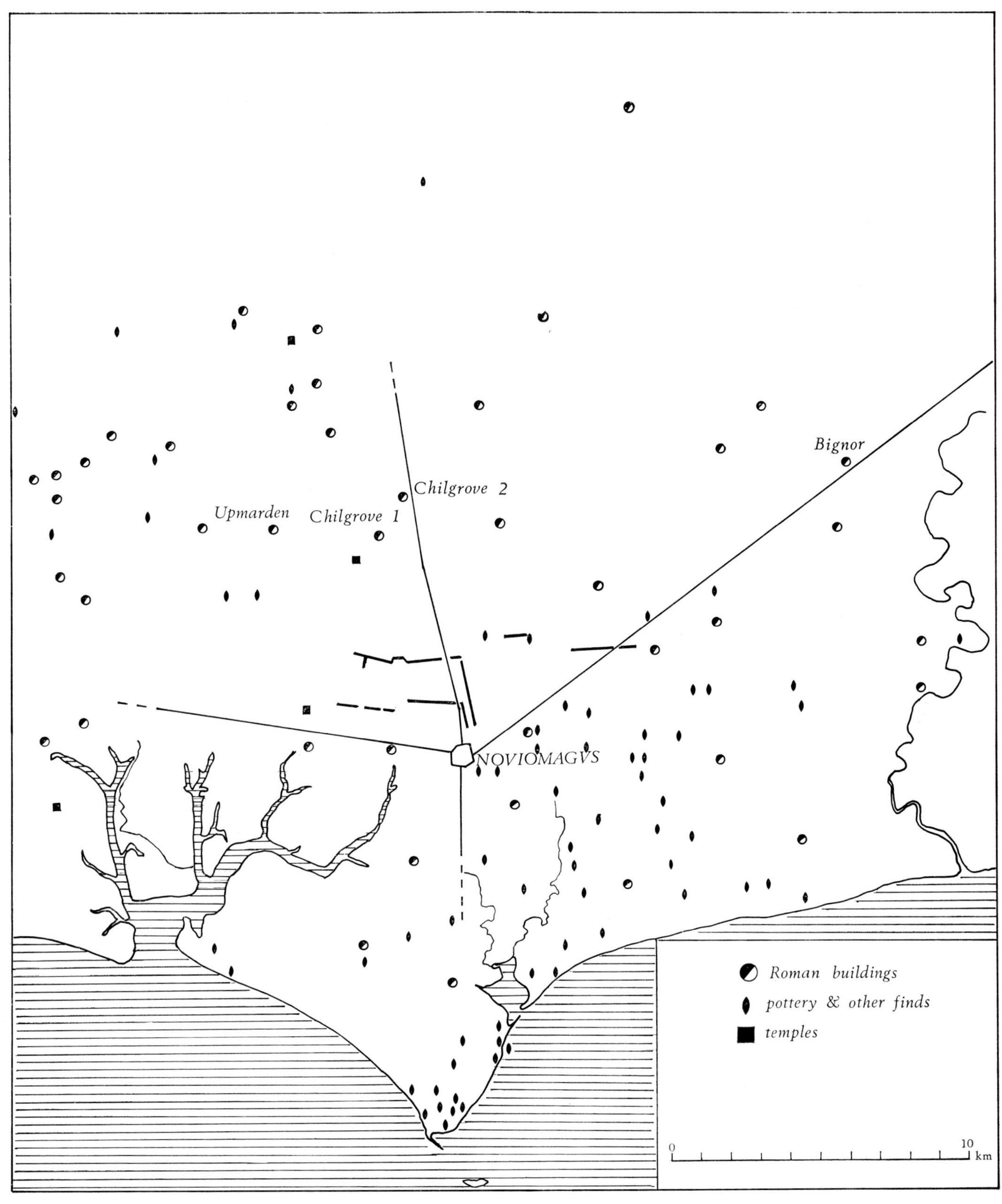

Fig 27   Distribution of Romano-British sites around Chichester and in the Chilgrove Valley

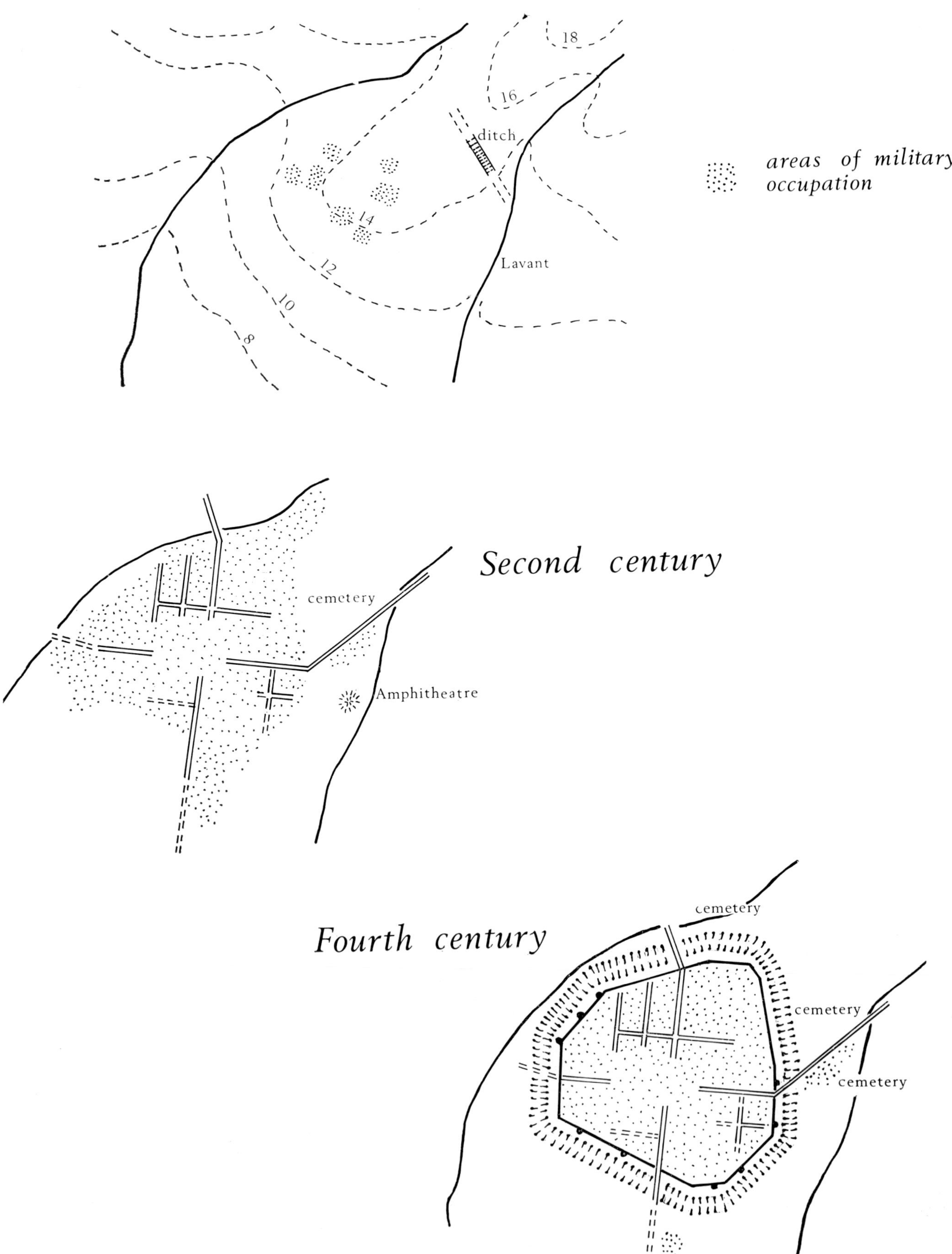

Fig **28**   *The development of Roman Chichester*

kingdom, and if it is accepted for Silchester it might well be considered for Chichester also. Certainly, the possibility of earlier defensive works cannot be entirely ruled out.

During the late 1st and 2nd centuries the town covered a wider area. Excavations outside the walls have produced evidence for 1st and 2nd century occupation along the south side of Stane Street; outside the Southgate for a distance of at least a quarter of a mile (*Chichester* **4**, forthcoming); outside the Northgate (*Chichester* **3**, 7, 8); and outside the Westgate (Holmes, 1959, 80–2).

At some time near the end of the 2nd century the town was enclosed by defences which delimited a much smaller area. The evidence was clear at Southgate in 1958 (Holmes, unpublished), and again on the west side of the town (*Chichester* **1**, 143–7). There is some evidence that the amphitheatre outside the Eastgate went out of use at the same time (White, 1936, 149–59), but this requires re-testing in the light of present knowledge. The defences consisted of a double ditch and bank (Fig 29), the latter being cut back at some time later and the masonry wall built. The gates (Fig 29) were probably constructed at the same time as the bank. No opportunity to excavate one of the gates has ever arisen, but information available from observation of public service trenches (Wilson, 1962, 75–7; Down, 1968, 122: *Chichester* **4**, forthcoming) suggests that the gates were of a simple re-entrant type. Grimm's drawing of the Eastgate (*Chichester* **2**, pl 10), which dates to 1782, shows the late medieval gate which was almost certainly built on the Roman foundations and probably followed the same design.

The construction of the defences at or near the end of the 2nd century was in conformity with other towns of comparable status in Britain, most of which appear to have received their defences at the same time. It may well have been in response to a threat to the security of the province; and since the defences imply a trained force to man the walls, either an army detachment or a local militia can be postulated. The constriction of the town limits may suggest that it was tailored for the available defence force, but the existence of the walls did not prevent suburbs from developing outside the gates. There is abundant evidence outside the East and South gates for 3rd and 4th century occupation, but at Northgate it appears that a cemetery was established which spread across part of the earlier town that had been abandoned when the walls were built. Opportunities are still awaited to examine the areas outside the Westgate.

The next modifications to the town defences took place towards the end of the 3rd or beginning of the 4th century, when a number of bastions were added to the walls to provide platforms for ballistae. The ditches, by then partially silted up (Holmes, 1959, 85), were filled in and a wider ditch dug further away (Fig 29). By this time Chichester must have been incorporated into the Saxon shore defence complex, and it was likely that it was garrisoned by a regular military detachment. A late Roman military belt buckle found in a silted-up sewer below County Hall (*Chichester* **2**, fig 5.6, 17) provides the only material evidence for this.

The cemeteries

Two cemeteries are known, one at Eastgate and another at Northgate, and a third is suspected at Southgate, where a burial was found when the canal basin was being dug in 1819 (*VCH Sussex* **3**, 16). Recent excavations (1976) near the site of the old gasworks have failed to locate a cemetery, and it is possible that the burial found in 1819

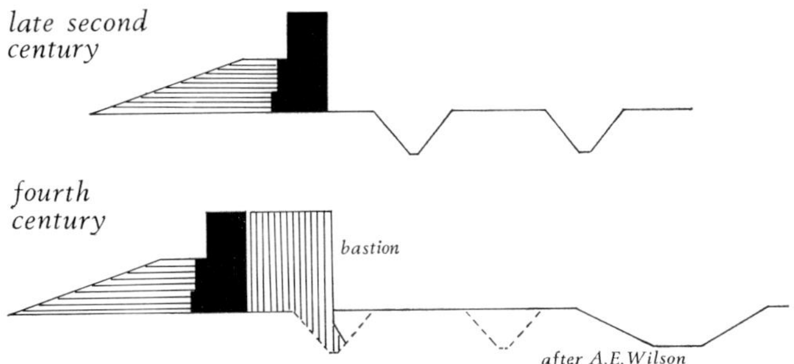

The Gates; conjectural plan

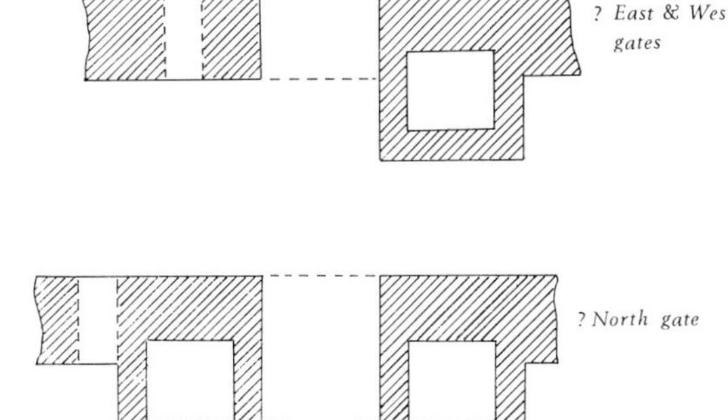

Fig 29   The defences of Roman Chichester

might belong to an estate outside the city limits. The cremation cemetery outside the Eastgate has been extensively sampled (*Chichester* **1**, 53–126) and dates from about the last quarter of the 1st century. Usage appears to have tapered off after the 3rd century, with only a few late inhumations being inserted in the 4th. By the early 3rd century it seems that another cemetery had been laid out at Northgate overlying earlier 1st century occupation (*Chichester* **3**, 7). The small sample of burials noted shows a high proportion of inhumations in contrast to the Eastgate cemetery, and it may perhaps be regarded as the successor to the earlier burial ground. A late Roman or sub-Roman inhumation cemetery was found on the south side of St Pancras (Stane Street) in 1976 (*Chichester* **4**, forthcoming). The burials, which were alongside the river Lavant, cut late Roman cess pits and at least two may have been buried in quicklime, which may suggest plague. There were no grave goods, and a 5th century date is postulated based on the relationship of the graves to the pits.

The civitas in the 4th to 5th centuries

During the early part of the 4th century there is clear evidence from the Chapel Street sites of a period of expansion. The two town houses excavated had been rebuilt on masonry footings and extended, and one of the town sewers which had fallen into disrepair was cleaned out and refurbished in timber, and the streets alongside the houses were resurfaced. Within 50 years, however, the picture had changed. There is evidence of decay and neglect; the timber revetment of the sewer collapsed through lack of maintenance; the streets became worn and unrepaired, and silt layers accumulated in hollows. Within the houses, signs of partitioning and ad hoc rebuilding are apparent, with hurdles driven into tessellated floors and hearths lit upon them (*Chichester* **3**, 43). The large sample of bronze coinage from the latest layers shows that no new issues were reaching the town much after about AD 378; and although this money may have remained in

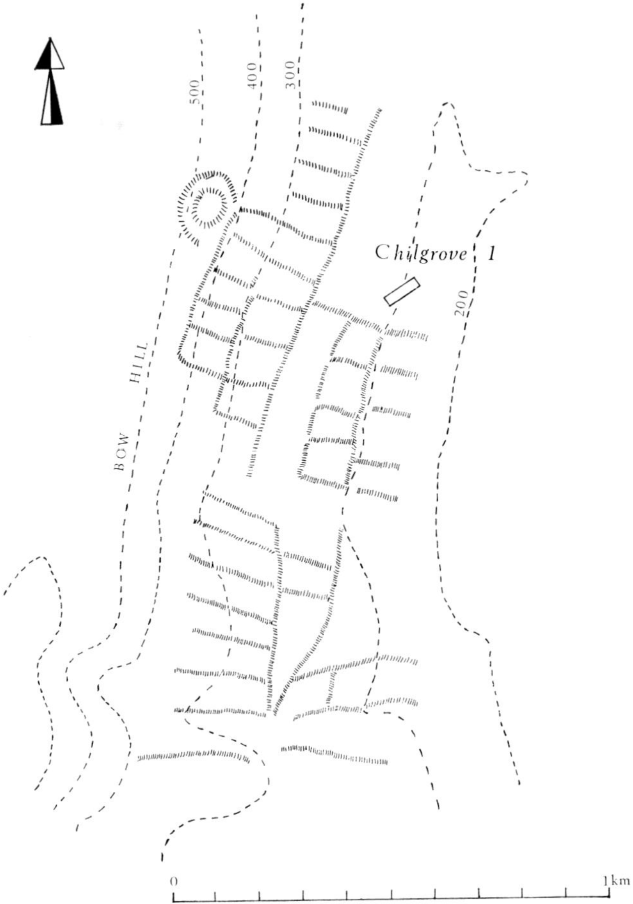

Fig 30   Field system around Chilgrove 1

circulation for some years, the citizens of Noviomagus are likely to have reverted to a barter economy by the second decade of the 5th century.

The end of the *civitas* is obscure. The absence of comment in the *Anglo-Saxon Chronicle* may be significant; if the town had been taken in open fighting or ceded to Ælle or his sons it is reasonable to suppose that this would have been claimed as a victory. The absence of any early Saxon cemeteries or artefacts in or near Chichester, as far as present knowledge goes, is another piece of negative evidence which may lead in the end to the conclusion that, for whatever reason, a sub-Roman enclave existed in and around the old *civitas*, possibly as late as the early 7th century.

Rural settlement in the Downs

The centre of Chichester is 3 miles from the 200 ft contour line marking the approach to the Downland, and the land between the Ems to the west and the Arun to the east, and north as far as the second line of hills has been taken as the area under discussion. Within these general limits the area of the Chilgrove valley and the parishes of West Dean on the east and Stoughton and Marden on the west has been the subject of a special study for some years. Two Roman villas have been extensively excavated and a third partly excavated. A detailed survey of the landscape around them has been carried out with the object of relating the countryside to the *civitas* with which it was interdependent (Down, forthcoming). A glance at the distribution map (Fig 27), which shows all the known sites and finds both

on the coastal plain and in the hills, indicates prolific occupation along the coastal strip, particularly in the region of Selsey, where the number of finds suggests a sizeable settlement. Sites are less numerous on the chalk, but the impression given by the distribution map may be misleading, representing the amount of archaeological and other activity rather than a true settlement pattern.

Before discussing in detail the development of farming within the Chilgrove study area, it may be as well to look at the wider Sussex picture. Cunliffe (1973, 74–87) has already drawn attention to the strong element of continuity from late Iron Age to Roman in the rural settlement pattern in the Regni, and cites certain specific examples of 'early' villa development in the 1st century AD, eg the proto-palace at Fishbourne, the Angmering villa and, rather less certainly, the villas at Borough Farm, Pulborough and Southwick. There is no good dating evidence for the latter two but their design and plan suggests a 1st century date. Another possible 'early' villa is the one at Eastbourne, and here the similarity of the flue tiles to those at Fishbourne may suggest a Neronian date. Cunliffe has suggested that these may represent the large estates of the local aristocracy who, it may be assumed, would have continued to hold their land after the death of Cogidubnus and the absorption of the Regni into the Roman administrative system. With the exception of Fishbourne, where the proto-palace was incorporated into the Flavian palace, none of the early villas has been excavated under modern conditions, so that it is not possible to trace their further development and eventual decay, or yet relate them to their estates. Nevertheless, this small number of villas is an important reminder that romanization began early in Sussex due to a unique situation at the time of the conquest, and the emergence of a number of wealthy estates must have had a significant impact on rural development within the area served by the *civitas*. Without a detailed study, it is not possible to be certain from where these early villa owners derived their wealth; but perhaps for some the exploitation of Wealden iron may have proved a profitable venture, at least in the early years while Cogidubnus was alive. After his death it is likely that the control of ironworking would have passed to the state.

In the Chilgrove study area, modern cultivation has largely destroyed the old field systems except where they have been preserved high up on the chalk, or beneath old woodland. Recent field work has shown 'Celtic' type field boundaries in areas of recently cleared ancient woodlands, hitherto unploughed and standing to a considerable height. Elsewhere, along the Chilgrove valley bottom near Chilgrove 1 (Fig 30), part of the field system belonging to a small Iron Age settlement below the stockyard of the later villa was mapped from the 1947 RAF survey and later confirmed on the ground. The villa appears to be intrusive into the field pattern, but there seems little doubt that the fields were cultivated by the Romano-British successors to the Atrebatic farmers who may have been their ancestors. Both at Chilgrove 1 and 2 (Fig 31) the earliest ceramic evidence suggests an early 2nd century date for the Period 1 buildings. In both instances they developed from a simple range of rooms with a corridor along one side. At Chilgrove 1 the first building was on narrow sleeper walls of flint and it was later rebuilt with wider masonry walls on almost exactly the same plan. At Chilgrove 2 there is slight evidence for a timber-framed building with a small barn at one end; this was also rebuilt on a much more substantial basis with a large aisled barn 80 ft by 50 ft wide on the north side.

Nothing is known of the system of land tenure among the Atrebates during the period just prior to the invasion, but it is likely that there was little change while Cogidubnus ruled as client king. Nor is there any reason to suppose that there would have been drastic changes after his death, although the tax burden might well have increased. It seems evident from a study of the development of the Chilgrove villas that agriculture in the valley gravels and chalk uplands was always prosperous throughout the Roman period. There was a big expansion early on in the 4th century when, after a long period of disturbance and civil strife, settled times began again under Constantine. By then the farms in the Chilgrove valley must have been enjoying boom conditions, and sufficient surplus was available to enlarge the buildings and indulge in luxuries like heated rooms, mosaics and bath suites. This prosperity is paralleled at Bignor, where the modest 3rd century single-range villa was transformed into a very large courtyard house with elaborate bath suites and splendid mosaics. Although most of the Upmarden villa (Fig 31) lies below the modern farmhouse, an examination of the wing containing the baths shows that this was also constructed in the 4th century, and the solid workmanship is clear proof that the owner could afford to pay for high-quality buildings.

By the third quarter of the 4th century a dramatic change had taken place. Chilgrove 1 was partially destroyed by fire and a similar disastrous occurrence at Chilgrove 2 gutted the aisled barn and part of the main villa. After that time there is some evidence that occupation of the buildings continued, but at a much reduced level of comfort. Unburnt beams from the roof of the barn at Chilgrove 2 were salvaged; the nails were extracted and left in heaps on the floor. Several of the roofless rooms were provided with makeshift roofs with a central supporting post; hearths were built on the tessellated floors and against corridor walls, and a massive bread oven was constructed in the barn. There is also some evidence which might be interpreted as a conversion of the *caldarium* and *praefurnium* of the bath house to a corn drying oven at this time. The picture can be paralleled at Chilgrove 1, and may also be compared with the evidence from the two town houses in Chapel Street, Chichester at about the same date.

The coin series ends with Magnentius (AD 353) for Chilgrove 1, and Valentinian 1 (AD 375) for Chilgrove 2. The absence of any Valentinian coins from Chilgrove 1 may indicate that it had ceased to be occupied before 375 by people using money, as Valentinian coins are so common that their absence, in this context, may be significant. The suggestion is that first Chilgrove 1 and then Chilgrove 2 were vacated by the owners or tenants, possibly for the greater safety of the town, during or just before the last quarter of the 4th century, but that the deserted buildings at Chilgrove 1 continued to be used. A large ironworking furnace was erected in the corner of one of the rooms, and a wide range of tools, nails and other implements made, while in the stockyard a number of small corn drying ovens testified to the fact that the land was still in production. At Chilgrove 2 there seem to have been people squatting in the ruins of the villa. It may well be that they worked the land, either for the owners, possibly under a bailiff, or for themselves. It is quite conceivable that both villas were under one management for part of the time, with the workpeople living at Chilgrove 2; and it is tempting to see the large bread oven constructed in the barn as evidence for communal feeding arrangements.

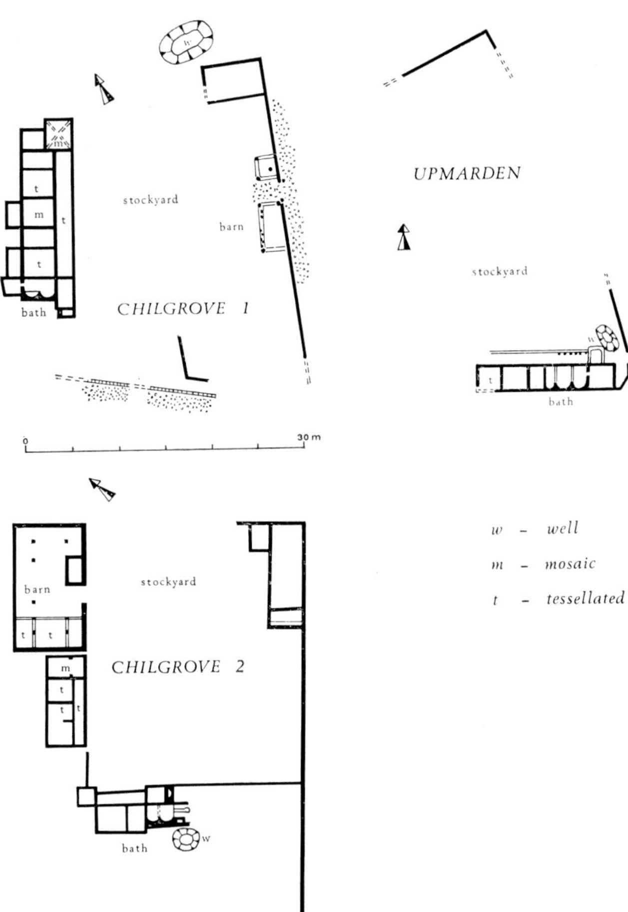

Fig **31**   *Plans of Roman Villas at Chilgrove and Upmarden*

The latest pottery cannot be dated after late 4th century, but with the slow decline and final abandonment of a money economy there would have been no wares coming in from the great fine-ware production centres of New Forest, Alice Holt and Oxford. A certain amount of wheel-turned sandy wares are present in the latest layers, but some of these could well have been made on site. There would always have been a tradition of pottery making within the villa communities and a strong tendency towards self sufficiency, with the fine table wares being bought or exchanged on market days in the *civitas*.

The end point for these two villas is uncertain. The latest coins and pottery can shed no light on the date when the people living in the old buildings ceased to do so. However, it is likely that the land continued to be worked until well on into the 5th century, and it may indeed have never gone entirely out of production. Towards the latter part of the period there may have been a greater emphasis on the rearing of cattle and sheep. The preliminary report on the animal bones found in the stockyard at Chilgrove 1 shows a significant increase in the number of sheep remains in the latest layers. Animal husbandry is less labour-intensive than arable farming, and the chronic shortage of manpower that afflicted Britain in the late 4th century may have been partly responsible for a shift in the balance of farming economy.

No other form of settlement has so far been identified within the study area, but Cunliffe (1976) has demonstated that late Romano-British settlements, possible villages, were present at Chalton, and there may have been a tenuous link between these and the earliest pagan Saxon settlements nearby. The Chalton communities appear to have started in the 2nd century; but it is not known whether the people living there were freemen who hired out their labour to neighbouring farms, or whether the house platforms and tofts belonged to labourers tied to a particular estate. Two other settlements have been recognized, both outside the main study area, at Arundel Park and Park Brow. There must have been others, and it is important that these should be identified and studied in depth. We need to know the relationship between these small settlements and the villas, and whether the settlements expanded as the villas declined.

The picture emerging from the Chilgrove study is likely to be a true reflection, in part at least, of the development and decay of Romano-British farming in the adjacent downland. There are many gaps to be filled; as in the nearby *civitas*, the missing elements are the absence of datable artefacts of the sub-Roman period and those of the early pagan Saxon period of the late 5th and 6th centuries.

By the 7th century, Saxon occupation in Chichester is recorded, and one of the most important and fascinating tasks for the future is the quest for evidence of the earliest Saxon settlements in the Downland villages, relating these, if possible, to the sub-Roman peasant communities which commonsense if nothing else tells us must have survived. Only when this has been achieved will the fate of the old *civitas* in the late 5th century become, perhaps, a little clearer.

References

Boon, G C, 1974   *Roman Silchester*, London

Cunliffe, B W, 1971   *Excavations at Fishbourne 1961–9*, London

Cunliffe, B W, 1973   *The Regni*, London

Cunliffe, B W, 1976   'A Romano-British village at Chalton, Hants', *Proc Hampshire Field Club Archaeol Soc*, **33**

Down, A and Rule, M, 1971   *Chichester excavations* **1**

Down, A, 1974   *Chichester excavations* **2**

Down, A   *Chichester excavations* **3**

Down, A   *Chichester excavations* **4** (forthcoming)

Down, A, 1968   'Excavations in Chapel Street, Chichester', *Sussex Archaeol Collect*, **106**

Down, A   *Excavations at Chilgrove and Upmarden* (forthcoming)

Holmes, J, 1959   'The defences of Roman Chichester', *Sussex Archaeol Collect*, **100**

VCH   *The Victoria County History of Sussex*

White, G M, 1936   'The Chichester amphitheatre; preliminary excavations', *Antiq J*, **16**

Wilson, A E, 1962   'Chichester excavations 1958–60, North walls and Northgate', *Sussex Archaeol Collect*, **100**

Henry Cleere

The Weald on the eve of the Roman invasion

The settlement pattern in the Weald on the eve of the Roman invasion of AD 43 is summarized in another contribution to this volume (Money, above). It was a pattern of sparse occupation based on major defended enclosures lying on the northern edge of the forest (Dry Hill, High Rocks, Castle Hill) and smaller enclosures deeper into the High Weald (Philpots, Garden Hill, Saxonbury). This penetration may be ascribed to pressure from Belgic tribes to the north; however, the association of both Garden Hill and Saxonbury with ironmaking suggests that the reasons may be economic rather than political.

There is no evidence of penetration into the Weald in this way from the South Downs. However, the ironmaking settlements at Crowhurst and Footlands in the region to the north of Hastings have yielded pre-Roman pottery, and it is not inconceivable that other sites of this group may have pre-Roman origins. The source of this exploitation of the iron ores in the Hastings-Battle-Sedlescombe area is unknown. However, it is tempting to see a link between this activity and the Chichester dedication slab by a *collegium fabrorum* (*RIB*,1, 91) and to assign this enterprise to the Regni.

It is clear that the Weald was seen by its Iron Age colonizers primarily as a source of iron, and Caesar's reference (*BG*, v, 12) corroborates its significance as early as the mid 1st century BC. An awareness of this important economic resource on the part of the Roman authorities will doubtless have influenced the subsequent pattern of settlement and development in the Weald.

The pattern of Roman occupation

Standard works on Roman Sussex (eg Winbolt, in *VCH Sussex*; Curwen, 1954; Margary, 1969) are very summary in their treatment of the Weald: it is described as being devoted exclusively to ironmaking. Thus Winbolt (*VCH Sussex*, III, 2) sums up Roman occupation in the following sentence: 'The coastal plain, the Downs, and a slight encroachment on the Weald give the sum of Roman Sussex . . . The iron district stands absolutely by itself to the north–east of a line drawn from Pevensey to Crawley Down.' A survey of the literature of the past quarter-century on Sussex archaeology suggests that this view requires little, if any, modification: a distribution map of ironmaking sites (Fig 32; Cleere, 1974) differs from Curwen's map (1954; fig 88) only in the number of ironmaking sites recorded.

Work by the Wealden Iron Research Group in the past dozen years has made it possible to increase the number of confirmed Roman ironmaking sites very considerably. These have been listed in a recent paper by the present author (Cleere, 1974), and excavations have been carried out in the past decade on several of them, which will be briefly summarized.

Ironmaking sites

A site at Bardown (Wadhurst) covering about 3 ha was excavated by the present author during 1960–8. It appears to have been founded around AD 140 and to have continued in operation for about a century. A large timber-framed building is reminiscent in plan of a military barrack block; this lay to the east of a central roadway, which appeared to separate the 'residential' area from the 'industrial' part of the settlement, where smaller timber-framed buildings housed forging hearths. No smelting furnaces were found, but there is abundant evidence of this primary process, in the form of a bank of slag and other refuse measuring 100 m × 50 m × up to 3 m deep along the south bank of the river Limden, together with ore-roasting furnaces of a distinctive type.

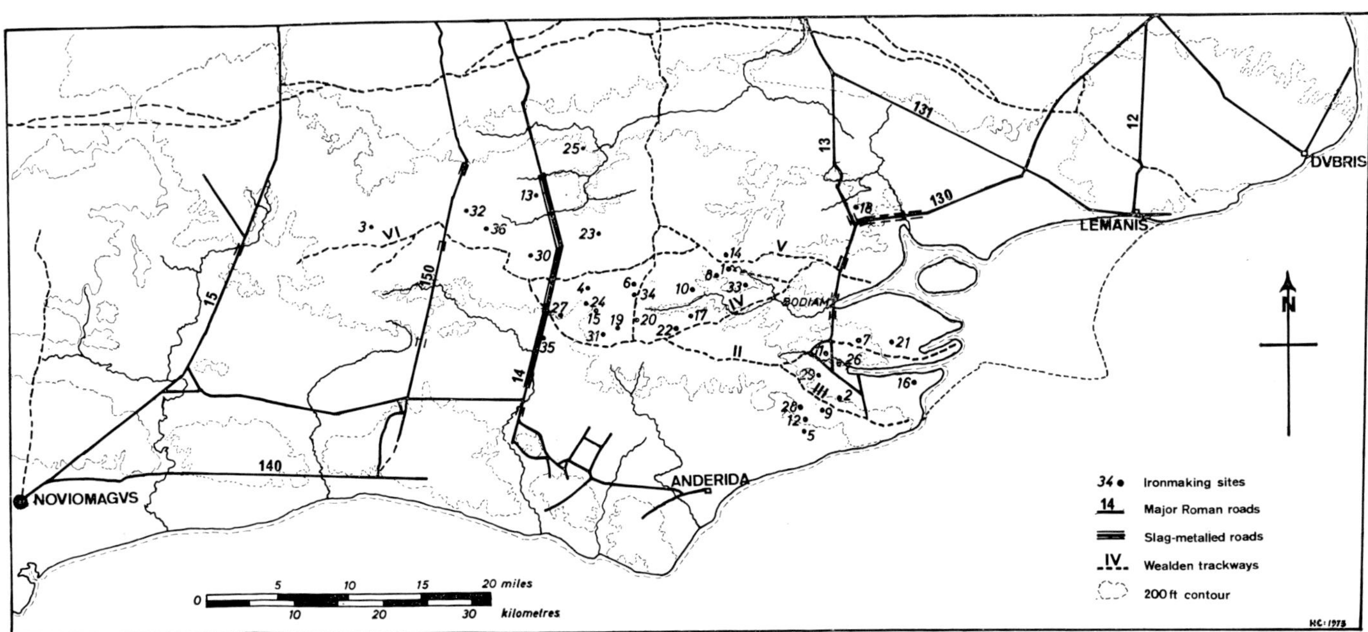

Fig 32 Distribution of Roman ironmaking sites in the Weald

Industrial operations appear to have ceased at the settlement around the end of the 2nd century, being transferred to a series of 'satellite' workplaces some 2·5 km on average from the main settlement. This was probably due to progressive deforestation and ore exhaustion closer in (this process is discussed in a recent paper by the present author: Cleere, 1976).

One of the 'satellite' sites, at Holbeanwood (Ticehurst), was also excavated by the author. Twelve smelting furnaces, of the shaft type known elsewhere in the province to be purely Roman, were found, in two groups of six, and a third group is postulated in an unexcavated area of the site. There was no evidence of any permanent settlement: the only buildings on the site were timber-framed structures erected over the two groups of furnaces. Examination of the slag deposits suggests a maximum life of this workplace of ten years.

Continuous observation of the Beauport Park (Battle) site has been carried out by A G Brodribb for many years. The building of a new golf course led to a rescue excavation in 1971–2, which revealed a well built and exceptionally well preserved bath-house of military type (now taken into guardianship by the Department of the Environment). Coins found in association with this building range from Trajan to Severus Alexander, indicating a date range similar to that of Bardown, though perhaps starting a little earlier; pottery analysis confirms this evidence. An initially four-roomed establishment was expanded during the 2nd century to six rooms. There are signs of a period of abandonment at the end of that century, followed by reconstruction (to a lower standard of building); a fragmentary inscription from the main entrance ascribes this rebuilding to the *vilicus* Bassus.

Beauport Park was a very large ironmaking establishment, judging by the amount of slag quarried away for road metalling in the mid 19th century; it is estimated to cover at least 10 ha. There are surface indications of a considerable 'residential' area lying to the east of the bath-house, which was built at the edge of the industrial area furthest from the dwellings.

Minepit Wood (Rotherfield) was excavated by J H Money, and revealed a small smelting site based on a single well preserved domed furnace of a type distinct from those at Holbeanwood, but familiar in the Germanic lands lying outside the Rhine *limes* (Money, 1974). Pottery evidence gave a 1st century date, spanning the Roman conquest. The relatively small amount of slag suggested a short life, possibly not more than a decade.

A similar furnace was found at Pippingford Park (Hartfield), with pottery of the same period (Tebbutt and Cleere, 1973). The slag dump here was even smaller, and a shorter span of use seems to be indicated. Recent work by WIRG members led by C F Tebbutt at another site nearby has produced three further examples of this type of furnace. The most extensive investigation of a Roman ironmaking settlement was that carried out at Broadfields (Crawley), where a very large settlement covering about 12 ha was excavated on a rescue basis for a number of years. The furnaces found totalled over 40, of which a number were of the Minepit Wood–Pippingford Park domed type, but the great majority were shaft furnaces of the Roman type known from Holbeanwood (Gibson-Hill, forthcoming). The settlement was shown on pottery evidence to date from before the Roman invasion and to have continued in use throughout the Roman period.

Earlier excavations, on a more limited scale, were carried out at Bynes Farm (Crowhurst: Lucas, 1950–3), Footlands (Sedlescombe: unpublished apart from a short report on pre-Roman pottery, in Chown, 1946–7), Icklesham (Homan, 1936–7), Petley Wood (Battle: Lemmon, 1951–2), Ridge Hill (East Grinstead: Straker, 1928), and Walesbeech (East Grinstead: Straker, 1931, 239–40).

Sites connected with the iron industry

Two major sites have been excavated in the Weald which appear to be connected directly with the Roman iron industry—Garden Hill (Hartfield) and Bodiam. The earlier phases of the Garden Hill defended settlement are discussed elsewhere in this volume (Money, above). Ironmaking was carried on at the settlement itself during the 1st century AD, but in the early Roman period the industrial workings were levelled and later buildings of a non-industrial character were erected. These were of timber construction with the exception of a simple three-roomed bath-house in stone. This phase of non-industrial occupation appears to have lasted, on pottery evidence, throughout the 2nd century. However, the bath-house was dismantled towards the end of the century and thereafter the settlement fell into disuse, probably becoming abandoned finally by the mid 3rd century.

At Bodiam (Lemmon and Hill, 1966) 'exploratory' trenching revealed evidence of continuous occupation from the mid 1st century to the mid 3rd century, and established the existence there of a substantial Roman port on the banks of the Rother. Although no direct evidence of any connexion with the iron industry in the form of slag or furnaces was discovered, the presence of tiles stamped with the CL BR mark of the *Classis Britannica* and the road system in this area are interpreted as linking this port with ironworks elsewhere in this part of eastern Sussex (see below). Recent (1978) fieldwork by the Robertsbridge and District Archaeological Society has revealed an extensive bloomery just above the port.

The possibility of waterborne transportation in the Weald should not be ruled out. Some years ago occupation and rubbish deposits were discovered on the west bank of the Rother at Robertsbridge. This site has not been excavated, but an examination of the pottery indicates a 2nd century date. A similar site was recently discovered by C F Tebbutt at Boreham Bridge.

Non-iron sites

The majority of known Roman sites in the Weald were either directly or indirectly associated with the iron industry. However, there is a handful of other recorded sites where no such connexion is demonstrable.

The best known is the posting station at Alfoldean, where Stane Street crosses the river Arun (Winbolt, 1923; 1924). Whether this qualifies as settlement proper is debatable: it was a simple rectangular enclosure on Stane Street lying between Chichester and London, and would have served solely for overnighting travellers. It is, perhaps, worthy of comment that no larger settlement developed here during the Roman period, as was the case at many analogous road stations, such as Towcester and Alcester. Not far from the Alfoldean site was a substantial Roman tileworks at Itchingfield (Green, 1970). This industrial operation appears to have flourished during the 2nd century, making the full range of tile types. The absence of stamps on any of the fragments examined makes it unlikely that there was any military connexion with this works. The excavator very properly draws attention to the similarities between the building at Itchingfield and one of the workshops of the XX Legion at Holt (Grimes, 1930);

the fact that military tiles appear not to have been stamped during the 2nd century as a matter of course means that the possibility of military operation of the Itchingfield tileworks cannot be ruled out. However, petrological examination of CL BR stamped tiles from sites in Sussex and elsewhere (Dr D P S Peacock, *pers comm*) shows that the Fleet was not making tiles from the clays that formed the basis of the Itchingfield tilery.

A more enigmatic site is the prehistoric Money Mound (Lower Beeding), where Roman coins, beads, and pottery were buried, presumably as votive offerings (Beckensall, 1967). The site lies roughly equidistant from Alfoldean and Broadfields, and so the votive deposits may be attributable to either of these communities (with a preference for the latter, where there was demonstrably a large community in permanent residence). However, the function and purpose of Money Mound will remain mysterious until more is known of Roman settlement on this part of the Weald Clay.

Apart from the relatively short-lived tileworks at Itchingfield and the 'encroachment' referred to by Winbolt, which is in effect an extension of the Downland settlement and so has been dealt with in another contribution to this volume (Down, above), there is almost no evidence of any kind of settlement in the Weald apart from ironmaking establishments. However, there is one site at Uckfield (Tebbutt, 1968–71) where a corn-drying oven associated with 1st century pottery was found during building work, which may be significant. It is the only known site that gives any hint of agriculture being carried on in the Weald. The traditional view has been that the heavy clays and dense forest cover of the Weald in prehistoric and Roman times made it impossible for early farmers to clear and till with their limited technology, and that it was not until the Anglo-Saxons arrived with the heavy plough that clearance and cultivation could begin. The immense tracts of woodland that must have been felled for charcoal burning by the Roman ironmakers (Cleere, 1976) demonstrate the apparent ease with which the timber could have been cleared, whilst the current view (Fowler, 1976) is that the heavy plough reached Britain with the Romans. Moreover, there is plenty of evidence from, for example, the Midlands, of the clearance and cultivation of heavy soils comparable with those of the Weald by the Romans. It would appear, therefore, that another explanation must be sought for the apparent absence of agriculture in most of the Weald during the Roman period (see below).

The Roman road system

Consideration of the road system in the Weald is fundamental to any survey of the Roman settlement pattern. It is, of course, known in detail thanks to the work of Margary (1965; 1973, 59–74). The main features are the three north–south trunk roads—Stane Street (Margary's route 15), the London–Brighton road (route 150), and the London–Lewes road (route 14). These are linked by an east–west road along the South Downs, but there is no major east–west connexion between this group of roads and the next major north–south road to the east (route 13). They are, however, connected by a series of what Margary (1965, 262–4) calls prehistoric trackways, running along the main Wealden ridges.

It is convenient to see these trackways as having been in use in the Roman period, since they appear to link a number of the ironmaking settlements in the central (or High) Weald, as Fig 32 shows. However, their existence at this time should not be taken as proven, as a study of the Bardown-Holbeanwood complex shows. Bardown lies in the Limden valley below Margary's Track V, and Holbeanwood lies above it to the north, just over the ridge. A track leads directly from Bardown to the satellite workplace, cutting across the ridgeway. It would appear, however, that this ridgeway was not used for the export of Bardown products, since aerial reconnaissance has clearly shown the existence of a Roman road running down the Limden valley from Bardown for at least three miles parallel to the supposed ridgeway for much of its length. It seems somewhat unlikely that a new road would have been constructed had a prehistoric track existed only 1·5 km from the main settlement.

Nevertheless, it is certain that there was a network of minor roads in the eastern part of the county, usually found to be metalled with iron slag, and that they linked the High Weald ironworks with the estuarine port at Bodiam, with another possible port on the Brede estuary at Oaklands Park (Sedlescombe), and conceivably also with a now submerged or eroded port in the Hastings area. There are thus two distinct Roman road systems in the Weald—the north–south trunk roads, linking London with the South Downs and the coastal plain, and a network of minor contour roads orientated towards a group of ports between Bodiam and Hastings. Their significance is discussed in the next section.

The Roman iron industry of the Weald

The present author has examined the industry in detail in a recent paper (Cleere, 1974); what follows is a short summary of the conclusions of that paper.

All the Roman sites lie within 4 km of a known or presumed Roman road. This suggests a classification of the sites based on their relationship to land and sea communications and their potential markets. This classification distinguishes two groups of sites: a *western* group, orientated on the major north–south highways, and an *eastern* group, with a primary outlet by sea from the estuaries of the small rivers Rother and Brede (and perhaps also a lost coastal port near Hastings).

The western group of sites such as Broadfields, Great Cansiron, Oldlands, and Ridge Hill may have been set up to exploit ore bodies discovered during road building operations (although in the case of Broadfields the road alignment may itself have been influenced by the existence of a pre-Roman ironworking settlement). This is particularly likely in the case of Great Cansiron, which lies less than a mile from the London–Lewes road, and where there is little indication of the ore body having been found in any other way. Figure 32 indicates those sections of the Roman roads which, according to Margary (1965) were metalled with iron slag. Only one patch of slag metalling is recorded on route 15, at Alfoldean, and here a connexion may be indicated with Broadfields. Route 150 shows patches south of Ardingly, around Selsfield Common (in the vicinity of the Ridge Hill ironmaking site), and to the north of Felbridge. It is route 14 that produces the greatest amount of slag-metalled sections. Wherever sections were cut between Cowden and Isfield a thick surface of slag was found, and there is another patch further south, beyond Barcombe Mills.

Routes 15 and 150 connected the prosperous and densely populated agricultural areas of the South Downs and coastal plain with London, the mercantile centre of the province; both ends of these roads would be potential markets for iron in large quantities. During the 1st to 3rd centuries there were hardly any military establishments in the south, and only the Cripplegate fort in London, and so it can be safely assumed that the civilian market would have absorbed the bulk, if not all, of the products of this group of sites. It is not inconceivable that the large works, such as Great Cansiron and Oldlands, with their relatively long periods of operation, were set up by entrepreneurs, either individuals or corporate groups similar to the *collegium fabrorum* of Chichester.

The eastern group of sites can be sub-divided, both chronologically and geographically. The earliest sites are those in the Battle–Sedlescombe area: Beauport Park, Chitcombe, Crowhurst Park, Footlands, and Oaklands Park (two of which date to before the Roman invasion). The later sites, which seem to have started up in the first half of the 2nd century, such as Bardown, Knowle Farm, etc, lie further north, in the High Weald. There appears to have been a northward shift some time between AD 100 and 140 (at the same time satellite sites, such as Bynes Farm, Forewood, and Pepperingeye, may have been established around the large Crowhurst Park establishment).

It would seem reasonable for the military to have secured a major source of iron fairly promptly after the conquest of Britain began, in order to supply the field armies, and that a number of the early sites in the eastern group began producing on a very large scale in the mid 1st century. There is no indication as to who was responsible for the operation of these works. However, it was essentially a sea-based operation from the beginning, based on ports at Bodiam and Oaklands Park on the Rother and Brede estuaries respectively. Margary's routes 130 and 131, which appear to provide a land-based route running into the heart of this eastern group of sites, are considered by him to be considerably later than route 13, which was contemporary with the more westerly trunk roads in Sussex. These roads appear to have been built at a time when the estuarine ports were beginning to silt up, and also when it was becoming increasingly hazardous to navigate across what is now Romney Marsh, because of both sandbanks and raiders.

To summarize, therefore, the iron industry is seen as comprising two distinct groups. The western group, which is related to the north–south trunk roads, was civilian in character, serving markets in London and to the south, and operated continuously from the period immediately following the conquest to the end of the Roman period. The eastern group, served by a network of minor roads, exported its products by sea. It was probably state-owned and operated, and started immediately after the conquest but, unlike the western group, was abruptly terminated in the mid 3rd century.

The Weald as an Imperial estate

The existence of tiles stamped with the CL BR mark of the British Fleet on four sites of the eastern group— Bardown, Beauport Park, Bodiam, and Little Farningham Farm (Sissinghurst, Kent)—introduces a new element into the interpretation of the Roman settlement of the Weald. There seems to have been a direct connexion between the ironmaking sites of the eastern group, with their seaborne export of products, and the Fleet, with its main base during the 2nd and early 3rd centuries at Dover. The finds of stamped tiles at Bardown, Bodiam, and Little Farningham Farm were not large, although in terms of the total tile fragments recovered they represent a significant proportion, but at the Beauport Park bath-house almost every tile was stamped.

The role of the Fleet is discussed in another paper by the present author (Cleere, 1977). It was essentially a support arm rather than a fighting force, and its involvement in industrial operations is in no way inconsistent or unusual. It seems reasonable to postulate that the Fleet secured this important resource base for the Army early in the Roman period—perhaps within a year or two of the invasion. A pre-existing industry in the Hastings area was in effect 'nationalized', and was greatly expanded, perhaps in due course supplying Roman armies on the other side of the Channel through the Fleet's base at Boulogne. For some reason that so far remains obscure, this operation was shut down abruptly in the mid 3rd century, perhaps being transferred to the Forest of Dean.

The western group of sites, however, remained in private hands: the entrepreneurs who first set up the Broadfields and Garden Hill settlements were allowed to continue their operations, although perhaps in return for substantial royalty payments, and new establishments were set up as fresh ore deposits were revealed by road building or prospecting. Garden Hill seems to have failed as an economic unit, but Broadfields, Great Cansiron, and Oldlands continued producing iron for civilian markets until the end of the Roman period.

It remains only to consider the administrative background to this pattern of industrial settlement. The virtual absence of settlements owing their raison d'être to any other activity than ironmaking has already been remarked. It is also apparent that there are no major urban or domestic settlements anywhere in this region, a somewhat surprising fact in view of the density of villa and town distributions in the regions surrounding the Weald—and indeed in the Lowland Zone generally during the Roman period. These indications taken together point strongly to the existence of an Imperial estate over most of the Weald.

It is generally accepted that the state owned the mineral rights in all Roman provinces during the early Empire: in practice they were vested in the Imperial patrimonium and thereby made an important contribution to the coffers of the Emperors. A study of other major metals-producing provinces, such as Dacia, Spain, Noricum, and Dalmatia, reveals a fairly consistent development pattern after absorption into the Empire.

All these provinces show massive increases in mining and ironmaking activities following annexation or conquest— even in Noricum, where the iron industry, already under royal control, was large at the time of the province's annexation. Nominal State control was asserted over all mineral resources, but in the earliest phase there was direct Imperial exploitation only of precious metal production, other types of mining being left in private hands in return for royalty payments. The iron industry tended to be in the hands of rich entrepreneurs (*conductores*) or limited companies (*collegii*) during this phase, which lasted until the end of the 1st century in Spain, the mid 2nd century in Noricum, and the end of the 2nd or early 3rd century in Gaul and Dalmatia.

The next stage involved the assumption of direct responsibility for mining and ironmaking operations by Imperial officials (*procuratores ferrariarum*), most probably working either through small concessionnaires (*coloni*) or managers (*vilici*). This development is borne out by epigraphic evidence, the most impressive of which is represented by the series of altars dedicated to Terra Mater, patron deity of miners, from the Briševo-Ljubija region of Dalmatia (Wilkes, 1969, 267–8).

A number of metal-producing regions have been identified as Imperial estates in these provinces, notably the Sana valley in Dalmatia, the Styrian Erzberg region in Noricum, and the Vipasca region of Spain (whose laws are known through the survival of the Aljustrel tablets: *CIL*. II.5181). In these estates there were no (or very few) towns, and those which existed had no citizenship rights or *territorium*; there was, however, a considerable degree of social protection for the inhabitants, as the *lex metalli Vipascensis* shows. In Imperial estates devoted to mining agriculture seems to have been forbidden; similarly, in estates devoted to, for example, corn production in North Africa no other activity was permitted.

On the ground the existence of an Imperial estate is testified by the absence of major urban settlements or establishments of the villa type, and the presence of settlements dedicated to a single activity. This is clearly the case in the Weald, as Fig 32 shows. The pre-Roman opening up of the Weald by ironmakers seems to have marked it out as a candidate for designation as an Imperial estate immediately. The lack of urban development in the later 1st century would argue an early date for this designation. The first phase seems to agree with that revealed in Noricum and elsewhere: entrepreneurial exploitation on a rapidly developing scale. At some time in the late 1st or early 2nd century the richer ore deposits of the eastern group of sites were taken over by the Imperial officials for direct operation—perhaps to increase supplies of iron to the Army at a period of great pressure (the takeover in Noricum can be related directly to the increased demands created by the Marcomannic Wars). The role of the Fleet is not clear, however. It may be that technicians from the Fleet were personally involved in ore winning and iron smelting, but it might be argued that their role was one of supervision, and that the professional metal-producing element was still civilian, in the form of members of the procurator's staff (the *vilicus* Bassus referred to on the Beauport Park inscription seems to lend support to this view).

A case might be made out for the putative Imperial estate covering only that part of the Weald where direct State intervention is attested, the eastern group of sites. However, the absence of any kind of urban development—even at Alfoldean, on its extremity—in the western sector would seem to indicate that the estate boundary came right up to Stane Street, but that direct Imperial control was not extended to this sector. Private operations seem to have been allowed to continue, though doubtless considerable royalties were paid into the *patrimonium* by franchise holders.

The circumstantial evidence for the existence of an Imperial estate covering most of the Weald seems to be strong. Unfortunately we lack the rich epigraphic sources of other Roman provinces: the lone Beauport Park inscription is not enough to sustain an unqualified assertion. However, the Imperial estate hypothesis seems to be the best explanation of the somewhat enigmatic settlement pattern of the Weald and it introduces a new element into consideration of the Roman administrative structure in Britain.

References

Beckensall, S G, 1967   *Sussex Archaeol Collect*, **105**, 13–30
Chown, E, 1946–7   *Sussex Notes and Queries*, **11**, 148–51
Cleere, H, 1974   *Archaeol J*, **131**, 171–99
Cleere, H, 1976   *Bull Inst Archaeol*, **13**, 233–46
Cleere, H, 1977   in *The Saxon Shore* (ed D E Johnston), CBA Res Rep **18**, 16–19
Curwen, E C, 1954   *The Archaeology of Sussex*, 2 edn
Fowler, P J, 1976   in *The Archaeology of Anglo-Saxon England* (ed D M Wilson), 23–48
Gibson-Hill, J   (forthcoming)
Green, T K, 1970   *Sussex Archaeol Collect*, **108**, 23–38
Grimes, W F, 1930   *Y Cymmrodor*
Homan, W M, 1936–7   *Sussex Notes and Queries*, **6**, 247–8
Lemmon, C H, 1951–2   *Trans Battle Dist Hist Soc*, 27–9
Lemmon, C H and Hill, J D, 1966   *Sussex Archaeol Collect*, **104**, 96–102
Lucas, B H, 1950–3   *Sussex Notes and Queries*, **13**, 16–19
Margary, I D, 1965   *Roman Ways in the Weald*
Margary, I D, 1969   *Roman Sussex*, Sussex Archaeol Soc
Margary, I D, 1973   *Roman roads in Britain*, 3 edn
Money, J H, 1974   *Bull Hist Metall Group*, **8**, 1–20
Straker, E, 1928   *Sussex Archaeol Collect*, **69**, 183–5
Straker, E, 1931   *Wealden Iron*
Tebbutt, C F, 1968–71   *Sussex Notes and Queries*, **17**, 25–6
Tebbutt, C F and Cleere, H F, 1973   *Sussex Archaeol Collect*, **111**, 27–40
Wilkes, J J, 1969   *Dalmatia*
Winbolt, S E, 1923   *Sussex Archaeol Collect*, **64**, 81–104
Winbolt, S E, 1924   *ibid*, **65**, 112–57

AD 477. In this year Ælle and his three sons, Cymen, Wlencing and Cissa, came into Britain with three ships at the place which is called Cymenesora, and there killed many Britons and drove some into flight into the wood which is called Andredeslea.

This account marks the beginning of Saxon Sussex as described in the *Anglo-Saxon Chronicle*. Following it are accounts of Ælle's battle with the British in AD 485 near the bank of Mearcredesburna, and his siege of Pevensey in 491 after which the inhabitants were massacred. Such is almost the limit of direct historical reference to Sussex until the period of its conversion to Christianity. It is, however, supplemented by what we know of events elsewhere in southern England, and by a growing body of archaeological evidence.

As pressure on the Roman Empire mounted, troops were steadily withdrawn from Britain until by AD 410 probably few remained, and those remaining would have been predominantly garrison troops. Simultaneously Saxon raids on the channel coast became more intense, and the expedient adopted by Romano-British leaders was to enlist the help of Anglo-Saxon mercenaries to whom they ceded territory. Groups of mercenaries may have arrived in Sussex early in the 5th century, but of this there is no incontrovertible evidence. It is likely that their first major territorial gains came with the arrival of Ælle: not in AD 477, the *Anglo-Saxon Chronicle* date, but some twenty years earlier. Recently a correlation of dates from various sources has indicated that those in the Chronicle are probably all twenty years too late (Morris, 1965).

The main area settled during the 5th century can be identified by the distribution of cemeteries of that period (Fig 33a). All the known examples, except Highdown, are between the lower Ouse and Cuckmere rivers. This was an area apparently devoid of Romano-British villa estates and thus likely to have been selected for a treaty settlement of Anglo-Saxon mercenaries (Welch, 1971). Subsequently Ælle seems to have tried to break out of the treaty area and in about AD 465 he fought the battle of 'Mearcredesburna', one translation of which is 'river of the frontier agreed by treaty'. The Chronicle does not tell us who won the battle, but with the taking of Pevensey in *c* AD 471 Ælle extended his territory up to the Pevensey Levels. East of the Levels was an area independently settled by the Hæstingas, a people whose territory continued to be regarded as an area apart from the rest of Sussex as late as the 11th century. No pagan Germanic cemeteries are known from their territory, and Welch (1977) has interpreted this as an indication that they were already Christian when they arrived, perhaps during the 7th century.

Concerning the area west of the Arun, evidence is largely negative. The only known pagan Saxon burials are at Pagham (7th or 8th century AD) and Bow Hill. This has led some writers to suggest that an area centred on Chichester remained in sub-Roman hands, throughout the 5th century and perhaps longer (Morris, 1973). Equally, however, there is no archaeological evidence from Chichester or its surroundings of a sub-Roman population during this period.

Six Anglo-Saxon cemeteries provide the bulk of the archaeological evidence for the early period; these are

Highdown, near Worthing, and the group between the rivers Ouse and Cuckmere: Alfriston, Selmeston, South Malling, Beddingham and Bishopstone. They all seem to have been of moderate size: those which have been fairly fully excavated are Highdown, with over 170 graves; Alfriston, 150–160; and Bishopstone, 118. Inhumation was the predominant rite in each case, but a proportion of cremations was present at Highdown (about 28) and Bishopstone (6). Most burials were furnished with grave goods; in the case of Highdown and Alfriston these were particularly rich. In addition to the usual knives, buckles, brooches, beads, spears, etc, objects were found which established the 5th century origin of these cemeteries (Evison, 1965). Quoit Brooch Style buckles or belt fittings, many of them inlaid with silver or bronze, were found at Highdown, Alfriston and Bishopstone, and the first two sites produced vessels with facetted carinations (Myres, 1969). Of special interest is the occurrence in all these cemeteries of artefacts of Romano-British origin, in particular the fine glasses from Selmeston, Alfriston and Highdown, the most beautiful of these being the inscribed goblet with a hunting scene from the latter site.

Burials continued to be made in most of these cemeteries during the 6th century and at Highdown probably to the beginning of the 7th (Welch, 1976).

Cemeteries where the objects seem largely to be of 6th century date are Saxonbury, near Lewes, and St Anne's Road, Eastbourne. Throughout the pagan period many burials were made in barrows, both reused prehistoric examples like that which formed the focus of the Bishopstone cemetery, and newly constructed mounds, examples of which were excavated on New Barn Down and found to contain individual burials (Curwen, 1934). Clusters of numerous small barrows are known at Firle Beacon; the Bostal, Rottingdean; and Mill Hill, Rodmell (Meaney, 1964). The first two sites have been dug into, but finds were few and the clusters can only tentatively be assigned to the latter part of the pagan period. The latest cemeteries appear to be those at Jevington (Holden, 1969) and Willingdon Road, Eastbourne, where the west–east alignment and very small number of grave goods is consistent with either a late pagan or early post-conversion date.

Until recently no settlements were known which could be associated specifically with these pagan cemeteries. It was believed that they served still surviving villages, generally on lower ground in the valleys and vales. All this was changed in 1967 by the finding of a settlement (Fig 33b) beside the Bishopstone cemetery (Bell, 1977b). The site was an exposed spur crest overlooking the mouth of the Ouse, a spot which had been occupied from the Neolithic and where a Romano-British settlement had been in existence until the late 4th or early 5th century. The Saxon settlement was on the site of its predecessors, but being rather larger, some 3 ha in extent, it spread over the surrounding 'Celtic' field system. Twenty-two buildings have been excavated: three of them sunken huts, one large 'boat-shaped' building, a foundation-trench building, a group of eight large posts, and the remainder rectangular buildings founded on individual posts. The structures were in an orderly layout, all but one aligned east–west along the contours. Between them were six hearth pits and postholes which were presumably the remnants of fences.

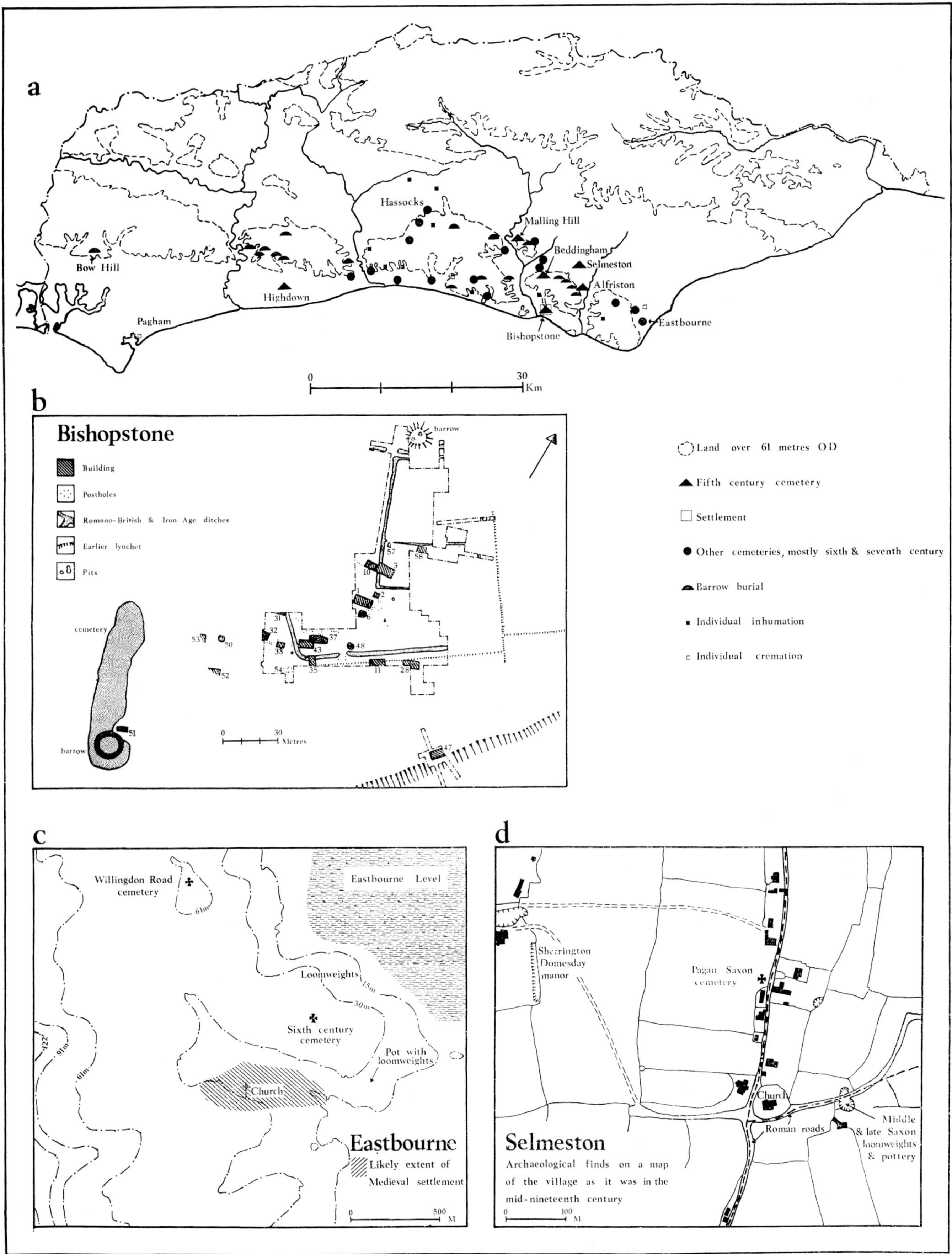

Fig 33 Early Saxon Sussex

In the light of this discovery, and others made elsewhere in England recently, it seems that early Saxon cemeteries were often closely associated with the settlements they served. There are indications that this was the case at Highdown where a quantity of Saxon sherds came from the vicinity of wooden buildings excavated in 1939. Originally the buildings were dated to the Roman period, but they now appear remarkably similar to Anglo-Saxon building types.

A further hilltop site, this time without a known cemetery, has been very extensively excavated just over the Hampshire border on Church Down, Chalton. This sizeable nucleated settlement seems to have been occupied within the 6th and 7th centuries. Professor Cunliffe (1972) has suggested that its abandonment led to the foundation of surviving villages such as Chalton, Blendworth, and Idsworth in the surrounding valleys. Much the same could have happened at Highdown, for below it on the Coastal Plain are a group of settlements with typologically early *-ingas* place-names.

Other early Saxon settlements may have survived on their original site; Selmeston is a possible example (Fig 33d). The 5th century cemetery is only 230 m north of the church which is situated at the crossing place of two Roman roads. Sand extraction close to this junction has brought to light intermediate and bun-shaped loomweights and pottery, suggesting occupation in the middle and late Saxon periods. Surviving settlements may frequently have obscured all trace of early Saxon origins, and there is some evidence that pagan cemeteries have sometimes been covered by Christian graveyards. For instance, a cinerary urn of 7th or 8th century date was found, together with parts of two other vessels, in the churchyard at Pagham; a large pot was found on the supposed site of the now vanished church of West Marden, and at Steyning burials have been found below a cottage near the church.

The only later Saxon settlement to be scientifically investigated is Old Erringham, a Domesday manorial site, near which a sunken floored hut has been excavated (Fig 34b). The hut is dated to the latter part of the middle and late Saxon period, and over 70 loomweights on the floor testify to its use as a weaving hut (Holden, 1976). Late Saxon loomweights and coins were also found under a defensive bank of the later manor. Chance finds point to the existence of similar sites (Bell, 1977a). Cliff erosion at Medmerry revealed sunken huts and floors with wattles and woodwork preserved by being waterlogged. This settlement was deserted, probably during the Saxon period, but traces of possibly sunken huts have been found in surviving settlements at Upwaltham, Thakeham, and Chichester. Even where a settlement has survived it may have undergone considerable change in orientation, morphology, and even location. This may have been the case at Eastbourne (Fig 33c) where Saxon evidence comes from Upperton ridge, the site of a 6th century cemetery and find-spot of two groups of late Saxon loomweights, one from Enys Road in a pot decorated by strapping (Figs 34d and 34e). During the medieval period the main focus of settlement seems to have shifted to the adjoining ridge, the site of the present parish church and Old Town. Hangleton is another settlement which underwent a fairly drastic change of location. The earliest finds from extensive excavations in the deserted medieval village were 12th century, and no trace was found of the settlement mentioned in Domesday Book (Holden, 1963).

Within the late Saxon settlement pattern there developed central places, some of which were to become towns. They were the result of two factors: one a state of emergency created by Scandinavian raids, the other the growth of market centres. Viking raids are recorded by the *Anglo-Saxon Chronicle* during AD 892, 894, 994, and 1009 and Scandinavian style objects, whether lost or traded, are known from Falmer, Hamsey, Westergate and Coombs (Ordnance Survey, 1973). Alfred responded to this threat by reorganizing the defences of southern Britain around a series of fortified burghs; those in Sussex were Lewes, Chichester, Burpham, and Hastings. The first two have produced evidence of late Saxon occupation, and recent excavations within the promontory fort at Burpham have revealed two large rectangular buildings and sizeable pits. There is also numismatic evidence for a reoccupation of the Cissbury hill-fort with a mint during the time of Aethelred II and Cnut (Dolley and Elmore Jones, 1955). It seems likely that this may be associated with a post-Roman refortification identified in the 1930s. Late Saxon occupation might be represented by platforms for rectangular buildings and large pits which overlie Celtic fields in the interior (Curwen and Ross Williamson, 1931). Other, perhaps undefended, towns seem to have developed, largely in response to economic factors. These were all ports. Steyning and Pevensey had mints before the conquest, Rye and Arundel were of lesser importance until the Norman period.

Archaeological sources enable us to document the genesis of individual settlements, but a more general framework is provided by place-name and historical studies. As yet no type of place-name has been identified which can be associated with the initial invasion phase. The earliest groupings, according to Dodgson (1973), are those with the suffix *-ham*, eg Patcham, which appear to have been founded in the 5th and 6th centuries AD. He attributes to a slightly later date places with the suffix *-ingas*, eg Hastings (Dodgson, 1966). With the foundation, in some numbers, of these surviving places the settlement pattern begins to resemble that of the medieval period, and henceforth the bulk of potential evidence is in historical sources. Land charters appear at the time of Bishop Wilfred's conversion of Sussex in AD 681. Generally present as later copies, they document grants of land usually by the king to ecclesiastical establishments or loyal servants. Charters record the existence of about 111 Sussex places and in some cases the boundaries are described (Barker, 1947; 1948; 1949). They also provide a record of those who granted land, and this gives an historical framework for Sussex which had been largely absent since the time of Ælle. During most of the interim it had been an independent kingdom, but from the beginning of the 7th century it was alternately under the domination of Wessex and Mercia. Finally the last vestiges of independent status were lost under Offa, who extended his influence to the territory of the Hæstingas in AD 771. The most comprehensive historical source is the Domesday survey (Morris, 1976; Haselgrove, 1977), made just after the Norman conquest. It lists 337 places, the majority of them in the Coastal Plain, downland valleys, and at the scarp foot of the Downs. Much of the Weald, except for the Rother valley and the environs of Hastings, appears to have been rather sparsely settled, but this is an anomaly to which we will return. The vast majority of Domesday manors and places listed in the charters have survived to become the villages of today. But what of their nature in the Saxon period? It is for the archaeologist to establish whether they were nucleated villages or manor farms.

Three classes of data, archaeological, documentary, and place-name, combine to give an impression of the economy of Saxon Sussex. Animal husbandry at Bishopstone was represented by sheep, numerically the most important

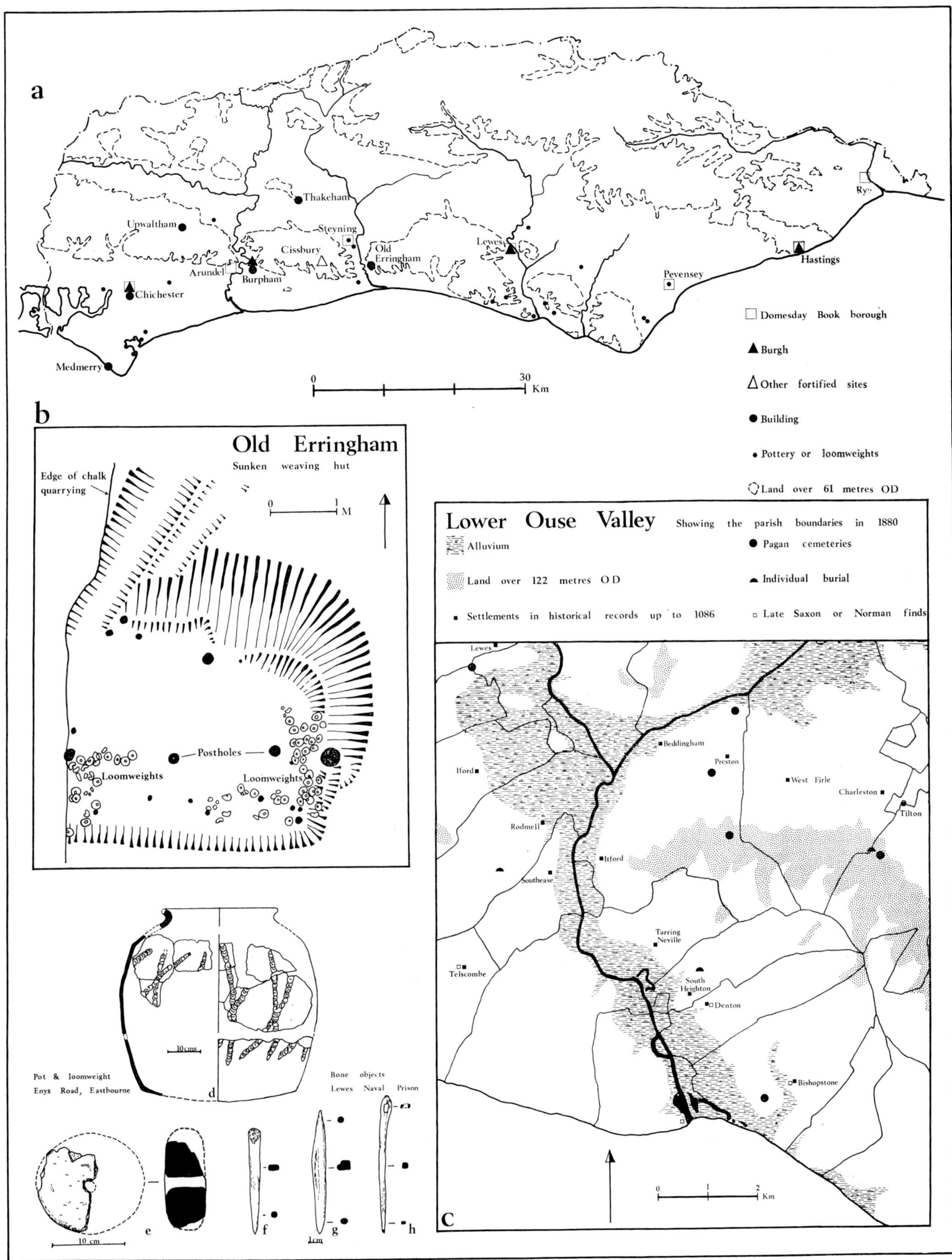

Fig **34**   *Middle and late Saxon Sussex*

species, cattle, pig, horse, domestic fowl, goose, and cat; the inhabitants also fished and collected marine molluscs in some quantity. Arable aspects of the economy were poorly represented, but this may not be an accurate reflection of their original importance since few contexts suitable for the recovery of plant remains were discovered, and no systematic attempt has yet been made to locate contemporary fields.

The Medmerry settlement (White, 1934) produced bones of horse, ox, pig, sheep/goat, and domestic fowl; a number of fish bones; two middens of sea shells and six rotary querns. Animals associated with the Old Erringham weaving hut were cattle, sheep, horse, fox, pig, bird, dog, fowl and rabbits; there were also marine and estuarine molluscs and quern fragments (Holden, 1976). Particularly interesting is the evidence that the hut provided for textile production; this was evidently a major craft activity in Saxon Sussex. Loomweights (Fig 34e) are known from thirteen sites. None was found at Bishopstone but here, and on a number of the later sites, there were spindle whorls, combs, pin-beaters (Figs 34f and 34g), and needles (Fig 34h).

The Domesday survey provides evidence of a range of economic activities far more extensive than the archaeological record (King, 1962); 87 watermills are recorded; coastal and riverine fisheries; quarries, in one case for millstones; and one ironworking site. Salt production is recorded in connexion with 34 settlements, particularly those on what would have been tidal estuaries like the Adur and Pevensey Levels. The sites of salterns are marked by groups of low mounds on the alluvium, and recently one of these, at New Monks Farm, Lancing, has been dated by excavation to the late Saxon period. Arable agriculture emerges from the Domesday Book as an important element in the late Saxon economy, and the record of plough-teams gives some idea of the extent and location of cultivated land. Most are enumerated under holdings on the Coastal Plain and downland margins, but there was a scatter in the eastern Weald, and some Wealden place-names imply clearances for cultivation. It is, however, the contribution of the Weald to the pastoral side of the economy which emerges most significantly from the late Saxon charters and Domesday Book. On superficial examination these sources seem to reflect the limited archaeological evidence from the Weald. This is partly an illusion created by the fact that the Weald formed part of an integrated economic system with the area to its south. The system was one of multiple estates with centres mostly on the Coastal Plain, downland valleys and in a zone just north of the Downs, but with scattered dependent territories many of which were in the Weald. Place-names given to the dependent territories testify to a fairly specialized function, for example Palinga Schittas: a swine cott of the people of Poling; Shipley: the sheep clearing; and the numerous *denn* endings, meaning swine pastures. The importance of the dependent territories as areas for pannage and grazing is further emphasized by drove roads linking them with estate centres in the south (Brandon, 1974). Economic specialization such as this should not, however, blind us to the fact that settlement in these territories might have developed quite early on, their existence being disguised in the documentary record by assessment under estate centres (Sawyer, 1976). An unfortunate tendency in the past has been to regard this economic system simply as the result of assart and colonization during the Anglo-Saxon period. More probably the origins of the system lie in patterns of seasonal transhumance which might have evolved in prehistoric times. This need not necessarily imply continuity within individual estates. A substantial

measure of continuity is, however, envisaged by Jones (1976), who claims that multiple estates and dependent territories of the Saxon and medieval periods were linked by obligations and rights which show similarities to estates in the Celtic west.

A complex economic strategy such as this surely presupposes an environment more intensively exploited than has generally been assumed, and one in which clear territorial boundaries had already been established. Descriptions of bounds are appended to some Saxon charters, and when they are sufficiently detailed and refer to distinctive topographical features it is possible to trace them by careful fieldwork. This has been done for a charter of AD 957 relating to South Heighton, where it could be shown that the estate was essentially the same area as the 19th century parish, though the boundaries are slightly different near the crest of the Downs. Saxon estates, or sometimes portions of them, seem to be quite frequently preserved in parish boundaries which would have become established once a church had been provided at the estate centre. If the South Heighton boundary was established by the 10th century, so probably were those of many of the surrounding territories also, thus making possible a very tentative reconstruction of the settlement pattern and territorial boundaries in the Lower Ouse Valley (Fig 34c). The settlements in this area, and in Saxon Sussex generally, were sited to exploit the varying land-use potential of different ecological environments.

This found its expression in long strip parishes running, for instance, from the river alluvium across a band of good arable, near which the main settlement lay, up on to extensive downland pastures. But when did these territories originate? There is some evidence from Wiltshire that they may be of considerable antiquity. Pagan Saxon burials are frequently concentrated on parish boundaries, which in certain instances seem to reflect boundaries of Roman or Iron Age date (Bonney, 1972). Some Sussex boundaries may go back at least to the early Saxon period. A notable proportion of pagan burials in the Worthing area are on parish boundaries (Ellison and Harriss, 1972), as are a number of those in the Lower Ouse Valley (Fig 34c).

An impression of continuity emerges from the history of Saxon Sussex. By the end of the period a settlement pattern was established which is recognizable in that of today; economic systems and territorial boundaries were in existence which, in some cases, survived into medieval and modern times. Occasionally there are hints that what we observe in the Saxon period may have originated much earlier. However, a closer look through archaeology at individual settlements reveals that the period was also one of change. No good evidence has been found of continuous occupation from late Roman to Saxon times. Many archaeologically attested Saxon settlements failed, and were deserted. Those that survived often shifted location, and we should not suppose that because a Domesday Book settlement is a nucleated village today it need necessarily have been more than a manor farm then. Historical and archaeological sources are therefore interdependent in achieving a balanced view of the period. Future researches must adopt a multidisciplinary approach for documenting specific instances of settlement and landscape evolution.

Acknowledgements

I am grateful to Messrs M G Welch and D C Haselgrove for their helpful comments on an earlier draft of this paper and to Mrs B Westley who typed it.

References

Barker, E, 1947   'Sussex Anglo-Saxon Charters, Part I', *Sussex Archaeol Collect*, **86**, 42–101

Barker, E, 1948   'Sussex Anglo-Saxon Charters, Part II', *ibid*, **87**, 112–63

Barker, E, 1949   'Sussex Anglo-Saxon Charters, Part III', *ibid*, **88**, 51–113

Bell, M, 1977a   'Saxon settlements and buildings in Sussex', in *The South Saxons* (ed P Brandon), Chichester

Bell, M, 1977b   'Excavations at Bishopstone, Sussex', *Sussex Archaeol Collect*, **115**

Bonney, D, 1972   'Early boundaries in Wessex', in *Archaeology and the landscape* (ed P Fowler), London, 168–86

Brandon, P, 1974   *The Sussex landscape*, London

Cunliffe, B W, 1972   'Saxon and medieval settlement pattern in the region of Chalton, Hampshire', *Medieval Archaeol*, **16**, 1–12

Curwen, E C, 1934   'A Late Bronze Age farm and a Neolithic pit-dwelling on New Barn Down . . .', *Sussex Archaeol Collect*, **75**, 137–70

Curwen, E C and Ross Williamson, R P, 1931   'The date of Cissbury Camp', *Antiq J*, **11**, 14–36

Dodgson, J McN, 1966   'The significance of the distribution of the English place-name in -ingas, inga, in south-east England', *Medieval Archaeol*, **10**, 1–29

Dodgson, J McN, 1973   'Place-names in *hām*, distinguished from *hamm* names, in relation to the settlement of Kent, Surrey and Sussex', *Anglo-Saxon England*, **2**, 1–50

Dolley, R H M and Elmore Jones, F, 1955   'The Mints "æt Gothabyrig and æt Sith (m)estebyrig"', *Brit Numis J*, **28**, 270–82

Ellison, A and Harriss, J, 1972   'Settlement and land use in the prehistory and early history of southern England: a study based on locational models', in *Models in archaeology* (ed D L Clarke), London, 911–62

Evison, V I, 1965   *The fifth-century invasions south of the Thames*, London

Haselgrove, D, 1977   'The Domesday record of Sussex', in *The South Saxons* (ed P Brandon), Chichester

Holden, E W, 1963   'Excavations at the deserted medieval village of Hangleton, Part I', *Sussex Archaeol Collect*, **101**, 54–181

Holden, E W, 1969   'Anglo-Saxon burials at Crane Down, Jevington', *ibid*, **107**, 126–34

Holden, E W, 1976   'Excavations at Old Erringham, Shoreham, West Sussex. Part I: a Saxon weaving hut', *ibid*, **114**, 306–21

Jones, G R J, 1976   'Multiple estates and early settlement', in *Medieval settlement* (ed P Sawyer), London, 15–40

King, S H, 1962   'Sussex', in *The Domesday geography of south-east England* (eds H C Darby and E M Campbell), Cambridge, 407–82

Meaney, A, 1964   *A gazetteer of early Anglo-Saxon burial sites*, London

Morris, J, 1965   'Dark Age dates', in *Britain and Rome* (eds M G Jarrett and B Dobson), Kendal, 145–85

Morris, J, 1973   *The Age of Arthur*, London

Morris, J, 1976   *Domesday Book: Sussex*, Chichester

Myres, J N L, 1969   *Anglo-Saxon pottery and the settlement of England*, Oxford

Ordnance Survey, 1973   *Britain before the Norman Conquest*, Southampton

Sawyer, P (ed), 1976   'Introduction: early medieval English settlement', in *Medieval settlement*, London, 1–7

Welch, M G, 1971   'Late Romans and Saxons in Sussex', *Britannia*, **2**, 232–7

Welch, M G, 1976   *Highdown: and its Saxon Cemetery*, Worthing Museum publication, no 11

Welch, M G, 1977   'Sub-Roman Sussex', in *The South Saxons* (ed P Brandon), Chichester

White, G M, 1934   'A settlement of the South Saxons', *Antiq J*, **14**, 393–400

Saxon and medieval mints and moneyers in Sussex — Caroline Dudley

The outstanding facts and statistics relating to the Sussex mints have long been known to numismatists, chiefly through the work of Dr Horace King, who published the corpus of known examples in the *Brit Numis J* (King, 1957–8, 61ff). However, recent insights into the workings of the mint at Winchester (Biddle, 1976, 396–422), and the detailed analysis of the output of the mint at Lincoln (Mossop, 1970), prompted a fresh attempt to gain a little more information from the bare facts available on the Sussex mints. Accordingly tables of all the moneyers known from each of the Sussex mints were compiled, together with the issues each moneyer struck, and a comparison was made between each mint in terms of duration of activity, numbers of moneyers and productivity at different periods. An attempt was also made to evaluate the correlation between the pattern of activity in the mints and recorded historical events. It soon became clear that this approach would repay more detailed analysis, but even so some interesting trends begin to appear.

The period during which mints are known to have operated in Sussex falls between AD 924 and *c* 1205, from the reign of Æthelstan until the reign of Henry II. The coin which was the only form of legal tender in England was the broad-flan penny, first introduced in East Kent some time between AD 765 and 786 as a replacement for the debased and discredited silver sceatta. Numismatists still disagree as to whether the new penny was introduced by Offa, or whether coins issued in the names of two little-known Kentish kings, Heaberht and Ecgbert, preceded Offa's coins. At any rate, it is agreed that the new penny did not really become established until *c* 786, after which the standard of the Saxon coinage never seriously faltered until its mangling at the hands of the moneyers of Henry I. The penny was a silver coin; there is a very rare example of a gold penny minted at Lewes (Æthelred II, *BMCat*, VIII Hild E), but so few of these have survived that it is impossible to judge what its status was in the monetary system. The prevailing opinion is that these gold pennies were offering pieces.

That there was a monetary system under the Saxons, and one which was firmly controlled and frequently manipulated by the government, is demonstrably true. The realization that a stable currency and political stability went hand-in-hand is reflected in the early and repeated injunctions against forgery and coining of bad money. It is most clearly expressed in the laws of Cnut (issued between 1020 and 1023: Whitelock, EHD, **I**, 420) which read:

'And let us take thought very earnestly about the improvement of the peace and the improvement of the coinage; about the improvement of the peace in such a way as may be best for the householder and most grievous for the thief, and about the improvement of the coinage in such a way that one coinage is to be current throughout all this nation, without any debasement, and no man is to refuse it'.

Control was exercised by issuing dies only from approved die-cutting centres, which in Sussex's case would either have been Winchester or London, and only to approved moneyers, who had to pay every time the type changed. Foreign coin had to be reminted or exchanged for the coin of the realm as soon as it was imported. It is possible that export of bullion was also controlled, as this passage from the 13th century Greater Chronicle of Matthew Paris illustrates:

'In the meantime the castellan of Dover, who kept a careful watch over the coast and was an unfailing scrutiniser of travellers, found many laden with the much desired coin, which they were taking out to the aliens; these he quickly relieved of their burdens, that they might travel more easily'. (EHD, 3, 103).

Certainly as early as the reign of King Alfred there is good evidence that the weight standard was raised in order, one authority suggests, to bring the accounting system of Wessex into line with that of Mercia (Lyon, 1976, 189); and throughout the Saxon and Norman period it seems that reducing the weight of coins was a means by which the mints could meet increased demands for revenue from the authorities or compensate for a scarcity of bullion (Lyon, 1976, 174–5). It is also clear that fixing the weight standard was not the prerogative of individual moneyers—experiments carried out show that the weights of individual types appear to show a remarkable uniformity within fairly narrow limits of tolerance, although the weight of one type and the next may be markedly different and standards may vary from one region to another (Lyon, 1976, 174). These variations were possible because under the Anglo-Saxon monetary system it was accepted that the penny was overvalued, ie its face value was greater than its bullion value. A specific example of this for Sussex during the late Saxon period is the entry for Bosham in Domesday, which states that during the time of King Edward, it took 65 pounds of money at 240 pence to the pound 'burned and weighed' to equal the levy due, which was 50 pounds of silver, bullion weight. In other words, the coins were individually so light by then that it took 25% extra in number to make up the correct bullion weight, and yet they were obviously in circulation as normal legal tender.

The reform of Eadgar in 973 may have been a measure to ensure the good quality of the coinage by instituting regular changes of type; but the possibilities for raising revenue must have been equally attractive, both to moneyers and the authorities, bearing in mind how many mints there were in the country as a whole, all of whom had to pay a levy each time the type changed before they were allowed new dies. Domesday tells us, for example, that in Lewes 'when the money is renewed, each moneyer gives 20 shillings; of all these two parts were the King's and the third part the Earl's' (then William de Warenne).

Eadgar appears to have envisaged a sexennial or septennial cycle of types, but this gradually gave way to a two- to three-year cycle after 1035, which must have placed quite a burden both on the moneyers who had to pay for the dies and the public from whom they had to recover their outlay. It may be that this increase in the frequency of changes of type is a factor in the decrease in the number of moneyers operating in Sussex after *c* 1035–40, but before attempting to reach any conclusions we should first look at the evidence for the mints in more detail.

The first documentary reference to the Sussex mints comes in Æthelstan's decree issued at Grately, Hampshire (II Æthelstan: EHD, **I**, 381), which states that:

'In Canterbury (there are to be) 7 moneyers, four of the

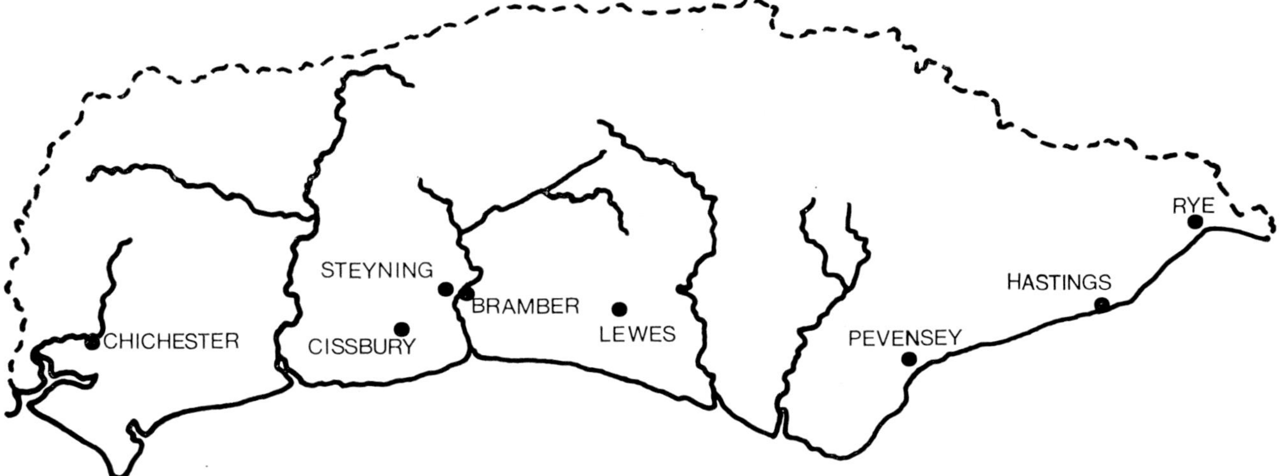

Fig 35 Pre- and post-Conquest mints in Sussex

king, two of the bishop, one of the abbot: in Rochester 3, 2 of the king, 1 of the bishop; in London 8; in Winchester 6; in Lewes 2; in Hastings 1; another at Chichester; at Southampton 2; at Wareham 2; at Dorchester 1; at Exeter 2; at Shaftesbury 2; otherwise in the other burhs one'.

The evidence of the coins bears out this allocation with regard to Chichester and Lewes. The first type to be minted in Sussex is Æthelstan's third type, the Circumscription Cross, struck by Iohan at Chichester and Wilebald and Eadric at Lewes. Æthelstan's previous two types, however, had not carried the mint name, only the moneyer, and among the moneyers' names recorded for Æthelstan's first issue, the Two-line type, are the names Iohan and Wilebald. It may be, therefore, that these mints were operating from the very beginning of his reign. No coins from the reign of Æthelstan are known from Hastings, however, although there is always the possibility that they were operating without using a mint name.

The quota of moneyers allowed for each burh in Sussex proves to have been decided on economic grounds rather than according to status, reflecting, one imagines, the local demand for coinage created by brisk trade and rich burgesses who needed coins to pay taxes. In spite of being a simple 'urbs' according to Domesday, Lewes rapidly outstrips its 'civitas' neighbour in this respect.

After Æthelstan's reign there is a gap of about 20 years in which no coins are attributable to Sussex mints. Again, however, the majority of coins from this period did not carry a mint name, so it is possible that coins may have been struck in Sussex. The moneyers whose names appear first when coins begin to carry the mint name again are Flodwyn, Cynsige and Sideman at Chichester, and Goldstan, Sexbyrht and Theodgar at Lewes; but the only one who may be identified in the previous anonymous issues is Sideman, who may be represented by the name Sedeman in Eadwig's Two-line type, issued between 955 and 959. There is some evidence, therefore, for thinking that the gap in the activities of the Sussex mints was more apparent than real.

By the beginning of Eadgar's reign in 959, and up until his reform in 973, it was still not commonplace to carry the mint name on the coin, although Flodwyn of Chichester used it on the Circumscription Cross type, but from 973 onwards the mint name almost always appears. Chichester and Lewes both mint the Reform Portrait type, and two out of the three Lewes moneyers also strike the Reform Portrait type for Edward the Martyr (975–8).

Chichester, however, does not strike this issue, nor the following First Small Cross type for Æthelred II; and it may be an indication that the mint really was out of commission between 975 and 979 that when they did begin minting again, the old moneyers do not reappear.

The next issue, Æthelred's First Hand type (c 979–985) is struck by Aethelm and Heawulf at Chichester, and Theodgar, Herebyrht, Eadgar and Leofstan at Lewes, and marks the beginning of a period of conspicuous stability and continuity for the mints of Lewes and Chichester. From now on they mint practically every type until the end of Cnut's reign, and after a few years during which they were clearly affected in some way by the confusion surrounding the reigns of Harold I and Harthacnut, they continue to mint without a break until the aftermath of 1066. Coins of Æthelred's Second Hand issue are also the first recognized from Hastings. As to why it did not begin to mint in 924 as the Grately decree allowed is still not clear. Once it opens, sometime between 985 and 991, its progress is extremely steady and its output in terms of issues struck and moneyers in business is remarkably regular.

The pattern of productivity at the Sussex mints is extremely interesting from this point onwards and calls for a detailed analysis of the facts for each burh, but the following conclusions seem to hold good. Lewes definitely emerges as the major economic centre in Sussex. Although it starts with only two moneyers as per Grately, and allowing for the gap when no coins are definitely attributable to Sussex mints, by 973 three moneyers are known to be working in Lewes, five between 979 and 985 then six, and between 1009 and 1017 eleven and in 1017–23, Cnut's First Quatrefoil issue, there is a maximum of twelve moneyers striking for Lewes. According to Biddle's evidence for Winchester (1976, 397) each moneyer represented a separate workshop, and in Winchester at least, some workshops had as many as six forges in them (Biddle, 1976, 422). Until 1180 it was expressly forbidden for moneyers in Winchester to work under the same roof (Biddle, 1976, 422, n6); although there is no evidence that this ban existed in other mints, it indicates a possibility that Lewes at this point would have had twelve separate moneyers' establishments. Moreover, again on the evidence of Winchester (Biddle, 1976, 421), moneyers were occupiers of prime sites in the commercial areas of the town, with a large group owning workshops and separate private houses right on the High Street. It would be fascinating to discover whether a similar situation existed in Lewes.

Although one has to bear in mind that even though the names of twelve moneyers appear on the coins of one particular issue, they need not all have been in business simultaneously (a moneyer might die or pass on his business to a man of another name in the space of a single issue), the evidence for a 'boom' period, albeit nowhere else as marked as in Lewes, also holds good for the other Sussex mints. Chichester starts with one moneyer, jumps to three for Eadgar's Reform coinage, drops to two again during 1003–9, then reaches a peak of six between 1017 and 1023. Hastings seems to share the same peak period; five moneyers work there between 1017 and 1023, as opposed to a 'normal' quota of two or three.

As for the minor mints, it is surely significant, with the examples of Chichester, Lewes, and Hastings before us, that the opening of the mint at Cissbury between 1009 and 1017 coincides with this peak period of activity. This increases the probability that the peak is related in some way to economic demand. Cissbury is generally referred to as an 'emergency' mint, but with a military emergency in mind rather than a temporary response to a demand. This theory has arisen, I believe, chiefly because the site we know as Cissbury is an inhospitable site known to have been fortified in the past, and by analogy with other 'emergency' mints such as Wilton, which was adopted because of the sack of Winchester and the destruction of the mint there. As there was no decline in production of the other Sussex mints at this time, and certainly none of them ceased operations altogether, the only logical reason for opening a new mint in the centre of Sussex seems to me to be because they needed one. Cissbury struck two consecutive issues between 1009 and 1023 in the names of three moneyers, Ciolnoth, Godwine, and Leofwine, none of whom appears to have transferred to Steyning when that mint opened *c* 1023–9, as they surely would have done if Cissbury was just the temporary home of the mint. Steyning certainly strikes the next issue due after Cissbury closes, but the moneyer is Wudia. It would appear most likely that a demand for a mint arose in central Sussex at this time, and that it was tried out at Cissbury first, but that later Steyning was preferred.

Pevensey did not open until 1077 and had a constant quota of one moneyer until its closing years between 1150 and 1158, when it had two, Alwine and Felipe. Rye opened in 1135, and only ever had one moneyer, while Bramber only struck coins between 1150 and 1158, the Awbridge type of Stephen. There seems to have been a definite revival of effort at the mints for this issue. It was struck at Pevensey, Rye, Bramber, Lewes, and Hastings, but proved to be something of a last gasp for all of them except Lewes, who struck the following type—the Tealby penny (1158–80), for Henry II—and Chichester, who after a gap of almost exactly fifty years struck the Short Cross type for John between 1199 and 1216, which proved to be the last coins issued from a Sussex mint.

The question as to what was the nature of that demand must arise, if the multiplication of moneyers in the operational mints between *c* 991 and 1036, with an apparent peak around 1009–23, is accepted as evidence of an economic demand. The evidence from Winchester makes it clear that moneyers were citizens of high status in that city, many of proven burgess rank (Biddle, 1976, 422). If the same is true for Sussex, surely Lewes could only have attracted twelve such men, and supported them, if there were rich pickings of some sort at this time. Moneyers needed a hinterland—they were basically changers as well as moneyers, and had to have bullion or old coins brought to them in order to produce new coinage.

Was Sussex, therefore, very busy and prosperous during this period? It seems a real possibility that it was. However, another possibility is that the monetary activity was connected by way of fiscal demands with the Danegeld. The first tribute was paid in 991—a first demand of £10,000, according to the *Anglo-Saxon Chronicle*. The year 1005 is recorded as the year of the great famine—not necessarily affecting Sussex, of course. The year 1009 seems a most unlikely time to begin a boom; the *Anglo-Saxon Chronicle* records widespread burning and harrying in Sussex, Hampshire, and Berkshire, although again not necessarily in central or east Sussex. In Chichester there is possibly a drop in the number of moneyers between about 1003 and 1017, which is contrary to the pattern in the rest of the county, and it is more likely that Chichester would have suffered periodic raids by the Danes, because of its nearness to one of their favourite strongholds, the Isle of Wight. The largest demand of all was in 1018 for a sum of £72,000, which seems to come right in the middle of the Sussex 'boom'. Therefore one is forced to ask whether the moneyers were making money out of raising these sums, or whether it was simply that Sussex was better off than many parts of the country. There is no doubt that moneying was a lucrative occupation, and the need to raise revenue created opportunities for making profits.

After *c* 1036–7 the boom, if such it was, seems to have levelled out fairly abruptly, although there are other short-lived peaks which affect individual towns. Danegeld was abolished in 1051, but it is noticeable that from *c* 1040 onwards the *Anglo-Saxon Chronicle* complains increasingly about bad weather, poor harvests, and rising prices. The other factor which may have had a significant effect on the situation is the increased frequency of changes of type, following hard upon a period of confusion and uncertainty created by the conflict between Harold I and Harthacnut. This leads me to my other preoccupation in this enquiry—to discover how far one can see known historical events reflected in patterns emerging from this analysis of the mints.

For example, at the end of Cnut's reign in 1035, Harold I became joint king with Harthacnut for two years. During this period Harold issued the Short Cross type in 1035, and his Jewel Cross type between Spring 1036 and Autumn 1037. Harthacnut issued the First Jewel Cross type between November 1035 and Spring 1036, both in his own name and in Cnut's, and the Second Jewel Cross type between Spring 1036 and Autumn 1037. In 1037 Harold became sole king, and *c* 1038 issued a Fleur-de-lys type. In 1040 Harthacnut became sole king, and his first short issue was another Fleur-de-lys type, struck between March and June 1040, a *mule* so far only known from London, which is a combination of the obverse of a Harthacnut First Jewel Cross type and a reverse from Harold's Fleur-de-lys type. In June 1040 came Harthacnut's final issue, the Arm and Sceptre type, which was also issued in Cnut's name.

In Sussex Cnut's own last issue was struck at Hastings, Lewes, and Steyning. Harold's first type was not struck in Sussex at all, but his Jewel Cross type (1036–7) was struck at Chichester, Lewes, and Hastings. Harthacnut's First Jewel Cross type, however, was struck at Chichester, Lewes, Hastings, and Steyning, and as its currency runs from 1035, when Harold's issue does not appear, it seems as though Sussex may have recognized Harthacnut first. As his die-cutting centre is thought to have been at Winchester, while Harold's was in London (Lyon, 1970), it may also have some significance in pointing to the natural focus of the area. Whether they continued to strike for Harthacnut when they began striking for Harold in 1036 cannot be distinguished yet, as the types seem to be concurrent; however, it is certain that Chichester, Lewes, Hastings, and Steyning all strike Harold's Fleur-de-lys type (1038–40) and all but Steyning strike the following Arm-in-Sceptre type in Cnut's name (1040–2). Only Lewes, however, struck Harthacnut's own Arm-and-Sceptre type, also issued between 1040 and 1042. One wonders whether the pace did not become too frantic for the smaller mints during this period. Steyning does not mint at all regularly during this time, although it may be that they continued to operate but carried on with old dies. The question as to whether a new type demonetized the previous type is one which still has not been settled, but there seems to be an indication that in the less central mints some dies may have continued in use for longer than they ought to have done, especially since it is generally agreed that a discontinued type may not have been finally demonetised until a few years after the introduction of its replacement (Dolley and Metcalf, 1961, 158; Archibald, 1974, 247–8). The fact that the moneyer at Steyning remains the same throughout this period of irregularity reinforces this possibility, in the writer's opinion.

On the accession of Edward the Confessor the situation stabilizes, but none of the mints in Sussex ever attains the same number of moneyers again, presumably partly as a result of the increase in frequency of changes of coin type, which must have increased the moneyers' overheads considerably.

Another period which is particularly important in Sussex history is of course around 1066, and a look at the pattern of productivity at the Sussex mints during this time seems to show some interesting and unexpected trends. Chichester, Lewes, Hastings, and Steyning have minted steadily throughout the Confessor's reign until 1065, when we have no example of the last type of the reign from Hastings. Edward died in the first few days of January, 1066, and Harold became king on 6 January. He had time to issue one type, the Pax penny, before his death on 14 October, 1066. This issue was struck at Chichester, Lewes, Hastings, and Steyning. By the end of the year William had issued his first type, the Profile-Cross Fleury. Now if there was one place in England where one would not expect this issue to have been minted it would be Hastings, and yet Hastings was the only mint in Sussex, apart from Chichester, which is known to have struck this type. Moreover, the coins appear to have been struck by the same moneyers, Dunninc, Theodred, and Colswegen, who had been moneyers in Hastings, striking every issue, since 1053, 1059, and 1062 respectively. So what happened? History says that Hastings and the surrounding villages were completely laid waste, and certainly this has never seemed unlikely. Was the Hastings mint provided with special protection, were the Saxon moneyers' dies used by the Normans, or were the moneyers a pragmatic lot, accustomed to changes of loyalty and indifferent to the source of their income? It may be that none of these theories provides the answer, but it may shed some light if we look at what was happening in the other mints in this and the subsequent issue.

In Chichester the Harold II Pax type had been struck by Aelfwine, whose name appears on coins without a break from 1044 until 1066. The first issue was also struck by Godwine, who had started operations in 1053. William's first issue, however, was struck by only one moneyer— Bruman, who was a complete newcomer. Moreover, he remained the only moneyer working in Chichester for about eleven or twelve years, until joined by another called Godwine. We never hear any more of Aelfwine, who had been working there for 22 years. Lewes and Steyning did not strike William's first issue at all. By William's second issue, things appear to be returning to normal— Lewes and Steyning strike again, and although Chichester misses this type, Bruman continues to strike the following type. At Hastings, however, the Bonnet type (1068–71) was only struck by Dunninc, and from then on the mint follows rather an erratic pattern. There is a gap of about six years during which no coins are known from Hastings; then between 1077 and 1080 a solitary issue is minted of the Two Stars type, again struck by Dunninc. There follows another gap of six years before William's last issue, the Pax type of 1086, in which Dunninc is apparently joined by Cipincc. He misses out the first type for William II in 1089, but strikes the second type; then nothing appears again until Henry I's reign in which he apparently strikes the 6th, 8th, and 9th issues. If this were all the same man's work, he would have been employed as a moneyer from 1053 to *c* 1125–30, a period of about 75 years, but this really does not seem likely. The answer is almost certainly that there were two consecutive moneyers of the same name, maybe even three, and that possibly they were from the same family. The evidence for Winchester is that moneying was a family tradition, and that continuity can be traced from generation to generation (Biddle, 1976, 416). One might suspect that Dunninc's name was retained posthumously, but there seems no reason for this when other moneyers came and went at Hastings in an apparently normal fashion. On balance, one would guess that during these years Dunninc and his family hung on determinedly to their occupation in Hastings and were enabled to do so because they were Norman sympathizers, or survived because they were practical people who knew which side their bread was buttered!

Although lack of space prevents further discussion of the subject, enough has, it is hoped, been said to show that an analytical approach to the sequence of moneyers and types struck in Sussex opens up some interesting possibilities, and that further analysis would undoubtedly reveal much more. In all discussions on this subject, however, one cannot forget that we are dealing with a subject where we are almost certainly not in possession of the full evidence, and a single hoard of coins from the Sussex mints could make nonsense of any analysis. It is also a fact that the sequence of coin types is neither as certain as one would like, nor are the dates for each type fixed beyond question. However, for the purposes of this paper, the author has chosen to follow the dates given by North (1963) in the hope that they will not prove too misleading.

References

Archibald, Marion M, 1974   'English medieval coins as dating evidence', *Coins and the archaeologist*, Brit Archaeol Rep, **4**, 234 ff

Biddle, M, 1976   'Organisation and society: iii The mint', *Winchester Studies I*, 396–422, Oxford

Dolley, R H M and Metcalf, D M, 1961   'The reform of the English coinage under Eadgar', in *Anglo-Saxon coins*, Chpt VIII

English historical documents, Vol I (ed D Whitelock), Vol III (ed H Rothwell)

King, H H, 1957   'The coins of the Sussex mints', Parts I–III, *Brit Numis J*, **28**, 61 ff

Lyon, C S S, 1970   'Analysis of the material', in Mossop, 1970, 11–19

Lyon, C S S, 1976   'Some problems in interpreting Anglo-Saxon coinage', in *Anglo-Saxon England 5* (ed P Clemoes), 173 ff, Cambridge

Mossop, H R, 1970   *The Lincoln mint c 890–1279*, Newcastle-on-Tyne

North, J J, 1963   *English hammered coinage*, **I**

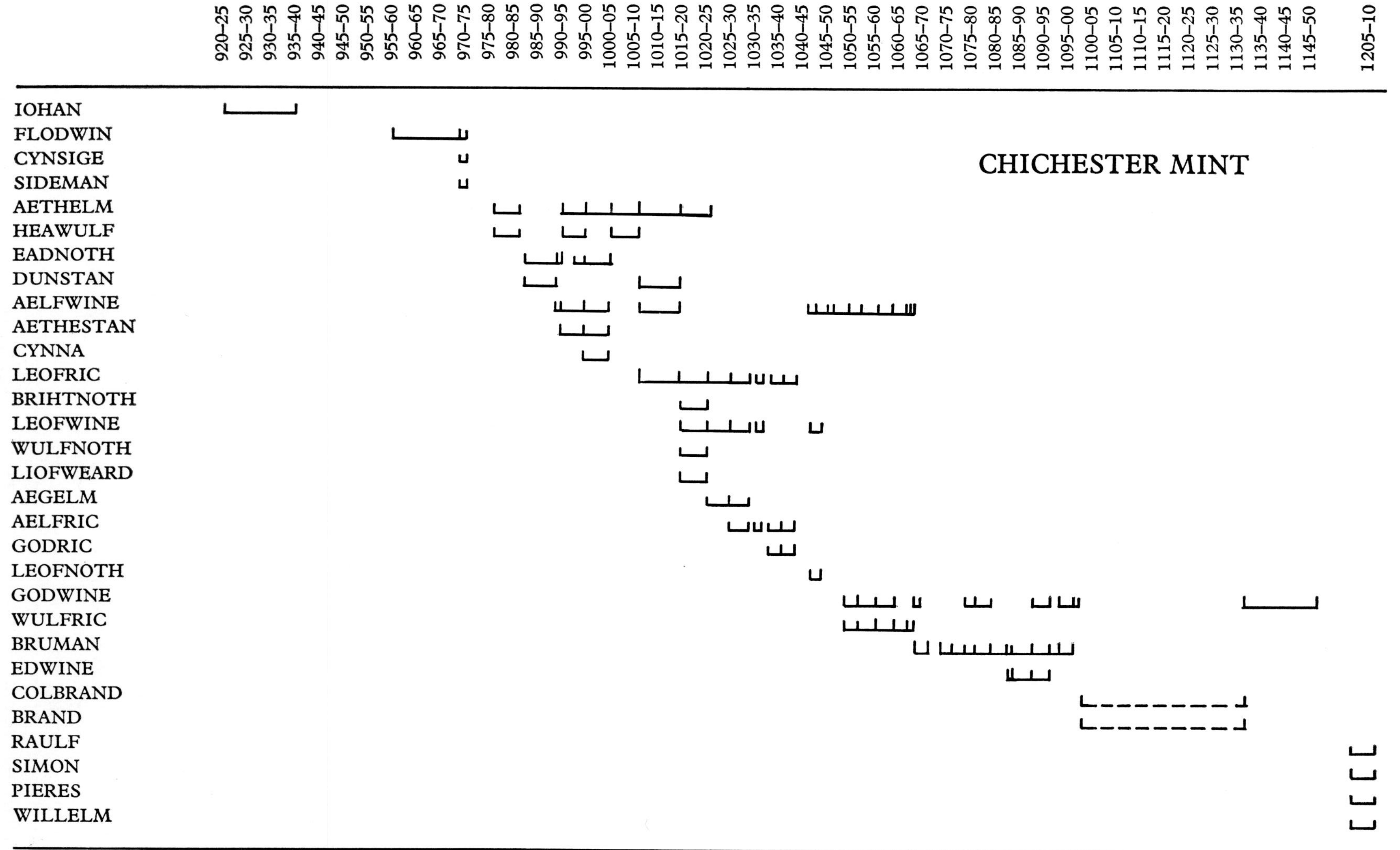

CHICHESTER MINT
920-25
925-30
930-35
935-40
940-45
945-50
950-55
955-60
960-65
965-70
970-75
975-80
980-85
985-90
990-95
995-00
1000-05
1005-10
1010-15
1015-20
1020-25
1025-30
1030-35
1035-40
1040-45
1045-50
1050-55
1055-60
1060-65
1065-70
1070-75
1075-80
1080-85
1085-90
1090-95
1095-00
1100-05
1105-10
1110-15
1115-20
1120-25
1125-30
1130-35
1135-40
1140-45
1145-50
1205-10
IOHAN
FLODWIN
CYNSIGE
SIDEMAN
AETHELM
HEAWULF
EADNOTH
DUNSTAN
AELFWINE
AETHESTAN
CYNNA
LEOFRIC
BRIHTNOTH
LEOFWINE
WULFNOTH
LIOFWEARD
AEGELM
AELFRIC
GODRIC
LEOFNOTH
GODWINE
WULFRIC
BRUMAN
EDWINE
COLBRAND
BRAND
RAULF
SIMON
PIERES
WILLELM

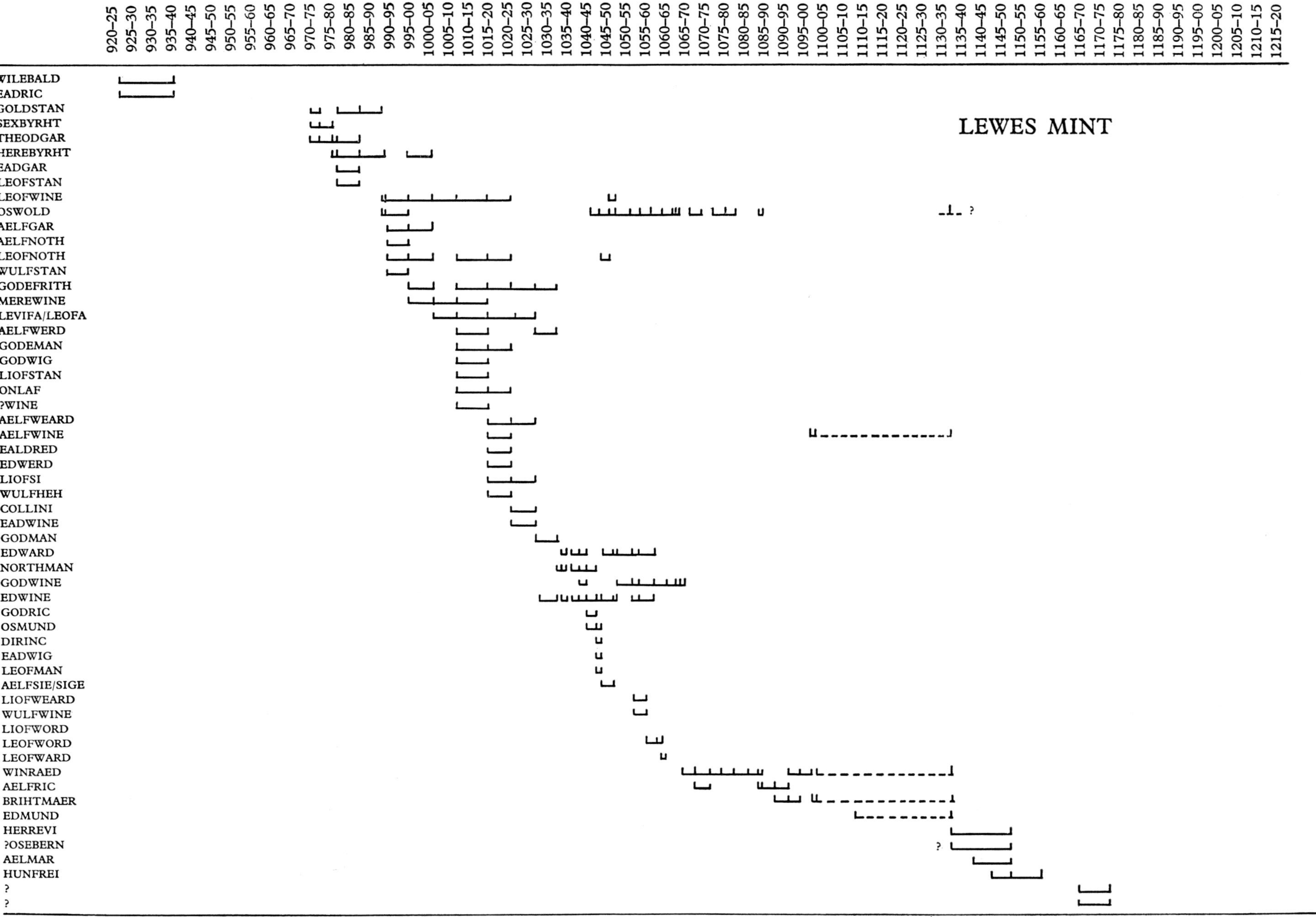

LEWES MINT
920-25 925-30 930-35 935-40 940-45 945-50 950-55 955-60 960-65 965-70 970-75 975-80 980-85 985-90 990-95 995-00 1000-05 1005-10 1010-15 1015-20 1020-25 1025-30 1030-35 1035-40 1040-45 1045-50 1050-55 1055-60 1060-65 1065-70 1070-75 1075-80 1080-85 1085-90 1090-95 1095-00 1100-05 1105-10 1110-15 1115-20 1120-25 1125-30 1130-35 1135-40 1140-45 1145-50 1150-55 1155-60 1160-65 1165-70 1170-75 1175-80 1180-85 1185-90 1190-95 1195-00 1200-05 1205-10 1210-15 1215-20
WILEBALD
EADRIC
GOLDSTAN
SEXBYRHT
THEODGAR
HEREBYRHT
EADGAR
LEOFSTAN
LEOFWINE
OSWOLD
AELFGAR
AELFNOTH
LEOFNOTH
WULFSTAN
GODEFRITH
MEREWINE
LEVIFA/LEOFA
AELFWERD
GODEMAN
GODWIG
LIOFSTAN
ONLAF
?WINE
AELFWEARD
AELFWINE
EALDRED
EDWERD
LIOFSI
WULFHEH
COLLINI
EADWINE
GODMAN
EDWARD
NORTHMAN
GODWINE
EDWINE
GODRIC
OSMUND
DIRINC
EADWIG
LEOFMAN
AELFSIE/SIGE
LIOFWEARD
WULFWINE
LIOFWORD
LEOFWORD
LEOFWARD
WINRAED
AELFRIC
BRIHTMAER
EDMUND
HERREVI
?OSEBERN
AELMAR
HUNFREI
?
?

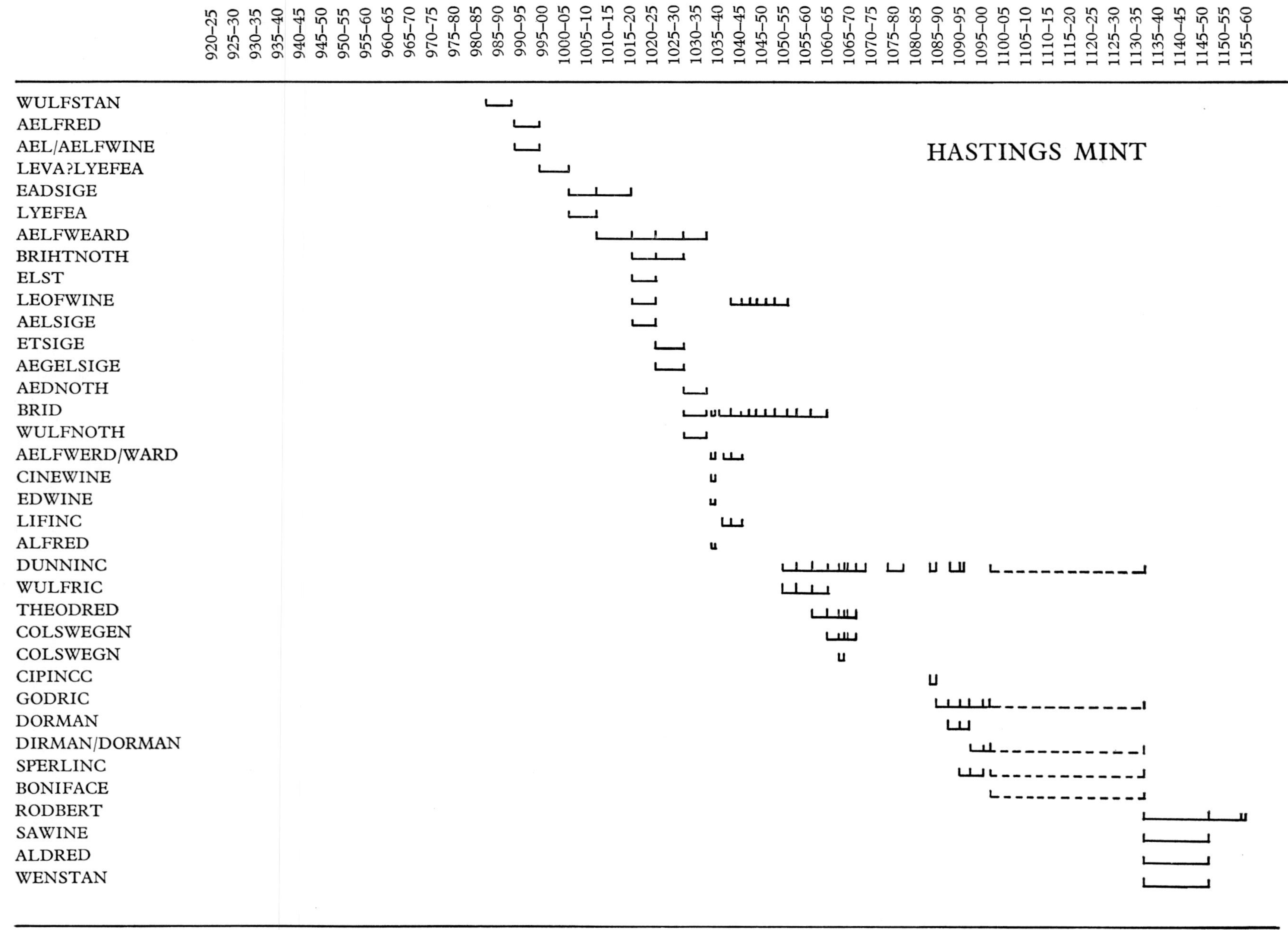

HASTINGS MINT
920-25
925-30
930-35
935-40
940-45
945-50
950-55
955-60
960-65
965-70
970-75
975-80
980-85
985-90
990-95
995-00
1000-05
1005-10
1010-15
1015-20
1020-25
1025-30
1030-35
1035-40
1040-45
1045-50
1050-55
1055-60
1060-65
1065-70
1070-75
1075-80
1080-85
1085-90
1090-95
1095-00
1100-05
1105-10
1110-15
1115-20
1120-25
1125-30
1130-35
1135-40
1140-45
1145-50
1150-55
1155-60
WULFSTAN
AELFRED
AEL/AELFWINE
LEVA?LYEFEA
EADSIGE
LYEFEA
AELFWEARD
BRIHTNOTH
ELST
LEOFWINE
AELSIGE
ETSIGE
AEGELSIGE
AEDNOTH
BRID
WULFNOTH
AELFWERD/WARD
CINEWINE
EDWINE
LIFINC
ALFRED
DUNNINC
WULFRIC
THEODRED
COLSWEGEN
COLSWEGN
CIPINCC
GODRIC
DORMAN
DIRMAN/DORMAN
SPERLINC
BONIFACE
RODBERT
SAWINE
ALDRED
WENSTAN

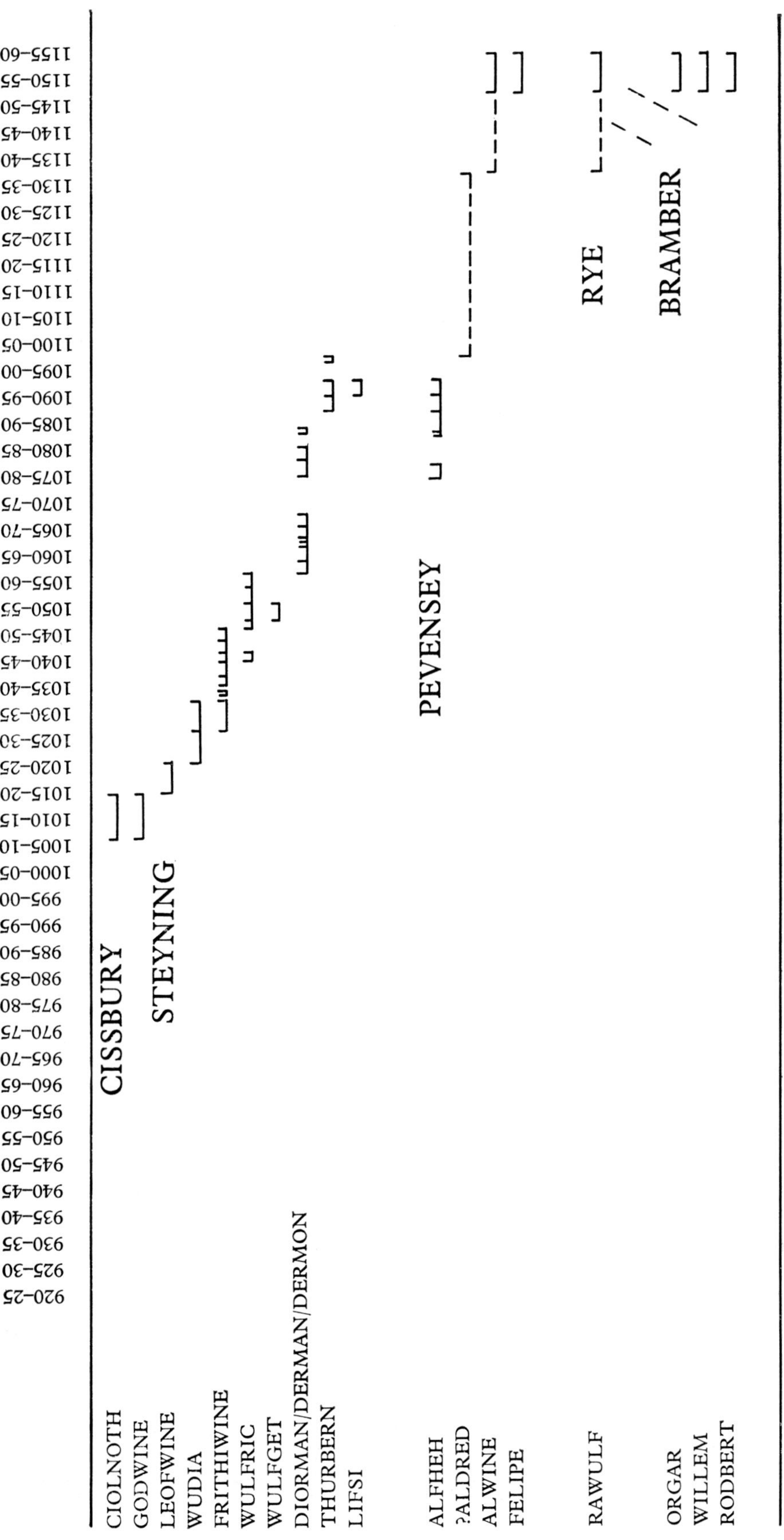

CISSBURY
STEYNING
PEVENSEY
RYE
BRAMBER
CIOLNOTH
GODWINE
LEOFWINE
WUDIA
FRITHIWINE
WULFRIC
WULFGET
DIORMAN/DERMAN/DERMON
THURBERN
LIFSI
ALFHEH
?ALDRED
ALWINE
FELIPE
RAWULF
ORGAR
WILLEM
RODBERT
920-25
925-30
930-35
935-40
940-45
945-50
950-55
955-60
960-65
965-70
970-75
975-80
980-85
985-90
990-95
995-00
1000-05
1005-10
1010-15
1015-20
1020-25
1025-30
1030-35
1035-40
1040-45
1045-50
1050-55
1055-60
1060-65
1065-70
1070-75
1075-80
1080-85
1085-90
1090-95
1095-00
1100-05
1105-10
1110-15
1115-20
1120-25
1125-30
1130-35
1135-40
1140-45
1145-50
1150-55
1155-60

Church archaeology in Sussex

Fred Aldsworth

Much has already been written about Sussex churches and further research may, at the outset, appear superfluous, but most previous writers have been concerned with church architecture and not with the historical information that a church and its churchyard may contain. The two, as I hope to demonstrate, are not necessarily the same. Not all writers, however, have given the same scant recognition of the historical importance of churches like the one dedicated to St Ledger (St Leodegar), at Hunston, near Chichester, which Ian Nairn and Nicholas Pevsner (1965, 249) describe thus:

'There are very few Sussex churches for which absolutely nothing can be said. Alas this is one of them. By A W Blomfield 1885'.

It is true that the church was entirely rebuilt in the late 19th century and no vestige remains of the earlier church on the site, but a description of the old church survives from 1776 (Pugh, 1953, 157–8) and an illustration of it was published in the *Gentlemen's Magazine* of 1792 (Urban, 1792, 805). These show that there was once a Norman church on the site, and it may have been an earlier form of this church that served the Domesday village of HVNESTAN (Morris, 1976, 11,43). The buried remains of the footings of this church may still survive. But where and what was the nature of the community that this church served? Why are the church and the adjoining 17th century manor-house surrounded by a moat, and why is the present village half-a-mile from the church? Are we dealing with a deserted village which has become repopulated a little away from the church in the recent past, or has the village migrated? These are some of the questions that the medieval archaeologist may ask of this church, and the answers are certainly not available within the published works on the church. It is clear that, as in all fields of archaeological study, we are unlikely to find the right answers in our research until we ask the right questions of our source material.

With the exception of the excavations on church sites at Angmering (Bedwin, 1975), Balsdean (Norris *et al*, 1953), Bargham (Barr-Hamilton, 1961), and Lullington (Barr-Hamilton, 1970), extensive archaeological investigations have not been undertaken on Sussex churches; and since previous writers have not been asking the sort of questions that I have presented, this paper, unlike the majority of others in this publication, will primarily be asking questions of the source material and suggesting avenues of research which, it is hoped, may help to answer some of them.

Church archaeology, as a subject in its own right, is a comparatively new field of study, for although the sites of a few churches have been the subject of archaeological excavation in the past, archaeologists have only recently begun to realize that both the buried and standing structure of a church and its graveyard, more than any other structure, are likely to advance the understanding of medieval settlement histories both in the rural and urban community. At the classic deserted medieval village site at Wharram Percy, in the Yorkshire Wolds, a long-term research project has related the surviving church and the buried population in the churchyard to the village and to the landscape around (Hurst, 1976). A similar project is now being undertaken at Deerhurst, in Gloucestershire (Rahtz, 1976). This work is demonstrating that the church, which often survives when all else has passed away, may provide, in its multiple architectural and archaeological periods, a microcosm of the history of the settlement it served.

To some extent, therefore, it is often difficult to separate church archaeology from medieval settlement studies; but because churches are generally excluded from the Ancient Monuments Acts and from planning legislation they often have to be considered as individual features separate from the community they served.

The rural church

The study of village origins, shape, form, and distribution is clearly fundamental to an understanding of the rural settlement patterns of the medieval period. William Hoskins (1955, 45) pointed out that the village can be found everywhere in England, but he noted that in certain areas, as for example in the Midlands, it is the predominant form of settlement. In medieval Sussex there was a mixed pattern of settlements—towns, villages, hamlets, and isolated farmsteads—although the towns were comparatively late foundations (Aldsworth and Freke, 1976). It was during the 600 years predating the Norman Conquest that Sussex became a county of villages and hamlets with their common fields. But precisely when did this change from the pre-existing settlement pattern occur and what were the social and/or economic factors that brought about the change?

Since the oldest surviving structure in a rural settlement is usually the church, it seems logical to commence investigations here although other factors, such as the date of the associated fields and roads, will undoubtedly also have to be considered. An isolated church may indicate the centre of a dispersed settlement or represent the sole surviving evidence of a deserted village, and within a nucleated settlement the position of the church may indicate the earliest area to be occupied. It is not acceptable to assume that in all cases any such relationship existed for the entire lifespan of a church. It may be that a church which originally served a dispersed community may have subsequently attracted a nucleated settlement.

Perhaps the best way to demonstrate the importance of the archaeology of a rural church is to examine some recent research in West Sussex. The Chichester Excavations Committee has been studying the evolution of one piece of Sussex landscape from the prehistoric period until the present day, and in attempting to understand the evolution of the medieval settlement pattern the churches clearly have an important role to play. The present parish of West Dean comprises the medieval parishes of West Dean and Binderton which were amalgamated during the 19th century. Binderton is mentioned in Domesday Book and it had a church in 1086 (Morris, 1976, 11, 4). This settlement appears to have survived at least until about 1680 when the church was taken down and replaced by a chapel nearby (Peckham, 1930). The village disappeared at the same time and its site is now occupied by a large house and landscaped grounds. There is now virtually no trace of the village although the foundations of the church have recently been located by excavation. In any

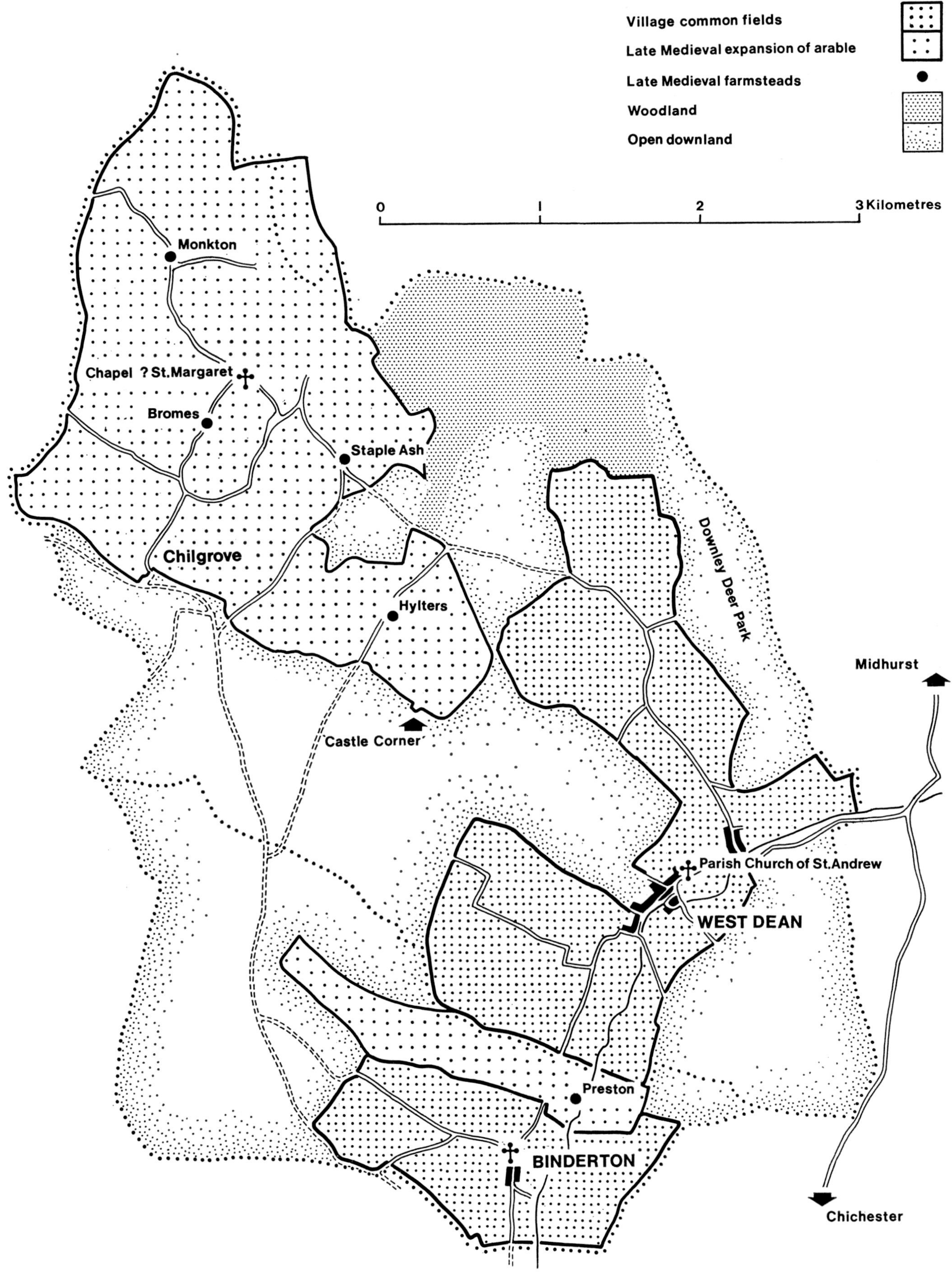

Fig 36   A reconstruction of the medieval landscape in the parishes of West Dean and Binderton based upon documentary research, archaeological excavations, and field survey. The parish boundaries are shown by the dotted lines

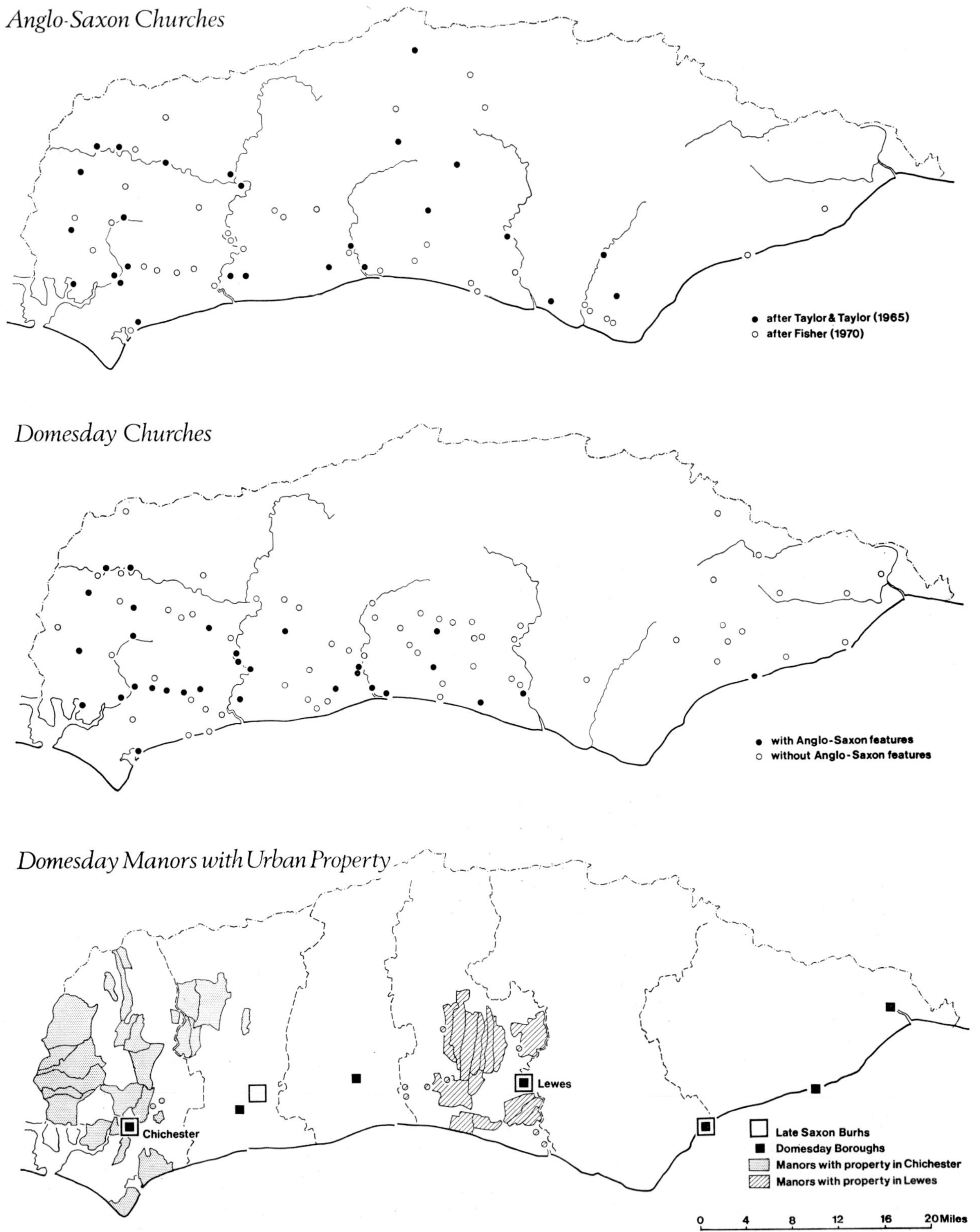

Fig 37   The combined East and West Sussex county boundaries are shown according to their alignment after re-organization in 1974. On the lower map the Rapes are shown by dotted lines and the Domesday manor boundaries are shown on the lines of the early nineteenth-century parish boundaries except where the place can be identified by name only

attempt to understand the early history of Binderton and the distribution of Saxon settlement in the area, it seems clear that the buried remains of this church may be the sole surviving evidence. West Dean is not specifically referred to as such in Domesday Book but there can be little doubt, bearing in mind the surviving north doorway in the nave of the church, which is built in pre-Conquest style, that the settlement is Saxon in origin. The form of the late medieval village and its common fields can be traced on an estate map of 1623, which is now in the West Dean Manuscripts in the County Record Office, and these have been reconstructed in Fig 36. The same estate map and early references indicate that a large area in the northern part of the parish was also arable by the early 13th century. This is today an area of dispersed farmsteads, but the site of a probable deserted medieval village or hamlet has been identified at Monkton by Eric and Hilda Holden. This area, usually referred to as the tithing and chapelry of Chilgrove, was served by a chapel, possibly dedicated to St Margaret, from about 1210 until between 1618 and 1636 when it was taken down. The chapel site was lost until recently when excavations, following the discovery of a possible site, demonstrated that it lay in what is now a copse to the south of Monkton Farm. The chapel appears to date at least from the middle of the 12th century and may be pre-Conquest in origin. It is the chapel that is most likely to provide evidence for the earliest post-Roman settlement in this area—which may be an extension to the arable land of West Dean parish, presumably made from woodland and open downland during a period of agricultural expansion.

Thus the medieval church is likely to provide some of the earliest evidence for rural settlement patterns and may also provide information concerning subsequent rural history.

Urban churches

The origins of these structures will be dealt with later, but first I want to concern myself with their role within the urban community, and I shall start by examining the results of recent work at Winchester, in Hampshire.

Documentary and archaeological evidence indicates that Winchester contained substantial blocks of property in 1148 which were held by 'great retainers'. These appear to represent the remains of an earlier arrangement in which these 'urban manors', each of which often contained a small private church or its rural counterpart, were a common feature (Biddle, 1976a, 340–5). It was not until later that some of these churches became urban parish churches. This arrangement of urban manors may have evolved as a direct result of Alfred's successful attempt to encourage urban living in the late 9th century. Two of the manors so far identified at Winchester were served by their own church and in the case of another church, that of St Mary in Tanner Street, archaeological evidence has shown that during the early part of its long sequence of occupation it had direct access only from the adjoining property and not on to an adjoining street (Biddle, 1975, 312–14).

It seems likely that the same pattern of urban manors may also have existed in the early 10th century Burghal Hidage towns of Chichester and Lewes which, like Winchester, also appear to have been replanned by Alfred in about AD 890 (Biddle and Hill, 1971). No evidence of this has come to light in excavations, but the Domesday Book appears to indicate that at least one possible example survived in Chichester in 1086. It refers to eleven sites or houses held by the rural manor of Bosham which were between the Towergate and the Crossgate in West Street; these were

probably adjoining tenements which represented one urban manor. Other examples are implied by groups of houses in both Chichester and Lewes. That the ownership of property in these two towns was once directly related to the areas of land which they once served can be demonstrated by examining the distribution of Domesday manors with urban property in 1086 (Fig 37). Of the seven Domesday boroughs, only Chichester and Lewes contained houses belonging to the surrounding manors—a pattern which probably relates back to their foundation as towns as well as defensible burhs by Alfred.

The establishment of urban manors with private churches is an aspect of urban foundation that should be examined if ever the opportunity arises for an extensive excavation to be undertaken on or near the site of a medieval church in either of these two towns.

Suburban churches are also important as they may provide information concerning the origins and development of the settlements which lay immediately outside the town walls.

The church and its origins

In addition to their role in providing evidence for rural and urban history, churches may also be capable of answering other questions. One aspect that the study of a church and its site may help to clarify is the question of continuity of occupation from the Roman to the sub-Roman and Saxon period. Perhaps the easiest to demonstrate is structural continuity for, although none are yet known in Sussex, examples of either ruined or near-complete Roman buildings being reused for the foundations of a Christian church do occur in Kent at St Martin's, Canterbury (Jenkins, 1965), Stone-by-Faversham (Fletcher and Meates, 1969), and Lullingstone (Taylor and Taylor, 1965).

Since Roman ruins are still to be found, it is not difficult to see how similar examples could have been used in the Saxon period as a source of building foundations. Many Sussex churches contain reused Roman material and some are known to lie close to the sites of Roman buildings, but no evidence has been found to demonstrate that a church occupies the same site as a Roman structure.

It is the continuity of site use or function that may be more difficult to account for. Martin Biddle (1976b) has drawn attention to the existence of martyr-graves located in a cemetery beside a road leading out of a major late Roman town. In the course of time they became sites for great churches, as at St Albans, with continental parallels at Xanten, Cologne, Trier, Mainz, and Bonn. He also notes that the only Roman buildings known in the western suburbs of the City of London have been found under churches, and suggests that the Roman buildings may have been incorporated into early churches on the same site. There appears also to be evidence of settlement continuity in certain areas. Saxon churches are often found within fortified Roman centres, but it is difficult to see why this should be so other than for defensive purposes. Of the 14 Saxon Shore forts twelve once contained churches and some of these, including the Sussex example at Pevensey, are of an early date. Elsewhere early churches appear to have been established on the sites of Roman settlements, as for example at Selsey, where Wilfrid established his church in the 7th century. Other examples which may warrant special attention are Wiggonholt and Hardham. Clearly there is a need here to examine the relationship between the earliest church on the site and the previous settlement for evidence of continuity of use. However, the answers will doubtless be difficult to find.

In addition to these problems of continuity, there is the additional problem of determining whether all churches were necessarily used as such in their original form. At Tanner Street, in Winchester, a long sequence of superimposed deposits included a Romano-Celtic temple, an Anglo-Saxon cemetery dating to about AD 700, an 8th to 9th century timber phase, and a rectangular stone building dating to about AD 900. The stone building was later converted into a structure which can certainly be identified as a church by the addition of a semicircular chancel. Its original function is not clear, but it may have been the workshop of a goldsmith or moneyer (Biddle, 1975, 303–10).

The structure of pre-Conquest churches

Much of what has already been stated in this paper has been concerned with the origins and earliest evidence for a church and the community it served, and since the study of standing post-Conquest churches can often be supported by substantial documentary evidence the author intends to comment here only upon the pre-Conquest churches.

A study of Anglo-Saxon architecture undertaken by H M Taylor and J Taylor (1965) has isolated several features which may indicate that a church is pre-Conquest in date. H M Taylor has revised some of his previous work, and in his paper (1976) he outlines his most recent thoughts on the subject. It is difficult to know quite how to add to what he has already said other than to emphasize the need for local research to isolate regional variations, to search for the timber phases which so far have proved difficult to find, and to examine his works on a local basis.

The four primary sources of evidence for architectural history are contemporary written records, the standing structure, the buried or hidden archaeological evidence, and the additional artistic enrichments such as sculpture and wall paintings. These are usually regarded as falling into four different fields of study, but it is often only as a result of using combinations of these sources that answers can be found.

Laurence Butler and Dorothy Owen have summarized the type of written records that may be available for evidence of the church fabric and the building history of churches (Butler, 1976; Owen, 1976); but few of these, apart from those churches mentioned in Domesday Book, provide evidence of the early history of a parish church. One exception, however, are the *Acta of the Bishops of Chichester* (Mayr-Harting, 1964), a collection from various sources of charters of the bishops, etc, which include a number of early references. Of particular importance also are the various collections of drawings and paintings of Sussex churches, notably those by Grimm and Petrie, which show the situation before Victorian 'restoration' and, as such, often include details that are no longer visible externally or have been destroyed.

The standing structure of a church may contain historical information of a typological form which may provide a sequence of periods of construction or alteration. Perhaps the simplest form of structural sequence is revealed when a feature, such as a tower, is heightened or when one feature is partially destroyed to accommodate another feature. When a stone building is erected walls are normally bonded to ensure against cracks, but this was not always the case when additions were made. For this reason straight joints often occur and these can provide useful information concerning the sequence of construction of the various elements of the plan of a church, but, as recently demonstrated at Romsey, Hampshire, they can reveal much more. At Romsey the chancel, crossing, and transepts of the present abbey were built to roof level in the first quarter of the 12th century whilst an earlier, Saxon, church was still standing to its full height on the same site. The Saxon church was then demolished to make way for the remainder of the Abbey which was completed in three clearly defined stages, being finally completed some time after 1230. The fabric of the demolished Saxon church was reused in the footings of the nave of the abbey, and a series of straight joints can be detected in the standing structure. This sequence of events revealed by the excavations and in the study of the standing building is being supported by a detailed study of the stones used in its construction. This sequence demonstrates the importance of continuity in the functional use of the chancel, at least in the greater churches, an importance which is also demonstrated at Winchester where the archaeology is supported by documentary evidence (Biddle, 1976a, 306–13). The east end of the cathedral was probably consecrated in April 1093, and on the feast of St Swithun in the following July the saint's remains were brought from the Saxon minster into the new cathedral. The demolition of the old church was commenced on the following day and the cathedral was completed some time between 1110 and 1124. In this case the new cathedral was not quite on the same site as the Saxon church but slightly to one side and on a different alignment. If continuity of the use of the chancel was so important, it may be that straight joints of the type found at Romsey could assist in the recognition of the former existence of earlier churches on the sites of some of our lesser churches. It is possible that such a situation may have existed at Chichester, but the restoration following the collapse of the central spire in the 19th century has obscured most of the areas where joints may have once been visible.

The archaeological evidence may include the exposure of areas or buried features which have not previously been seen, the provision of dating evidence in the form of pottery, coins, or burials, and evidence indicating the extent of time which a particular phase may have been in use.

Artistic enrichments, such as the paintings at Clayton, Coombes, and Hardham, provide additional dating evidence especially when they relate to particular components in the church plan.

As has already been noted, the study of post-Conquest churches is well founded and churches can often be dated on a comparative basis by recognizing characteristic features. A number of architectural techniques have now been recognized as being of pre-Conquest date and, where they survive in a primary context, they can be used to identify churches of Saxon origin although this is still only assigning a period of some 300 or so years during which they were constructed. Taylor and Taylor recognize four features: long-and-short quoins, triangular-headed openings, pilaster strips, and throughstone double-headed openings with baluster support—as distinctive of Saxon date although some of these techniques survived in use into the first few years after the Norman Conquest. They list 26 churches in Sussex which retain features of this type, and Fisher (1970) adds a further 35 examples which contain indications that they may also be pre-Conquest in origin (Fig 37). Domesday Book lists about 100 churches in Sussex, although the existence of some of these, not shown on the map, can only be assumed. Some of the Domesday churches appear to contain Saxon remains but some appear not to have survived to the present day. On the other hand, some of the Saxon churches are not mentioned in Domesday

Book. The distribution maps do not show a complete picture for the distribution of Saxon churches or for the churches that existed in 1086; what they do show is that few Wealden churches were listed in 1086 and that few of the Domesday churches in the eastern half of the county contain Saxon remains. It is within these local areas that identification and research is still required, for it may be that there was a form of pre-Conquest church in the eastern part of the county which has yet to be recognized.

Future progress in the study of Sussex medieval settlement history is likely to require considerable support from the study of churches. The techniques must include research in the written records, the standing structures, and the buried remains. The choice of which structures to examine may well be dictated by the extent to which they are threatened with redundancy and alteration. It is important that a survey of churches is completed and that a policy is determined to ensure that the best use is made of the limited historical and structural resources available.

Acknowledgements

I would like to thank the Chichester Excavations Committee for allowing me to publish information concerning the development of the medieval landscape in the parish of West Dean, and the director of the Test Valley Archaeological Committee, Mr Kevin Stubbs, for drawing my attention to the results of his recent work at Romsey Abbey.

References

Addyman, P and Morris, R, 1976   *The archaeological study of churches*, CBA Res Rep **13**

Aldsworth, F G and Freke, D, 1976   *Historic towns in Sussex: an archaeological survey*, Institute of Archaeology, London

Barr-Hamilton, A, 1961   'The excavation of Bargham Church site', *Sussex Archaeol Collect*, **99**, 38–65

Barr-Hamilton, A, 1970   'Excavations at Lullington Church', *ibid*, **108**, 1–22

Bedwin, O, 1975   'The excavation of the Church of St Nicholas, Angmering, 1974', *ibid*, **113**, 16–34

Biddle, M, 1975   'Excavations at Winchester, 1971', *Antiq J*, **55**, 96–337

Biddle, M, 1976a   *Winchester in the early Middle Ages: Winchester studies 1* (ed M Biddle)

Biddle, M, 1976b   'The archaeology of the church: a widening horizon', in Addyman and Morris, 1976, 65–71

Biddle, M and Hill, D, 1971   'Late Saxon planned towns', *Antiq J*, **51**, 70–85

Butler, L A S, 1976   'Documentary evidence and the church fabric', in Addyman and Morris, 1976, 18–21

Fisher, E A, 1970   *Saxon churches of Sussex*

Fletcher, E and Meates, G W, 1969   'The ruined church of Stone-by-Faversham', *Antiq J*, **49**, 273–94

Hoskins, W G, 1955   *The making of the English landscape*

Hurst, J G, 1976   'Wharram Percy: St Martin's Church', in Addyman and Morris, 1976, 36–9

Jenkins, F, 1965   'St Martin's Church at Canterbury: a survey of the earliest structural features', *Medieval Archaeol*, **9**, 11–15

Mayr-Harting, H, 1964   *The Acta of the Bishops of Chichester 1075–1207*, Canterbury and York Society, **56**

Morris, J, 1976   *Domesday Book: Sussex*, Phillimore

Nairn, I and Pevsner, N, 1965   *The buildings of England: Sussex*

Norris, N E S, *et al*, 1953   'Excavations at Balsdean Chapel, Rottingdean' and 'Report on pottery from ditch under Balsdean Chapel', *Sussex Archaeol Collect*, **91**, 53–68

Owen, D, 1976   'Documentary sources for the building history of churches in the Middle Ages', in Addyman and Morris, 1976, 21–7

Peckham, W D, 1930   *Sussex Notes and Queries*, **3**, 85–97

Pugh, R P, 1953   *Victoria County History: Sussex* 4 (ed R P Pugh)

Rahtz, P A, 1976   'Research directions at Deerhurst', in Addyman and Morris, 1976, 60–4

Taylor, H M and Taylor, J, 1965   *Anglo-Saxon architecture*, Cambridge

Taylor, H M, 1976   'The foundations of architectural history', in Addyman and Morris, 1976

Urban, S, 1792   *Gentlemens Magazine*, **805** (ed S Urban)

Peter Brandon

The medieval period has, until recently, been very unfashionable in Sussex archaeological circles. Large-scale intensive field-work has hardly begun. Settlement excavation is still in its infancy. Most aspects of medieval economy and society remain almost archaeologically unexplored. This limited effort contrasts with the relatively intense inquiry into agrarian questions by economic historians and historical geographers.[1] This has been too little directed to the management of the land, its resources and colonization. No one who has carried out field walking in the spirit of Allcroft and Crawford, and observed the countless, and at present, mystifying marks on the surface of the ground in almost every part of Sussex, can doubt the mass of striking medieval detail which cries out to be fitted into a meaningful pattern. Those who attempt to trace this medieval development from its faint stirrings in the twilight of the Dark Ages to the economic setbacks of the mid 14th century have some persistent misunderstandings to expunge, and frequently come to the realization that many 'facts' are no more than assumptions. In short, the meaning of layer upon layer of anonymous enterprise waits to be recovered before a general picture of medieval endeavour in Sussex can be fully understood. The problems are not all soluble, and as some are resolved so new aspects are revealed and fresh ideas and evidence are needed to test the validity of the older assumptions. The worker in this field thus needs the inclination to face big issues freshly, and to be ready to challenge received opinions and widely held theses with carefully constructed arguments based on his own continuously searching studies.

The medieval period should be studied against the division of Sussex into the Weald on the one hand and the Downland and coastal plain on the other, a fact of nature to which man in Sussex has had to adapt himself throughout time. The special blend of landscape and architecture which marked these regions off from one another and their contrasting challenges and potentialities make their study a fascinating one, and it is far from being completely written. The association of backwardness with the Weald and progress with the coastal belt holds good in many respects, but these generalizations may need qualification in the light of further research.

In the space available it is impossible to cover more than a few selected issues requiring study and discussion. Those relating to the coastlands may be summarized as follows:

1 Of the group of coast towns scattered along the sea-face of the English Channel, how many have roots in the Saxon or even earlier periods?

2 What was the nature and strength of the continental cultural links established by these ports through their trade in corn, wool, and timber?

3 What was their social and political role in their prime, when still full of enterprising shipowners of large fortunes?

4 From the second half of the 14th century many of the Sussex seaports were deserted and decayed. How abject was this decline?

In answer to this question it is necessary to stray a little into the 16th century in search of statistical evidence. The Elizabethan muster rolls of able-bodied seamen, the periodic Tudor surveys of harbours, the lists of ships and returns of trade, all imply a shabby village-like quality borne by once thriving coast-towns which had seen their trade carried away from them by silting and erosion. By way of example, the borough of New Shoreham and the village of Old Shoreham comprised only 46 households between them in 1566. Worthing and Heene together (but excluding Broadwater) were supporting 62 households and even the two Lancings comprised 45 households.[2] This bespeaks a melancholy decline at New Shoreham and makes rather more credible the stated population of 36 persons in a petition of 1432,[3] when both physical and economic conditions were probably worse. The 1548 muster rolls of Bramber Rape,[4] and a schedule of ships in the Channel ports on one occasion in 1577, both tally with the 1566 evidence. Hastings was also in a similar plight to that of New Shoreham. The State Lottery of 1567, intended to raise funds for the improvement of harbours, elicited a response from Hastings that:

> 'Never a poor fisher town in England
> of ye great lot hath more need'
> (Kempe, 1835)

Much more historical research and certainly more archaeological enquiry into the slow death of Sussex ports is clearly needed. In striking contrast to the general picture of decline is the population of Brighthelmstone in 1566, then comprising 200 households; it would seem that the fisheries there had grown at other ports' expense.

Turning to the Weald, its isolation, real or imagined, is a recurrent theme in its historical record. It is commonly envisaged as an indigenous, almost self-sufficient, farming country with regressive tendencies, grossly under-exploited, a sort of appendage of the more developed coastal zone until the late 14th century. Is this a rather fanciful extrapolation of conditions in the remote past when the Weald still defied human penetration, or a true appreciation of the forest society through most, if not all, medieval time? Only more detailed archaeological and historical study will provide the answer.

A central, even dominant, theme of medieval Sussex, is the story of man's reclamation of farmland from forest, heath, and marsh. The history of this achievement has yet to be fully written. It is probably realistic to conceive the Weald's course of development as being from that of a frontier, using this term in the sense it acquired in the United States during the 19th century to mean a sparsely settled district of pioneer farmers, miners, and traders beyond the older settled and more maturely developed areas. Such frontier zones were lands of hope and opportunity, places with elbow-room, where 'only the strong shall thrive, that surely the weak shall perish and only the fit survive'. It would, of course, be an exaggeration to regard as equal the natural conditions influencing the shaping of the Wealden and the harsher moorlands of upland Britain, or that of the Middle West of the United States at a much later period. Nevertheless the Sussex Weald has many characteristics of a 'region of difficulty' in which life was often sufficiently hard to cause distress. As the landscape is more minutely observed and early settlement sites are excavated, we shall be in a better position to assess how hard was the struggle to live.

Little research has yet been devoted to the men who faced the wildness of the Weald and sought to make something out of it. The would-be pioneering lords and peasants faced new conditions in which they could not ply their traditional farming skills inherited from the Downland and Coastal Plain, or live as they had been accustomed. In learning new ways of living, they were making a permanent contribution to civilization. These new lands, new men, and new thoughts warrant further study; so also does the extent to which the woodmen moulded the wild to their own needs and in turn were moulded by the nature of the environment with which they were in contact.

Tentative recent work by the present author suggests that four 'folk flows' contributed to the peopling of this Wealden frontier. Each sequential 'folk flow' can be related to a certain type of rural settlement and to a distinctive economy, so that each contributed to the rich medley of Wealden life and to the human environment. The evidence for the four 'folk flows' is based on early Saxon place-names and a detailed examination of the land tenures and rents recorded in 13th century and later medieval documents (Brandon, 1972).

The first men inhabiting the unenclosed woods and wastes were *drofmen*, drovers engaged in tending cattle and swine, who unlike other peasants grew no corn and had no oxen for the plough. They would have divided their year between their 'winter house', their permanent abode in the parent village, and their 'summer house' in the outlying woodland pasture. They followed the close network of north–south droveways which are still reflected with remarkable clarity by the surviving road system, and which were probably tracks already beaten in Roman times and earlier. Also relict features from this phase are the surviving patches of woodland-common, such as the Mens and Ebernoe commons in west Sussex. These *drofmen* introduced a stage of temporarily occupied huts and shelters associated with seasonal pastoral farming. Place-names embodying the OE element *(ge)sell*, meaning a group of shelters for animals, herdsmen or both; *scydd*, meaning shed, and usually now rendered by 'shot'; *wick* (OE *wic*), probably meaning 'dependent farm'; and *fold* (OE *falod*), denoting land staked off as a pasture-ground for cattle, record this early stage of the Weald's evolution (Brandon, 1978).

The second 'folk flow' comprised the small men owing labour services to the lord, including reaping on the distant demesne. It is through the efforts of these early farmers that the parish churches and water-driven mills were erected. When documentary evidence becomes available towards the end of the 13th century, we find them inhabiting not single isolated farmsteads but loosely grouped clusters of small family farms on shared named yardlands of customary land, and with a territorial organization and economy which Professor Glanville Jones has likened to the Celtic *clachan*. Some of the churches also subsequently founded subordinate chapels in the same period, eg Rotherfield had a dependent settlement at Frant which had its own chapel before 1100. The High Wealden churches are mostly on ridge-top sites, and were probably almost isolated from the pioneer farms being established at lower elevations along the sides of valleys where spring water, deeper soils, and narrow strips of water meadow were at hand. The churches would have stood almost alone as do the churches of Burstow, Worth, and Itchingfield to this day. We have, therefore, the somewhat unusual circumstance that many of the relatively outlying, peripheral settlements in Wealden parishes are older than the central nucleated village, the reverse of the 'normal' development in England generally. We must never assume that even a medieval village had been a village from the first.

These customary tenants were the forerunners of a new wave of pioneers who entered the High Weald region from about 1240 and held small parcels of 'assart' land for a money rent. The frontier of remaining Wealden waste was fast driven back, bringing into existence the familiar 'waste-edge' pattern of straggly rural settlement. These peasants began to supplement their hard-won living by various kinds of by-employment and initiated the long-standing custom of craftsmanship in the Weald.

The final medieval 'folk flow', initiated perhaps slightly later than the preceding one and overlapping with it, comprised tradesmen moving in to set up business and artisans building cottages when the supply of 'frontier' land had given out. These people added cottages to once-isolated churches, so creating the characteristic Wealden hill-top villages and built the Wealden towns.

It seems certain that this industrial development of the Weald in the 13th and 14th centuries has been much underrated. Professor Everitt has suggested (1969) that the numerous artisans in the 16th century Weald was a recent phenomenon. This Wealden characteristic is in fact traceable much further back in time. As early as the 13th century the Wealden peasants were deeply involved in craft activities. The scattered forest hamlets were alive with business, full of artisans supplementing their hard-won living from the land with various forms of by-employment. They grappled with local raw materials such as timber, clay, iron, water, wool, hides and sand (used in glass-making). Evidence of woodcrafts such as coopering, turnery, and tanning, is well preserved by the names of persons listed in medieval documents by surnames derived from their trade, such as William *Le Cupere*; surnames such as Fuller (a cloth finisher by trade) or Smith (used of an ironworker as well as a blacksmith) are also common. Tebbutt's recent work (1975) is beginning to shed light on this aspect of the Wealden economy.

This flow marks the climax of the colonization movement into the Weald, and it is terminated by the economic setbacks engendered by plague and famine from the beginning of the 14th century.

It is not suggested that every part of the Sussex Weald underwent an occupation of all four folk: eg the town of Battle was founded by the monks of Battle Abbey in the early 12th century and there was no marked 'assart' phase in that district. Nevertheless, its validity for the Sussex High Weald generally seems evident on the basis of the author's research. The Low Weald was invariably colonized before the poorer lands in the High Weald were taken up, and there is little sign of the third (assart) flow, but plenty of evidence for the fourth.

The assignment of a chronology to these several phases of evolution is at present a source of unresolved difficulty to which archaeologists may one day provide the key. The main question at issue concerns the appearance of the countryside the Saxons inherited and adapted. It is implicit in Professor Glanville Jones's hypothesis of Celtic territorial survivals in the Saxon countryside in which the multiple estate and its hamlet structure of settlement evolved around the focus of downland hill-forts, that the first two 'folk flows' are of pre-Saxon date (Jones, 1961; Sawyer, 1976). The other, and conventional view, sees the whole process of Wealden colonization as initiated by Saxons, probably in the 8th and 9th centuries, by which time it is considered that the original small communities had grown sufficiently to require further land for colonization in the backwoods. It is worth observing that the place-name evidence briefly considered above seems to lend rather more support to the 'conventional' view rather than the Jones hypothesis. That some, at least, of the hamlet-type pattern of settlement in the Weald was the response to the pressure of medieval expansion, rather than the survival of Romano-British dispersed patterns, is a matter discussed by the present author elsewhere (1978). Professor Sawyer's recent discussion on the fallibility of Domesday data on Wealden settlement (Sawyer, 1976) was anticipated by Reginald Lennard nearly twenty years ago (1959) in his *Rural England, 1066–1125*, and as a result Wealden scholars have been familiar with the problems Sawyer has raised. The main constructive argument of Sawyer's thesis is that the rural resources of England were almost as fully exploited in the 7th century as they were in the 11th. This may be true of large areas of the more developed parts of England but it is clearly invalid for the Weald, where the clearance of woodland in the 12th and 13th centuries, quite apart from Saxon clearings, was very extensive.

The road to prosperity in the Weald was an arduous one with many set-backs. A recurrent theme in the history of the Wealden landscape has been the temporary cultivation of land, which was subsequently taken over again by the forces of nature in the form of scrub or forest until its reclamation was once more attempted when the tide of settlement turned again. Place-names such as Hazlehurst in Ticehurst (documented from AD 1040), meaning 'earsh (arable) land overgrown with hazels', or the lost name of *Birchen ersh* in Cowfold, meaning 'earsh land grown over with birch trees', appear to be hinting at this transience. We may be able to link these *erse* names with *sænget*, a rare English element that went out of use soon after the English invasions, but which seems to occur in Singleton, mentioned in an 8th century charter. Deep in the heart of the Weald we encounter the element at two other places bordering Ashdown Forest, Saint Hill and St Ives in East Grinstead and Hartfield respectively. This element seems to confirm that the practice of burning the forest for cultivation was an established custom amongst the first invaders of the wilderness. At a later date war and epidemic may have periodically depleted the still sparse Wealden settlement to the point where farmland was sporadically abandoned, even within ring-fenced fields, throughout the medieval period to *c* 1480.

Although it is well known that the character of the Wealden landscape is due to the piecemeal enclosure of woodland into fields, the morphology and function of its field boundaries have still to be investigated in detail. Ancient hedges are amongst the oldest man-made features of the Wealden landscape and provide valuable evidence of the clearing and management techniques of early farmers, and also of later stages in the evolution of the countryside. They have, therefore, a direct bearing on the historical value of landscape and thus upon its conservation. The most striking way in which man has shaped south-east England is by shaws, the wooded strips serving a hedgerow function which still exists around many fields. These have captured the imagination of countless artists who have rightly conceived them as the synthesis of Wealden landscape, but surprisingly historical geographers and archaeologists have given them relatively little attention, though they are symbols of the former intense regionalism of Wealden life.

Speculation on the origin of shaws is traceable to

William Marshall (1798) who considered them as residual features from the period of the original woodland clearance by pioneer farmers. This explanation has long gone unquestioned by subsequent writers, including the present author. Fieldwork now being undertaken in various parts of the county makes it abundantly clear that Marshall's hypothesis is in need of drastic qualification. Shaws would appear to have come into being as a result of a variety of agencies operating over a long period of time. Some shaws are doubtless relics associated with the original intake of farmland from the waste, but these appear to have been largely confined to steep, unploughable, ground. In the parishes of Balcombe and Cuckfield, surveyed in detail by the present writer, shaws are invariably located on the sides of lynchets, or extend on one or both sides of a clearly defined earthen bank and ditch. Fences were evidently cut far closer formerly and kept within relatively narrow limits. Cartographic testimony also confirms that many once-hedged fields later came to be bounded by strips of woodland. Many shaws, therefore, appear to represent the encroachment of trees and woody shrubs on to previously cultivated land.

The development of most shaws probably occurred in periods when the valuation placed on timber in its own right, or as an amenity, exceeded that of farmland, eg during the peak of the charcoal iron industry in the late 16th century and again during the heyday of the late Victorian 'pleasure-farm' when park-like shaws were appreciated for ornament and for game preservation. Perhaps, however, the prime cause of the thickening of hedgerows into shaws is simply due to neglect during periods of agricultural depression. If we come to understand them as hedgerows that have run wild, that is as extremes of dereliction, we can more readily understand that farmers might put a match to them when economic conditions improve. Clearly the historical appreciation of shaws is overdue, for when we know more about how the Wealden scene has developed we shall be in a better position to accept practical advice on the means of changing or preserving it.

Notes

[1] There is no intention, of course, of underrating some excellent archaeological work already undertaken. Eric Holden's on Hangleton, G R Burleigh's on medieval deserted villages in general, Alec Barr-Hamilton's at Streatham, and David Martin's on moated sites and vernacular architecture, spring readily to mind.
[2] Public Record Office, London (hereafter PRO), SP12/39, f27
[3] PRO, E101/57.
[4] PRO, SP10/3, f117.

References

Brandon, P F, 1972   'Medieval clearances in the East Sussex Weald', *Trans Inst Brit Geogr*, **48**, 135–53
Brandon, P F, 1978   'The Saxon Andredesweald', in *The South Saxons* (ed P F Brandon), Chichester
Everitt, A, 1969   *Change in the provinces: the 17th century*, Department of English Local History, Univ Leicester, Occasional Papers, 2 ser, no 1, 22
Jones, G R J, 1961   'Settlement patterns in Anglo-Saxon England', *Antiquity*, **35**, 221–32
Kempe, A J (ed), 1835   *The Loseley Manuscripts*, 432
Lennard, R, 1959   *Rural England, 1066–1125*
Marshall, W, 1798   *The economy of the southern counties*, **1**, 48–50
Sawyer, P H (ed), 1976   *Medieval settlement*, 1–6
Tebbutt, C F, 1975   'An abandoned medieval industrial site at Parrock, Hartfield', *Sussex Archaeol Collect*, **113**, 146–50

Medieval urban archaeology in Sussex

David Freke

Current approaches to the study of urban places are discussed by Wheatley (1972), and of the five avenues he isolates, two in particular have proved attractive to archaeologists. The first is what Wheatley calls the 'trait-complex' approach (1972, 608), which attempts to define urban places by attributing particularly 'urban' characteristics to them. Some of these characteristics are archaeologically detectable, such as defences, craft specialization, size, trade and so on, and these attributes have been used as indicators of urban status and development (Childe, 1950, 3–17; Heighway, 1972; Schledermann, 1970; Trigger, 1972). Barley (1976, 83) has suggested listing 'urban' characteristics as an archaeological research project. A more dynamic version of this is the call for the search for the 'underlying logic' of urbanism (Haselgrove, 1976, 110). The modern town and ethnographic survivals would provide most of the available evidence for such a programme with archaeology relegated to the role of background scene painter.

The shortcomings of the first approach are its static view of an essentially dynamic situation and its inability to explain the phenomena it describes. The second, in attempting to set up a processual model against which to test the results of urban research, assumes that urbanism is a closed system governed by quasi-physical laws. This assumption is as unlikely to apply to urbanism as it is to any other facet of human behaviour. It is certainly archaeologically untestable (Leach, 1976, 164). The other major archaeological approach to towns has been connected with what Wheatley calls 'cities as centres of dominance' (1972, 613–19), first formulated by Christaller in 1933 and known as Central Place Theory (Christaller, 1966). The problems of applying Central Place Theory to the archaeological study of medieval towns in England have been outlined by Carter (1977), who concludes that 'the greatest care is needed in these sorts of studies to ensure that notions which are readily acceptable for the present are not uncritically used in very different technological and economic circumstances'. Carter especially stresses the difficulty caused by the unreliability of quantifiable data for comparative purposes.

The broadening of the traditionally site-orientated attitude of archaeology into the realms of anthropology and geography is an attempt to relate the necessarily selective and locally detailed data recovered from excavations to a wider understanding of human behaviour through time. The problem is particularly acute in urban archaeology because urbanization is an expression of the non-uniform distribution of human activities, making extrapolation from the tiny percentage of any urban settlement actually excavated enormously difficult. More traditional allies in the search for a context are documentary studies (eg Hassall, 1974; Keene, 1976), which constitute the chronological framework within which medieval archaeology continues to operate.

In this paper the years AD 900 to 1500 are divided into periods of roughly 150 years. An attempt is made to distinguish the characteristic features of medieval urbanism both through time and in terms of different types of settlement. This is in effect a study of urbanization, and it will be seen that towns acquired variable clusters of attributes related both to their own development and to the historical period of their acquisition. Viewed in

this way the confusing, and sometimes contradictory, tangle of 'urban features' such as nucleation, sprawl, walls, castles, markets, fairs, mints, etc can be unravelled into explicable sequences. The distribution maps of each period only show the acquisition of urban features, with the intention of demonstrating the changing pattern of town genesis and expansion. For reasons of clarity, and through the lack of precise information in many cases, not all urban features can be shown, for instance suburbs and craft specialization. At the end of each chronological section the main archaeological priorities for that period will be briefly discussed, and it will become clear that lack of data is a continuing major problem. For a more detailed review of the archaeology of individual Sussex towns, see Aldsworth and Freke (1976).

Late Saxon urbanization (Fig 38)

The earliest medieval towns in Sussex are late Saxon. They are known principally through documents, especially the *Burghal Hidage*, a 10th century list of Wessex fortresses (Hill, 1969). The four Sussex *burghs* are Hastings, Lewes, Burpham and Chichester. There is one other town of this early period not mentioned in the *Burghal Hidage*, the undefended *port* of Steyning. The locations of the *burghs* were presumably chosen for their strategic strength and they are not necessarily on previously occupied sites. In Sussex only Chichester had been previously settled, and even there, there seems to have been a hiatus in the pagan Saxon period (Down and Rule, 1971; Down, 1974). We are ignorant of the actual location of the *burgh* at Hastings, but it was not necessarily previously occupied by the *Hæstingas*, whose territory may have been as large as the present Rape of Hastings. Lewes appears to be a new establishment at the narrowest point of the Ouse, just opposite the earlier settlement at South Malling. Burpham was built on a promontory in the Arun valley across from Arundel, which seems to have been occupied at some time in the late Saxon period. These last three sites seem to have been chosen for their natural defensive advantages, but at Chichester the Roman defences were reused, a situation paralleled at Portchester, Winchester and elsewhere (Biddle, 1976). It has been suggested that the siting of some *burghs* had a commercial component (Aston and Bond, 1976) and Chichester, where sheer impregnability has been compromised by accessibility, may be one of these.

The valleys of the Adur and the Cuckmere are not covered by this defensive chain. In the Cuckmere gap the earthwork known as The Rookery has been claimed to be late Saxon on the basis of its shape, untypical for a Norman motte and bailey. Excavations in the 1950s proved inconclusive (Musson, 1955), and the matter must await further research.

The Adur gap is occupied by the late Saxon town of Steyning, where a settlement existed as early as the 8th century. Its omission from the *Burghal Hidage* may suggest that it did not achieve the status of a town until 1016 when it acquired a mint. This is not a necessary conclusion, however, because it does not seem to have been the *burgh* builders' policy to guard every vulnerable point on the Wessex borders, but merely to provide reasonably spaced garrisons or refuges. The average distance between the

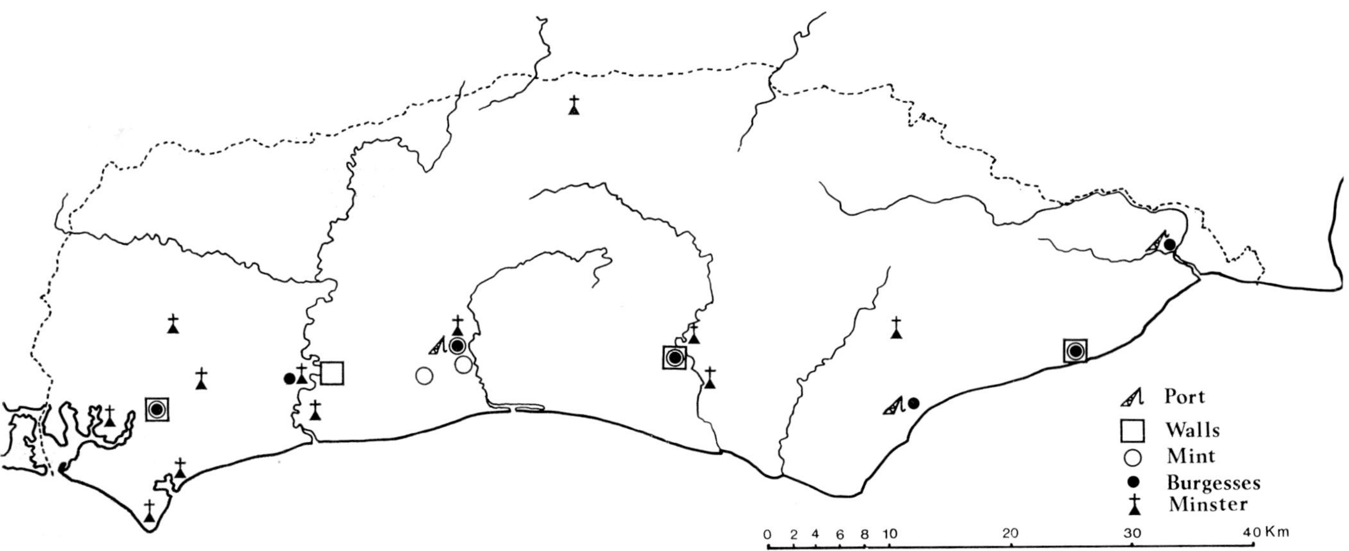

Fig **38**   *Late Saxon urbanization*

Sussex forts agrees very well with the average for the system. Its late acquisition of a mint may demonstrate that the primary condition for a 10th century mint was a defensible site. It is difficult to envisage the reused hill-fort at Cissbury generating the demand for the mint it enclosed (Dudley, this volume). Perhaps, when the threat of Danish incursions receded, this no doubt inconvenient site was abandoned in favour of the town it probably served. Three excavations carried out in Steyning in the last fifteen years (Evans, 1968; Freke, forthcoming) have confirmed late Saxon occupation and given some indication of the extent of the settlement; but more and better dated information is needed concerning its early economic status.

Archaeological work in the *burghs* themselves is patchy. The location of 10th century Hastings is still unknown and with only 500 hides it may have been quite small. Excavations and observations over several years in Lewes have indicated possible pre-Conquest occupation on a number of sites (Norris and Thompson, 1963; Thompson, 1967; Freke, 1976 and 1977a) and demolished some myths about the topography of the early town (Freke, 1975). The line of the Saxon defences has still to be proved, however, and until that is done its size remains conjectural. By the time of the Norman Conquest it was clearly very important economically, as numismatic evidence shows (Dudley, this volume). Its Domesday valuation was £26 as against Chichester's £12. There were also nine churches, some of them only 50 m or so apart along the High Street, a fact that supports the suggestion of small urban estates (Aldsworth, this volume). Burpham is particularly interesting because it had no mint and it never grew into a town. This has led to speculation that it was never permanently occupied. Certainly it lacks the good communications necessary for a successful trading centre and it is no surprise that Arundel, already a *port* with burgesses in the late Saxon period, was chosen by the Normans as the principal town of the Rape. A small rescue excavation in 1973 confirmed Saxo-Norman occupation within the defended area of Burpham, but the excavation was very small and the extent of the occupation is still unknown (Suter-meister, 1977).

In Chichester documentary evidence exists of some ecclesiastical activity in the 8th century and there have been many finds of late Saxon features and pottery. Enough information has been collected to enable a street map of late Saxon Chichester to be produced (Down, 1974). The overriding problem in all these late Saxon towns is the distinction between pre- and post-Conquest artefacts, particularly ceramics. The accurately dated late Saxon types from Thetford, Stamford, and Portchester do not seem to have penetrated into Sussex, except Portchester ware which has been found in Chichester. Chichester has also produced the only kilns making the local Saxo-Norman coarse ware so far discovered. The absence of pottery from Lewes which could pre-date the so-called Saxo-Norman wares inclines one to the view that although the forms and fabric seem to linger into the 11th, and even the 12th centuries, many of the contexts where it is exclusively found must be earlier. At Bramber Castle K J Barton's excavations under the motte in 1966–7 produced a handful of sherds dating to 1075 or earlier (Barton and Holden, forthcoming), but as they consisted of two types of fabric—rough and fine—no simple diagnostic trait can be deduced.

Once this problem of identifying pre-Conquest features is overcome, the number of historical questions for which archaeology could provide answers is greater than in subsequent periods. For instance: were the Sussex *burghs* originally markets as well as forts? All except Burpham housed burgesses by the time of the Conquest, as did Rye, Pevensey, and Steyning. When did this mercantile activity begin, was it merely local, and where were the markets actually held? Were there permanent settlements in all the forts and if so, how large were they and what were their characteristics? Was there zoning of activities within the walls as the pottery kilns at Chichester may suggest? Evidence of weaving and iron-working on the outskirts of Lewes and Steyning (Freke, 1977a; 1978) is inconclusive without information from other areas within these towns. The walls themselves have yet to be adequately investigated in any of the Sussex *burghs*. It is most likely that they had timber revetted earthen banks as at Tamworth, Wareham, Crick-lade, and elsewhere; but were they reinforced or refortified at any time as was Wareham at the time of the Conquest? Lewes seems to offer the best opportunities for research into this aspect as Chichester's wall has been shown to be too damaged (Hannah, 1934; Wilson, 1957). In Lewes

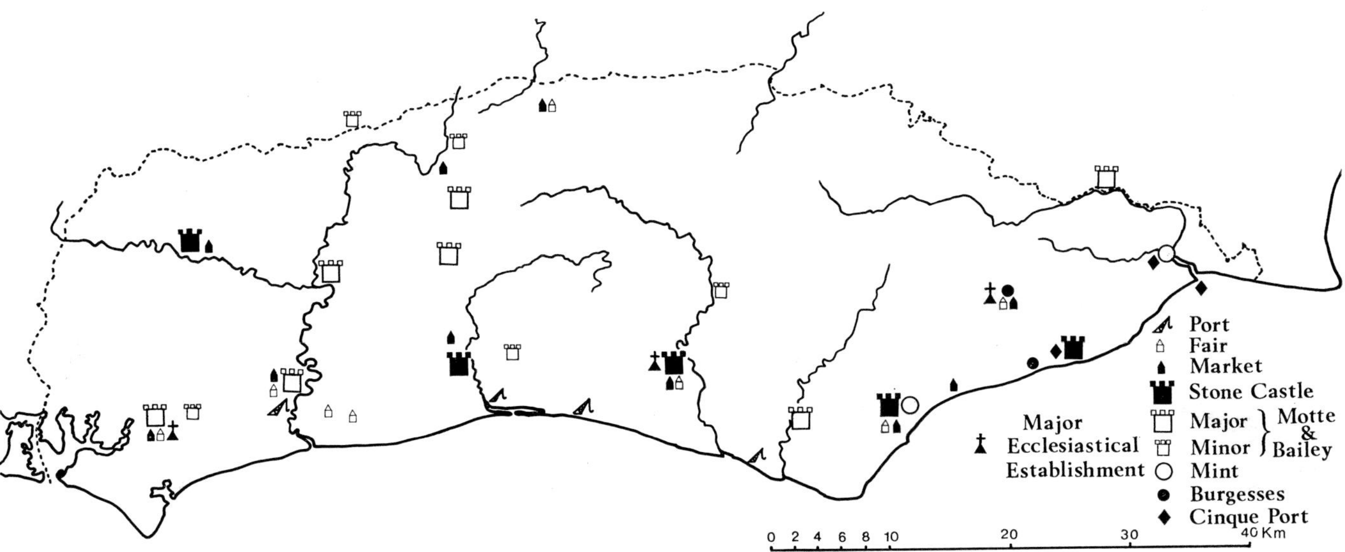

Fig 39   Norman urbanization

the length of wall calculated from the *Burghal Hidage* is smaller than the traditional line, which has in any case been shown to be erroneous in the north-east (Freke, 1975). The calculations for Chichester's wall seem to show that sometimes natural defensive features were left unmanned, presumably in this case the marshy area to the south of the town. Probably the most difficult problem to answer archaeologically, although there may be no other way of tackling it, is the question of pre-Conquest planned towns (Biddle, 1976). Chichester and Lewes may have been planned on a regular grid, although it has never been tested in Lewes and the constraints imposed by the Roman walls at Chichester may be misleading (Collis, 1976). There is evidence from Wareham and Winchester to suggest that areas within the walls were left free of buildings, perhaps to accommodate refugees in the event of a Danish attack. Large-scale area excavations may be the only way to answer many of the problems of late Saxon town planning.

Norman urbanization (Fig 39)

The distribution map of the features acquired by Norman towns immediately indicates administrative and economic expansion. The Saxon walls which protected the towns against external disorder are replaced by castles imposing internal discipline. These citadels are the visible manifestations of a foreign power, and the growth of the coastal towns is a less obvious consequence of the same fact. The feudal overlords and many of the ecclesiastical establishments maintained direct links with France. Each of the inland feudal towns established outports to handle their shipping as their defensive locations became a handicap to trade. The new towns of Seaford, New Shoreham, Littlehampton, and Winchelsea had no defences or administrative functions. In the two coastal towns which were also feudal strongholds, Pevensey and Hastings, the mercantile quarters apparently grew away from the castles towards the quays. The French connexion at Rye was provided by the Abbey of Fécamp, which owned the town from 1017 to 1247. Rye gave the Abbey direct access to the sea when their port at Steyning had been compromised by William de Braose's new harbour at Shoreham. Like the other mercantile towns Rye was not defended until much later.

Ecclesiastical power, albeit directed by the secular arm, was responsible for Battle, one of the new towns in the Weald. Battle Abbey, built on the site of William's victory, stimulated the growth of a small town at its gates, presumably to house the construction workers originally, but later to service the Abbey. Another divinely inspired settlement grew up at Southover to become a suburb of Lewes, and Chichester may owe much of its Norman development to the removal of the See from Selsey in 1071.

Norman castles are perhaps the most striking remnants of the period and as such they have been a focus of archaeological activity. Each of the major castles has been the subject of excavations as well as many of the mottes. Apart from their intrinsic interest, such datable structures can provide the sealed artefact sequences needed to date more anonymous sites (Barton and Holden, forthcoming). Some of the Sussex castles were imposed upon already established towns, their sites being chosen for strategic reasons that did not necessarily respect the layout of the previous settlement. At Lincoln 166 tenements were destroyed to make way for the castle. Did something similar happen at Lewes and Chichester?

The growth of Norman towns presents many problems, especially the growth of suburbs (Keene, 1976). From documentary evidence it seems clear that Lewes had spread across the river to Cliffe by 1086, and the suburb of Southover has already been mentioned. Excavations in north and east Lewes have begun to show the extent of the Norman settlement (Norris and Thompson, 1963; Freke, 1975; 1976; 1977a). The growth of the smaller Norman towns needs much more research. Did their first settlements huddle round the feet of castles in the classic way? This was probably the case at Battle in relation to the Abbey. At Pevensey, excavations in 1962–4 (Dulley, 1967) located a 12th century quay, and the excavator suggested that his sites were on the outskirts of the earlier town, implying a movement away from the castle. At Bramber, Holden has shown (1975) that a quay was in operation at the time of the building of the castle, but that it was buried under flood deposits by the end of the 12th century. Was this quay merely used to unload building material, or did an active merchants' quarter grow up along the causeway to the castle; if so, in which

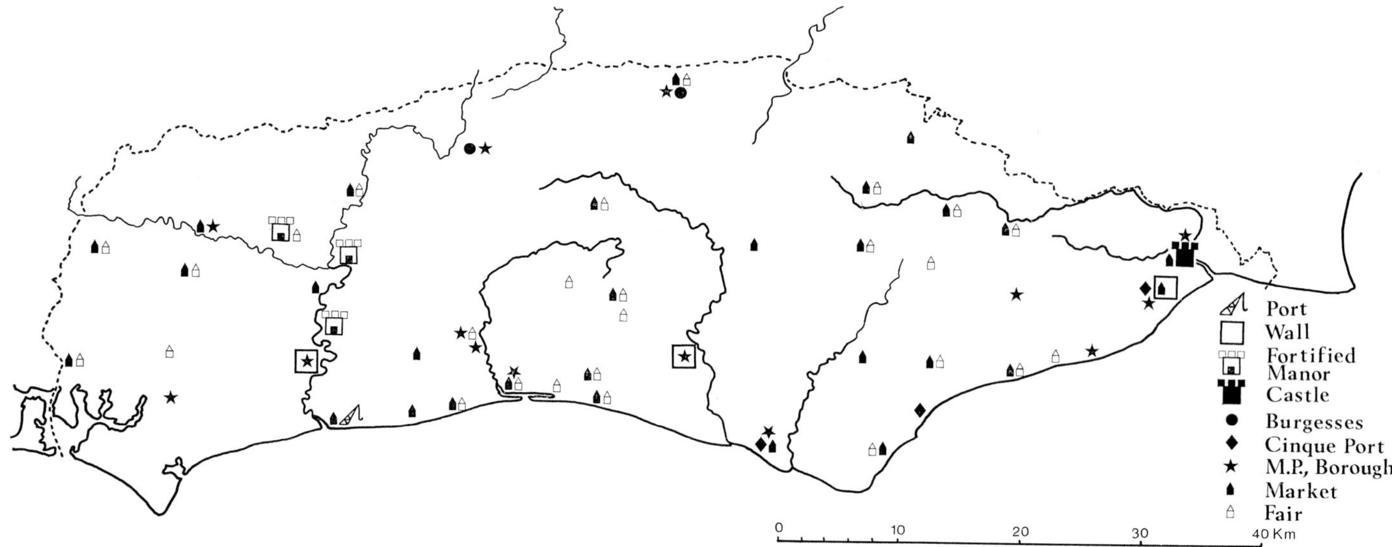

Fig **40**   *Urbanization 1200–1350*

direction? Sele Priory owned tenements just across Bramber bridge, so perhaps here is an example of Norman ribbon development.

Norman economic life generally seems to have been directly linked to the protection or patronage of major feudal or ecclesiastical powers. The ports are no exception to this, they are merely at one remove. The Wealden town of Crawley, however, is exceptional, having an early 12th century market and fair with no imminent fortress. Midhurst is more typical.

Urbanization 1200–1350 (Fig 40)

This period sees an enormous expansion in the number of towns. In the 150 years after the Conquest seven new towns were founded, but between 1200 and 1350 at least 26 new markets and fairs were established, double the total for the previous half-millennium. Very few of these new towns grew up under the walls of fortresses although some could boast a fortified manor. Perhaps it should not be called an 'urban' expansion, for some were undoubtedly speculative grants of markets and fairs to villages by lords who wanted more revenue. Many must have dealt solely in agricultural produce on a periodic basis, but even this must have meant a profound social change with a large increase in the entrepreneurial class throughout the county. It is interesting that the map showing all the markets and fairs operating *c* 1350 (Fig 42) shows the Weald well represented, although it remains true that the very rich towns are around the Downs.

Did this increase derive from the inhabitants of the former villages merely changing their status, or was there an influx from the countryside with a consequent enlargement of the urban communities? Excavations in Seaford have produced results which might suggest expansion (Freke, 1977b), and work in Winchelsea, a classic planned town of this period, has also shown the growth of one tenement in the 14th century (King, 1975). Chichester was growing beyond its walls in the 13th century, but the topographical results of such expansion cannot be taken for granted. In Lewes, for instance, the town seems to have withdrawn in the 13th century from areas occupied in the 11th and 12th centuries (Freke, 1976), presumably to grow in other directions.

During this period the feudal outports boomed. In Seaford, for instance, in 1330 there were more than double the number of wool merchants in Lewes although Lewes had the wool staple in 1364–5. However, Lewes still owned more ships. Shoreham's prosperity was even more spectacular, as demonstrated by the shipping totals for 1289–90 when she handled 23 ships as against Seaford's 9 and Chichester's 6 (Pelham, 1929; 1930). The rise of these ports should have left a fascinating archaeological record, particularly in the matter of imported goods. Little work has been done, however, although there is a complete 13th century French jug from Shoreham (Evans, 1969). Excavations in Seaford have produced pottery from north and south-west France and Germany, as well as more local goods from Cornwall (Freke, 1977b).

The archaeology of the Wealden towns has been a neglected area, especially that of Horsham, Crawley, and East Grinstead. Their northerly locations allow them access to markets to the north and London which must have left some mark in the archaeological record. There has been no systematic excavation in any of these towns, although from Horsham there is a large group of 13th or 14th century ceramics (Honeywood, 1868).

Late medieval urbanization (Fig 41)

Urbanization in this period almost stops, and many of the speculative foundations of the preceding 150 years fail or decline (Beresford, 1967). This seems to demonstrate Blouet's theory of the evolution of towns (1972) which suggests that in a period of competition the larger towns in advantageous positions offering more goods and services will survive and the smaller towns decline. (Compare Fig 42 showing towns in 1350 with Fig 43, showing 16th century towns.) The acquisition of walls by some of the coastal towns at this time is not the expression of a new sense of civic pride, as it might be in cities like Coventry, rather a reflection of the bare necessities of defence against the French. Rye, Winchelsea, Hastings, and Seaford all built or applied to build their walls after being sacked. A very few late markets were founded both with and without the protection of fortified manors, as at Bodiam and Alfriston.

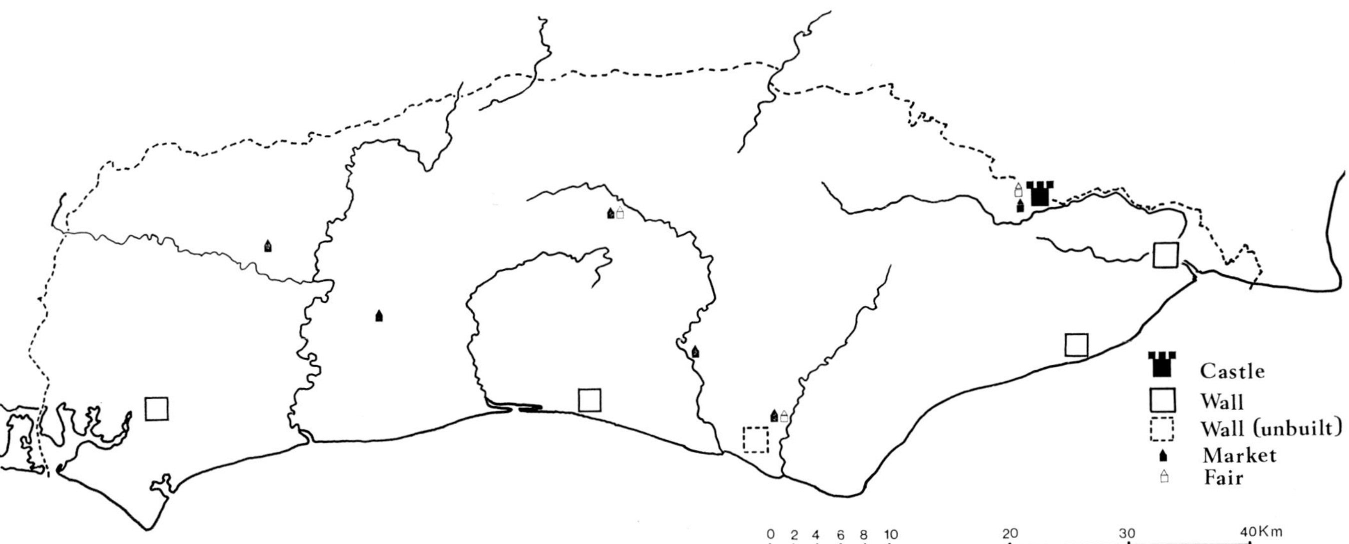

Fig **41**   *Late medieval urbanization*

Fig **42**   *Markets and fairs c 1350*

Fig **43**   *16th century market towns*

Very little archaeology has been expressly directed towards this period. Much of the evidence indeed lies inaccessible under present-day charming town centres or is still standing, and so has been left to historians and the students of vernacular architecture. This is a period where the disciplines of archaeology, documentary history, and architectural history have much to offer one another.

References

Aldsworth, F and Freke, D, 1976   *Historic towns in Sussex: an archaeological survey*, London

Aston, M and Bond, J, 1976   *The landscape of towns*, London

Barley, M W (ed), 1976   *The plans and topography of medieval towns in England and Wales*, CBA Res Rep **14**

Barton, K J and Holden, E W   'Excavations at Bramber Castle', *Archaeol J* (forthcoming)

Beresford, M, 1967   *New towns of the Middle Ages*, New York, 251–318

Biddle, M, 1976   'The evolution of planned towns before 1066', in *The plans and topography of medieval towns in England and Wales* (ed M Barley), CBA Res Rep **14**

Blouet, B W, 1972   'Factors influencing the evolution of settlement patterns', in *Man, settlement and urbanism* (eds P J Ucko et al), London, 3–15

Carter, H, 1977   *Networks and hierarchies*, Typescript of a paper delivered at a Conference of the CBA Urban Research Committee, London

Childe, V G, 1950   'The urban revolution', *Town Plan Rev*, **21**, 3–17

Christaller, W, 1966   *Central places in Southern Germany*, New Jersey, translated from 1933 German original edition

Collis, J, 1976   'Review', *Archaeol J*, **133**, 304

Down, A and Rule, M, 1971   *Chichester excavations* **1**

Down, A, 1974a   *Chichester excavations* **2**

Down, A, 1974b   *Rescue archaeology in Chichester*

Dulley, A J F, 1967   'Excavations at Pevensey', *Medieval Archaeol*, **11**, 209–32

Evans, K J, 1968   *Worthing Museum Society Newsletter*, January

Evans, K J, 1969   'A discovery of two unusual objects in New Shoreham', *Sussex Archaeol Collect*, **105**, 79–86

Freke, D, 1975   'Excavations in Lewes 1974', *ibid*, **113**, 66–84

Freke, D, 1976   'Further excavations in Lewes 1975', *ibid*, **114**, 176–93

Freke, D, 1977a   'Excavations in Lewes 1976', *ibid*, **116** (forthcoming)

Freke, D, 1977b   'Excavations in Seaford 1976', *ibid*, **116** (forthcoming)

Freke, D, 1978   'Excavations at Steyning 1977', *Bull Inst Archaeol*, **15** (forthcoming)

Hannah, I C, 1934   'The walls of Chichester', *Sussex Archaeol Collect*, **75**, 107–29

Haselgrove, C, 1976   'After civilization: archaeology, anthropology and the study of urbanism', in *Archaeology and anthropology* (ed M Spriggs), London

Hassall, T, 1974   'Urban surveys: medieval Oxford', in *Landscapes and documents* (eds A Rogers and T Rowley), London

Heighway, C M (ed), 1972   *The erosion of history*, London

Hill, D, 1969   'The *Burghal Hidage*–the establishment of a text', *Medieval Archaeol*, **13**, 84–92

Holden, E W, 1975   'New evidence relating to Bramber Bridge', *Sussex Archaeol Collect*, **113**, 104–17

Honeywood, T, 1868   'The discovery of medieval pottery at Horsham', *ibid*, **20**, 194–7

Keene, D J, 1976   'Surburban growth', in *The plans and topography of medieval towns in England and Wales* (ed M Barley), CBA Res Rep **14**

King, A, 1975   'A medieval town house in German Street, Winchelsea 1974', *Sussex Archaeol Collect*, **113**, 124–45

Leach, E, 1976   'A view from the bridge', in *Archaeology and anthropology* (ed M Spriggs), London

Musson, R, 1955   'Burlough Castle (the Rookery)', *Sussex Notes and Queries*, **14**, 19–22

Norris, N E S and Thompson, D, 1963   'Note', *ibid*, **16**, 1, 35

Pelham, R A, 1929   'The foreign trade of Sussex 1300–1350', *Sussex Archaeol Collect*, **70**, 93–118

Pelham, R A, 1930   'Some further aspects of Sussex trade during the 14th century', *ibid*, **71**, 171–204

Schledermann, H, 1970   'The idea of the town', *World Archaeol*, **2**, no 2, 115–27

Sutermeister, H, 1977   *Sussex Archaeol Collect*, **114** (forthcoming)

Thompson, D, 1967   'Greenwall Lewes', *Sussex Notes and Queries*, **16**, 337–9

Trigger, B, 1972   'Determinants of urban growth in pre-industrial societies', in *Man, settlement and urbanism* (eds P J Ucko et al), London, 575–99

Wheatley, P, 1972   'The concept of urbanism', in *Man, settlement and urbanism* (eds P J Ucko et al), London, 601–37

Wilson, A E, 1957   'The archaeology of Chichester City walls', *Chichester Papers*, **6**

Housing in eastern Sussex in the late medieval period — David Martin

Much has been written in recent years on vernacular architecture. The best book dealing with Sussex is undoubtedly *Framed buildings of the Weald*, a work which traces the general development of both medieval and early post-medieval housing (Mason, 1964). It is therefore intended here not to deal in general terms with medieval domestic architecture, but instead to try and assess the spectrum of medieval society represented by the surviving rural and semi-rural buildings, and to illustrate the ways in which their owners often designed them to impress.

The specific region studied here is the Rape of Hastings, an area at the extreme eastern end of Sussex. In 1665 the hearth tax gives a total of *c* 2,750 households for the Rape, though if the towns of Battle, Hastings, Rye, and Winchelsea are omitted, this is reduced to approximately 1,900. As is so often the case, a lack of earlier statistical information makes an assessment of the number of rural households in the late 15th century impossible, though it must have been below that of 1665, probably between 1,000 and 1,500. As to medieval survival, Vol 9 of the *Victoria County History of Sussex* is as yet the best general survey that exists. Unfortunately, many of the *VCH* descriptions are either inaccurate or superficial, whilst recent survey work has shown many omissions. To date, current research has swollen the number of known late 14th and 15th century rural and semi-rural dwellings from 64 to 110. As over 1,500 historic properties still await inspection, even this is unlikely to be representative of the actual survival figure.

For discussion regarding distribution and survival the dwellings have been divided into two main groups: (i) rural and (ii) major rural settlements.

The former classification includes any dwelling not located within a village or town, whilst the latter are houses within the rural trading centres, settlements which, in early documents, are often referred to as 'towns'. The smaller villages and major towns have here been omitted owing to present lack of knowledge.

Distribution and survival

The rural areas (Figs 44 and 45)

In rural areas it may be possible to estimate roughly to which class of person the surviving dwellings belonged by comparing the size of the house with its plain acreage (ie acreage excluding woodland). The probable medieval acreages have so far been ascertained for eleven houses surveyed, the information regarding these being shown in Table 1 and Fig 45.

(a) *Copyhold and freehold property.* No houses of pre 1500 date have yet been discovered on copyhold or freehold tenements with supporting lands of less than 50 acres, whilst seven of the buildings in Table 1 were situated on tenements of between 50 and 125 acres and two of over 125 acres. The remaining two houses included in the analysis were leasehold properties and are thus dealt with later. On the whole, the ground floor areas (GFA) of the buildings compare favourably with the acreages, with six of the seven tenements of 50–125 acres having houses of between 71 and about 150 m² GFA, and the two larger holdings having dwellings of considerably larger size.

The exception to these general guide-lines is Mill Cottage, Salehurst, a high-quality building which comprises only two rooms. The large medieval barn adjacent to this house illustrates that there must have been special circumstances for the dwelling to be of such a small size. This building emphasizes how statistical information can only be used as a guide and not as a rigid ruling. On the whole, however, the implication is that a substantially built house of between 70 and 150 m² GFA could be supported by a freehold or copyhold tenement of 50–125 acres, whilst larger holdings were capable of maintaining proportionally larger buildings. Although only a limited sample has been analysed, at present there are only three known rural houses of less than 70 m² GFA; furthermore, with the exception of Ruth Cottage (36 m² GFA), all are only marginally smaller and of good construction. What of the tenements comprising less than *c* 50 acres; and why are there no small or poorly built medieval houses surviving, as indeed there are for the 16th century? Unfortunately, these are questions to which, at present we do not have answers. Certainly by the mid 16th century many were of more than elementary plan, for the 1567 Robertsbridge Manorial Survey shows that over 50% of houses on holdings of between 10 and 50 acres contained detached kitchens (D'Elboux, 1944, 1–124).

The results of the above analysis would be of more use if it were known how common holdings of the various sizes were in medieval times. At present the only method of achieving this is by analysis of 16th century manorial rental surveys. By comparing the entries for the Robertsbridge Abbey Boroughs of Hothligh (mainly in Burwash and Ticehurst) and Stretfield (mainly in Ewhurst), it soon becomes clear that no generalizations can be made. In Stretfield, an area of poor survival, 88% of the holdings had plainlands of less than 50 acres, whilst in Hothligh, where survival is good, only 52% were under 50 acres. This variance is still further emphasized by the manorial records of Bodiam Manor (records held by the National Trust) which show that of the 18 freehold and copyhold tenements within Bodiam Parish, all but one were of less than 50 acres (ie 94%). It is probably these very marked regional variations which are chiefly responsible for the uneven pattern of surviving buildings shown in Fig 44.

Table 1 Plain acreages supporting medieval dwellings

Parish	Name	Ground Floor Area (m²)	Approx Plain Acreage
Copyhold and Freehold			
Burwash	Parkhill	78	59
Ticehurst	Bull Inn	81	60½
Ticehurst	Bakers Farm	97	60½
Salehurst	Mill Cottage	46	c70
Ticehurst	Dale Hill	83	75 or c100
Brede	Sowdens	71	108
Brede	Conster	100–c150	125
Northiam	Gt Dixter	c225	226½ or c360
Bodiam	Bodiam Castle	c1000	c1200
Farmed Out Lands			
Salehurst	Park Farm	75	c300
Etchingham	Ketchingham	74	c250

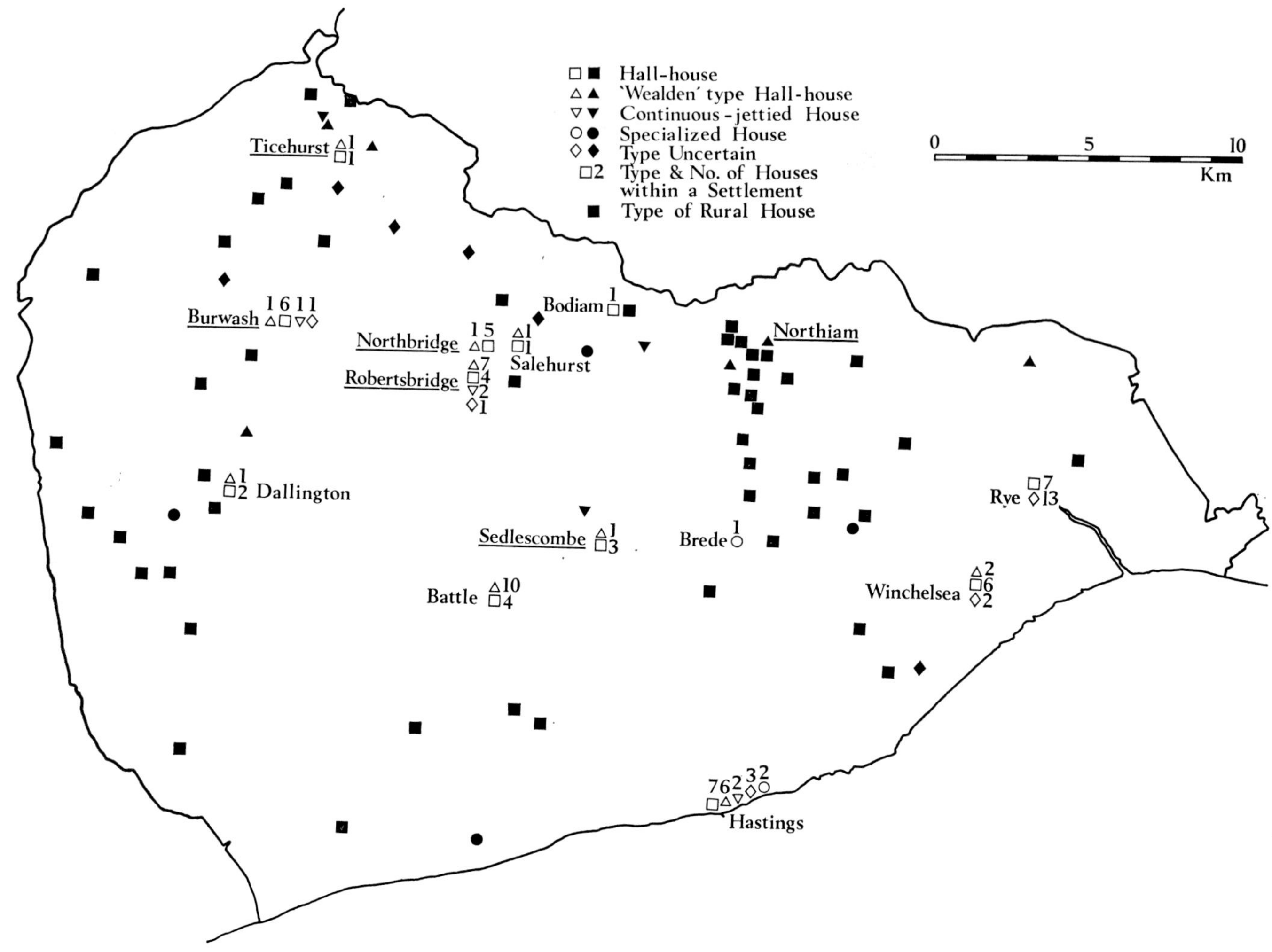

Fig **44**   *Known surviving medieval buildings within the Rape of Hastings*

(b)   *Property leased or 'farmed' out.*   The last two holdings given in Table 1 were farmed out on long-term leases during late medieval times. It will be noticed that whereas the acreage in both cases is high, both being around 250–300 acres, the GFA of the dwellings are comparable with copyhold and freehold tenements low in the 50–125 acre range. Furthermore, although well built, both houses are in fact of very plain nature. This is not surprising when one considers that few landlords are likely to build a large, high-quality house for a tenant. Only where a pre-existing dwelling is included in a new lease is the tenant likely to have lived in a house of exceptional quality. Both holdings analysed were demesne lands of monastic establishments; how often copyhold or freehold lands were leased is difficult to say. It is not rare for several manorial holdings to be held by one tenant, and it can only be assumed that these would have been leased out.

The major rural settlements (Fig 44)

These are the rural trading centres, quite different in appearance from the towns, having widely spaced houses and a large number of barns (Martin and Mastin, 1974, 9). There are only four rural centres within the Rape, these being Burwash, Robertsbridge, Sedlescombe, and Tice-hurst; in all of these agriculture played but a secondary role, and consequently acreage totals are of little use for analysis purposes.

Surprisingly, the settlements contain a very high survival of relatively large medieval houses. At present, Roberts-bridge, the largest of the four, is the one about which most is known (Martin and Mastin, 1974). The 'town' retains 14 houses dating to *c* 1500 or earlier; all are substantially built and most have a GFA of between 70 and 100 m², thus being comparable with the rural dwellings on holdings of 50–125 acres. There is strong evidence to indicate that at least 50% of the dwellings within the 'town' were of this general high standard (Martin and Mastin, 1974, 12). Although the smallest surviving building has a GFA of only 45 m², its construction is of a high standard.

A little to the north of Robertsbridge is the suburb of Northbridge, which in 1658 consisted of approximately 13 houses and 4 barns (abstracted from Vivian, 1953). Six medieval dwellings survive, whilst two others of substantial size are known to have been destroyed at the beginning of this century. Of the existing structures, the smallest is a three-roomed house with a GFA of 41 m², whilst the largest comprises seven rooms and has a GFA of 121 m²; the remainder vary in size between these two extremes. As in the main settlement, all (without exception) are substantially timbered and well built.

Far less is known of the other three principal settlements. Burwash was probably a little smaller than Robertsbridge, but retains at least nine medieval houses, the majority of these being both larger and of a superior quality to those which survive in Robertsbridge. A cursory inspection of the two much smaller settlements of Sedlescombe and Ticehurst suggests equally good survival.

From the above it would seem that these rural settlements had by the close of the 15th century attained a general high standard of living, almost certainly considerably better in overall terms than that enjoyed by the majority of the rural population. A word of caution should, however, be stressed, for it is known that standards slumped drastically in these settlements during the late 16th–19th centuries, with the majority of houses gradually being subdivided and leased out. As the early architecture was of a high standard, it seems likely that the new landlords would be inclined to update and modify rather than rebuild. In contrast, during the same period many of the rural farming units were combining to form larger, more economic farms. This in turn often meant the destruction of obsolete houses on now combined tenements, together with the reconstruction of the main house to meet its increased status. Whereas the reduction of standards in the villages tended to preserve the early architecture, in the rural areas the rate of destruction was probably high, thus resulting in an exaggeration of the imbalance in survival rates amongst buildings of equal quality.

Economies in building design

The general standard of construction attained both in the major rural settlements and in the country tells something of the money available for construction works in the 15th century. With very few exceptions, surviving medieval dwellings are both heavily timbered and well constructed; most unless either small or early, incorporate at least one moulded crossbeam. If finance was short, there were many ways in which the client could have built a house of comparable size on a much smaller budget. This could, for instance, have been achieved by reducing the scantling of the timbering, by omitting or simplifying the moulded beams, or merely by reducing the high quality of finish that is found in most houses. In the majority of cases these economies were not implemented, though it is true that in some instances economies can be noticed in houses of no mean size. Where these are found, they are usually made in such a way as not to be too obvious. One of the best examples exists at Chateaubriand in Burwash High Street, where the client has designed a building which appears at first sight to be both of considerable size and of heavy timbering (Martin, 1974, 21–9). Indeed, the building is long, measuring 16·8 m, but the general scale has been further emphasized by making the structure both tall and narrow. The width of the hall was enlarged to a respectable dimension by the addition of a short quasi-aisle at the rear. The timbering to both the main façade and the hall is heavy, but elsewhere, away from public view, it is of a much flimsier nature. Within the services further economies were made by utilizing poorly finished, waney joists.

A similar method of achieving economies was attempted at Church Farmhouse, Salehurst, though here they almost resulted in disaster (Martin, 1972a). In order to give the main façade style, the house was designed as a 'wealden' whilst, as at Chateaubriand, the timbering within the hall was both neatly finished and of respectable scantling. The hall also incorporated a high-quality moulded beam with moulded spere brackets and doorways with shaped heads. In order to afford these luxury items it was necessary to make severe economies; this was achieved not only by using smaller, poorly finished, waney joists and rafters within the service bay, but also by omitting the principal posts and

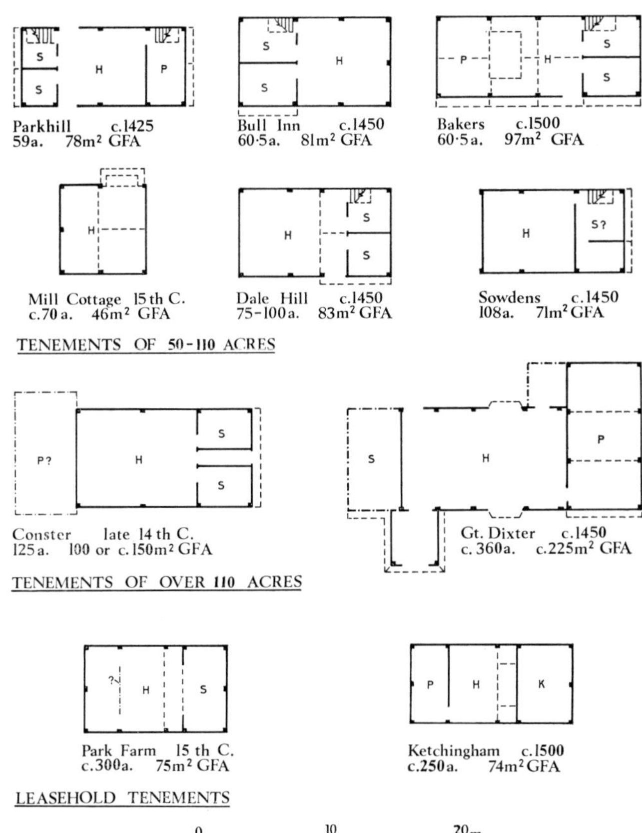

Fig 45   Plans of houses mentioned in Table 1

crossbeam from the central truss of the long service area. An intermediate tiebeam with a crownpost above was inserted, but the bay was seriously under-designed for its length, with the result that the principal longitudinal timbers failed. Only major repairs prevented the service end of the structure from collapsing. Dunsters Mill House, Ticehurst, is another building which incorporates skilfully disguised economies (Martin, 1975). The main house itself is well built, but the parlour end, added a short time afterwards, shows a marked lack of finance. The extension ought to have been constructed in two bays but, as at Church Farmhouse, the truss was omitted to save costs. In this instance, however, not only was an intermediate tiebeam included, but a principal post was also inserted into the main façade, thus simulating a two-bay extension when viewed from the road. The timbering internally is both rough and scanty and the span of the joists is excessive; even so sufficient money was made available to incorporate a jetty at the end of the building in order to give an impressive external appearance.

In the smaller houses, structural economies were sometimes made without any attempt at disguising them. In the small early 16th century dwelling at Haiselmans Farm, Salehurst, only the basic essential framing was used, whilst, at roof level, the spindly rafters were spaced so far apart that it has since been necessary to insert rafters into the spaces (Martin, 1971a). Ruth Cottage, Beckley, the smallest rural medieval house yet recorded within the Rape, is constructed entirely of reused material from an earlier building, thus achieving an obvious saving in cost (Martin, 1971b).

Although structural economies of the type described above are rare, one can often notice restriction being made on quality in order to conserve money. The most common of these is in the use of close vertical studding, an expensive form of wall infill used for aesthetic effect. With very few exceptions, where this is used externally it is limited to the front and side elevations, the rear wall being constructed with large daub panels. Windows with shaped heads and moulded mullions are rare in medieval houses, though again, where used these are normally restricted to the front and side elevations. The Preachers House, Ewhurst (*c* 1500) is an exception in that the rear window of the hall is also of elaborate type, probably because it was visible from within the hall itself (Martin, 1977a). The Old Post Office, Brede (late 15th century) on the other hand has conventional rear windows, but front windows with shaped heads (Martin, 1976). Another example existed at Portland Cottages, Burwash (early–mid 15th century) where, although shaped heads were not used, the windows on the front and end walls were fitted with moulded mullions (Martin, 1972b, 14–30).

The above are just a few ways in which costs could be cut without affecting the size of the structure. There were, however, clients who placed great importance on both structural quality and finer detail, people who in fact were willing to make sacrifices in the size of their home in order to obtain a high quality. A typical product of this school of thought is Bower Cottages, Burwash, where a relatively small house measuring 12·30 × 5·95 m incorporates moulded beams, panelling, shaped door heads, and a dais canopy; such attention to detail in a house of this size is rare (Martin, 1969). Sowdens, Brede, one of the fourteen rural households analysed earlier in this paper, is a highly finished structure incorporating massive timbering and a large amount of close vertical studding. Even so, it is small for the 108 acres of plainland which supported it, having a GFA of only 71 m² (Martin, 1977b). Whereas Bower Cottage is of standard plan with a storeyed bay at either end of the house, Sowdens has only one storeyed end with the hall located at the other. Furthermore, the daub infill to the end wall of the hall is set flush with the framing on the hall side, leaving the basic frame protruding externally. In this instance, although the client sacrificed overall size in order to achieve quality, he designed his house in such a way that it could easily be enlarged by the addition of a bay when funds permitted. He appears to have been over-optimistic, for it was about 150 years before the house was completed. Dunsters Mill House, another highly finished building designed to be constructed in two phases, was completed without much delay, though in order to achieve this it was necessary to make severe economies (see above; Martin, 1975).

Conclusions

As has been shown, research to date indicates that, on the whole, the rural late-medieval domestic architecture of Hastings Rape survives only on tenements in excess of 50 acres, holdings which may loosely be described as belonging to the yeoman classes. Although not proven, indications suggest that where survival is at its most dense (ie in the Northiam area), up to 50% of the dwellings would have been of the same general high standard as that found in the standing buildings, but that elsewhere the number is likely to have been considerably lower, perhaps below 10% in places.

The four major rural settlements of Burwash, Roberts-bridge, Sedlescombe, and Ticehurst appear at this period to have been prosperous, with at least 50% of the houses being of both reasonable size and sound construction. Present evidence suggests that these communities were peopled by families living largely on a dual economy, usually a craft or trade backed up by a small holding located on the periphery of the settlement. From the quality of the houses, this was obviously a successful combination.

In both the rural and semi-rural regions the surviving architecture was, on the whole, constructed to impress, often having high-quality features strategically placed to be visible either to the public or to visitors. Away from such areas the finish was often inferior, whilst in some cases the quality features could only be afforded by making major structural economies away from public view. This sort of careful planning aimed at impressing others is a feature commonly found in classes who had only recently, quite rapidly, obtained a position of some status. That this was the case here is surely to some extent proven by the virtual absence of buildings of submanorial class predating *c* 1350. As to the many households of lesser status, it is unlikely that we shall ever have a picture anything like as detailed as that which has emerged for the 'yeoman' class. With the absence of surviving examples, all information must come from either excavation or from documentary sources.

References

D'Elboux, R H, 1944   'Surveys of the manors of Robertsbridge, Sussex, and Michelmarsh, Hampshire, and of the Demesne lands of Halden in Rolvenden, Kent, 1567–1570', *Sussex Record Society*, **47**

Martin, D, 1969   'Burwash—Bower Cottages', *Rape of Hastings Architectural Survey. Report no 28* (unpublished—copy lodged with National Monuments Record, London)

Martin, D, 1971a   'Salehurst—Haiselmans Farmhouse', *ibid*, *Report no 56* (unpublished—copy lodged with Nat Mon Rec, London)

Martin, D, 1971b   'Beckley—Ruth Cottage', *ibid*, *Report no 72* (unpublished—copy lodged with Nat Mon Rec, London)

Martin, D, 1972a   'Salehurst—Church Farmhouse', *ibid*, *Report no 78* (unpublished—copy lodged with Nat Mon Rec, London)

Martin D, 1972b   'Portland Cottages, Burwash', *Sussex Archaeol Collect*, **110**, 14–30

Martin, D, 1974   'Chateaubriand, Burwash', *ibid*, **112**, 21–9

Martin, D, 1975   'Ticehurst—Dunsters Mill House', *Rape of Hastings Architectural Survey, Report no 182* (unpublished—copy lodged with Nat Mon Rec, London)

Martin, D, 1976   'Brede—The Old Post Office', *ibid*, *Report no 213* (unpublished—copy lodged with Nat Mon Rec, London)

Martin, D, 1977a   'Ewhurst—Preachers House', *ibid*, *Report no 269* (unpublished—copy lodged with Nat Mon Rec, London)

Martin, D, 1977b   'Brede—Sowdens', *ibid*, *Report no 267* (unpublished—copy lodged with Nat Mon Rec, London)

Martin, D and Mastin, B J, 1974   'An architectural history of Robertsbridge', *Hastings Area Archaeological Papers no 5*

Mason, R T, 1964   *Framed buildings of the Weald*

Vivian, Sir Sylvanus P, 1953   'The Manor of Etchingham Cum Salehurst', *Sussex Record Society*, **53**

Index